T0311480

German-American Relations in the 21st Century

German-American relations have become interesting again. U.S. President Donald Trump's lukewarm policy toward Europe has ensured that the relationship between Berlin and Washington is once again regarded as an important field of scholarship within global politics. And yet it was only a few years ago that German-American relations seemed to take second place to transatlantic relations in general, and the European Union (EU)–USA relationship in particular. The advent of Donald Trump as US President in January 2017 has made all the difference. Trump's difficult personal relationship with German Chancellor Angela Merkel, and his denigration of everything the Western world – including the USA itself – has stood for since 1949, have given a new significance to German-American relations in practice and theory.

This volume offers an empirical and conceptual analysis of German-American relations in the 21st century and highlights the serious and perhaps unprecedented challenges the two countries face at present. The authors discuss a number of aspects of the current, much more fragile state of German-American relations from different perspectives.

This book was originally published as a special issue of the journal *German Politics*.

Klaus Larres is Richard M. Krasno Distinguished Professor of History and International Affairs at the University of North Carolina at Chapel Hill, USA. He is Senior Fellow in the Center of Transatlantic Relations at Johns Hopkins University/School of Advanced International Studies (SAIS), Washington, DC, USA and a Visiting Professor at Schwarzman College/Tsinghua University, Beijing, China. He also serves as Counselor and Senior Policy Adviser at the German Embassy in Beijing, China. His research focuses on relations among the USA–Europe–China, US foreign policy and transatlantic relations and the Cold War and the politics of Winston Churchill.

Ruth Wittlinger is Associate Professor in the School of Government and International Affairs at Durham University, UK. She has published extensively on memory and identity in post-unification Germany and Europe. She is author of *German National Identity in the Twenty-First Century*. In 2017, she was awarded a Lady Davis Visiting Professorship at the Hebrew University of Jerusalem, Israel.

German-American Relations in the 21st Century

A Fragile Friendship

Edited by
Klaus Larres and Ruth Wittlinger

Routledge
Taylor & Francis Group

LONDON AND NEW YORK

First published 2019
by Routledge
2 Park Square, Milton Park, Abingdon, Oxon, OX14 4RN, UK

and by Routledge
52 Vanderbilt Avenue, New York, NY 10017, USA

First issued in paperback 2020

Routledge is an imprint of the Taylor & Francis Group, an informa business

British Library Cataloguing-in-Publication Data
A catalogue record for this book is available from the British Library

ISBN 13: 978-0-367-58452-8 (pbk)
ISBN 13: 978-1-138-35358-9 (hbk)

Typeset in Times New Roman
by codeMantra

Publisher's Note
The publisher accepts responsibility for any inconsistencies that may have arisen during the conversion of this book from journal articles to book chapters, namely the possible inclusion of journal terminology.

Disclaimer
Every effort has been made to contact copyright holders for their permission to reprint material in this book. The publishers would be grateful to hear from any copyright holder who is not here acknowledged and will undertake to rectify any errors or omissions in future editions of this book.

Contents

CONTENTS

Citation Information

The chapters in this book were originally published in the journal *German Politics*, volume 27, issue 2 (June 2018). When citing this material, please use the original page numbering for each article, as follows:

Preface
Karsten Voigt
German Politics, volume 27, issue 2 (June 2018) pp. 147–151

Introduction
A Fragile Friendship: German–American Relations in the Twenty-First Century
Klaus Larres and Ruth Wittlinger
German Politics, volume 27, issue 2 (June 2018) pp. 152–157

Chapter 1
The 2003 Iraq War as a Turning Point in German–American Relations: Political Leadership and Alliance Cohesion
Dieter Dettke
German Politics, volume 27, issue 2 (June 2018) pp. 158–173

Chapter 2
The End of Memory? German-American Relations under Donald Trump
Eric Langenbacher and Ruth Wittlinger
German Politics, volume 27, issue 2 (June 2018) pp. 174–192

Chapter 3
Angela Merkel and Donald Trump – Values, Interests, and the Future of the West
Klaus Larres
German Politics, volume 27, issue 2 (June 2018) pp. 193–213

Chapter 4
The Global Financial Crisis and the Euro Crisis as Contentious Issues in German-American Relations
Christian Schweiger
German Politics, volume 27, issue 2 (June 2018) pp. 214–229

Chapter 5
Different Approaches to Russia: The German–American–Russian Strategic Triangle
Stephen F. Szabo
German Politics, volume 27, issue 2 (June 2018) pp. 230–243

Chapter 6
Trading Places: Securitising Refugee and Asylum Policies in Germany and the United States
Joyce Marie Mushaben
German Politics, volume 27, issue 2 (June 2018) pp. 244–264

Chapter 7
More Similar Than Different: Of Checks, Balances, and German and American Government Responses to International Terrorism
D. Hellmuth
German Politics, volume 27, issue 2 (June 2018) pp. 265–281

For any permission-related enquiries please visit:
http://www.tandfonline.com/page/help/permissions

Notes on Contributors

Dieter Dettke is Adjunct Professor at Georgetown University, Washington, DC, USA and Senior Fellow of the American Institute for Contemporary German Studies, Washington, DC, USA. He is author of numerous articles and book chapters on US, German and European political, economic and security issues as well as the book *Allianz im Wandel*; and also served as editor and author of *The Spirit of the Berlin Republic*. His most recent works are "Hungary's Jobbik Party," "the Challenge of European Ethno-Nationalism and the Future of the European Project," published in 2014, and "Germany: From the Ashes of War to the Center of Power in Europe," published in 2016.

D. Hellmuth is Associate Professor of Politics at the Catholic University of America, Washington, DC, USA and serves as Academic Director of the Politics Department's parliamentary internship programs in Europe. She is Non-Resident Fellow at the American Institute for Contemporary German Studies (AICGS), Washington, DC, USA and serves as Fellow at the German Institute on Radicalization and De-Radicalization Studies (GIRDS). Her research and teaching covers world politics, particularly the study of transatlantic security, counterterrorism, counter-radicalization, homeland security, European and general comparative politics and American foreign policy.

Eric Langenbacher is Teaching Professor and Director of Honors and Special Programs in the Department of Government at Georgetown University, Washington, DC, USA, where he completed his PhD in 2002. Recent publications include *The German Polity*, 11th edition (co-authored with David Conradt, 2017), *The Merkel Republic: An Appraisal* (2015) and *Dynamics of Memory and Identity in Contemporary Europe* (co-edited with Ruth Wittlinger and Bill Niven), (paperback 2015). He is also Managing Editor of *German Politics and Society*, which is housed in Georgetown's BMW Center for German and European Studies.

Klaus Larres is Richard M. Krasno Distinguished Professor of History and International Affairs at the University of North Carolina at Chapel Hill, USA. He is Senior Fellow in the Center of Transatlantic Relations at Johns Hopkins University/School of Advanced International Studies (SAIS), Washington, DC, USA and a Visiting Professor at Schwarzman College/Tsinghua

University, Beijing, China. He also serves as Counselor and Senior Policy Adviser at the German Embassy in Beijing, China. His research focuses on relations among the USA–Europe–China, US foreign policy and transatlantic relations and the Cold War and the politics of Winston Churchill.

Joyce Marie Mushaben is CAS Professor for Global Studies and the Curators' Distinguished Professor for Comparative Politics & Gender Studies at the University of Missouri–St. Louis, USA. She has published extensively on East and West German identities, EU gender politics, citizenship, migration and integration policies, inter alia. Her books pertaining to migration and asylum include *The Changing Faces of Citizenship: Integration and Mobilization among Ethnic Minorities in Germany* (2008) and *Becoming Madam Chancellor: Angela Merkel and the Berlin Republic* (2017).

Christian Schweiger is Visiting Professor at the Chair for Comparative European Governance Systems at Chemnitz University of Technology, Germany. His research concentrates on the EU, especially the comparative politics and political economy of the member states, globalization and transatlantic relations.

Stephen F. Szabo was formerly Director of the Transatlantic Academy (TA) and is currently Senior Fellow at the American Institute for Contemporary German Studies at Johns Hopkins University, Baltimore, USA. He has written on German foreign and security policies, generational politics in Europe and transatlantic security and political relations. His publications include *The Changing Politics of German Security, The Diplomacy of German Unification, Parting Ways: The Crisis in the German–American Relationship* and *Germany, Russia and the Rise of Geo-Economics.*

Karsten Voigt served as Coordinator of German–North American Cooperation at the Foreign Office of Germany from 1999 to 2010 and is also a board member of the Atlantik-Brücke, an association to promote German–American understanding. Voigt had previously served as a member of the German Parliament from 1976 to 1998, member of the Parliamentary Assembly of NATO from 1977 to 1998 and as Chairman of Jusos, the Young Socialists in the Social Democratic Party, from 1969 to 1972.

Ruth Wittlinger is Associate Professor in the School of Government and International Affairs at Durham University, UK. She has published extensively on memory and identity in post-unification Germany and Europe. She is author of *German National Identity in the Twenty-First Century.* In 2017, she was awarded a Lady Davis Visiting Professorship at the Hebrew University of Jerusalem, Israel.

PREFACE

KARSTEN VOIGT

While transatlantic relations remain important, they are also subject to change. They need to change, because the world around them changes. Since the end of World War II, each generation has collected new experiences and insights regarding the German–American relationship. Overwhelmingly, these have been positive. However, there have also been crises and disappointments in this relationship. At present the statements and policies of President Trump are perceived by most Germans as a risk or even a threat to the values on which the transatlantic partnership has been based since World War II.

At the end of November 1989, a few days after the Wall came down, I was heading from the subway station towards the main train station on an escalator, which was blocked in front of me by a family with three children. Judging from their dialect, they came from East Germany, and it was their first time in Frankfurt. On their way up, they saw an advertisement for a flight to New York. When the mother saw this ad, she turned to her children and said: 'And next time we're going to New York.'

I was deeply moved, since this sentence expressed the longing of an entire people that had dreamed of escape from East Germany and to enjoy the freedom of no travel restrictions. Now their hopes had been fulfilled. Their first stop was West Germany, yet they wanted to see the world – and New York was a symbol as well as a travel destination for the wide world.

Many generations of Germans felt like this family. For the finance industry, New York was the centre of the world. German tourists were intoxicated by the rush of this big city. They crossed the US on Route 66 to experience life in San Francisco. And it was the highest honour for German students to study at an American elite university. For many German politicians, a reception at the White House was just as important as the audience with the Pope was for many Catholics.

Germans who strongly criticised the American government were nevertheless willing to learn from American role models in US society, education and music. The energy and power of self-initiative, stemming from the roots of US society, were and remain inspirational.

Each side remains inspirational to the other. Both sides learn from each other. And both sides will criticise each other and differ from each other, because since the founding of the US there has been criticism towards Europe and vice versa.

This also applies to the current cycle, where Trump sees German refugee policy as a frightening example, whereas President Obama saw it as a model for others. Whatever President Trump is saying and doing, the societies on both sides of the Atlantic will remain connected through shared interests and values. The United States is Germany's

1

most important partner outside the European Union. While the US is not a member of the EU, it nevertheless will continue to be a power in Europe.

Still, something is changing in our relationship. This doesn't have to be negative per se; to the contrary, in some fields a quicker development of change is necessary. For example, I am hoping for a faster move towards a more effective European foreign and security policy. And the overwhelming majority of American politicians hope for a Europe that can handle challenges in foreign and security policy when it comes to solving a crisis on their own turf. From an American point of view, European allies should ask for protection less, and export more security and stability themselves.

Germany was focused on the East–West conflict in Europe after World War II. Its overall policies in other regions of the world were influenced by this worldview. This has changed in recent years, with Germany becoming active outside of Europe as well, in Afghanistan, Mali and Congo and now in northern Iraq, Syria and even Jordan. This development has been welcomed by the US.

These changes also seemed to concur with the new situation in Europe after the end of the Cold War: Germany was no longer in the centre of global competition of systems and powers. Since the 1990s it has been surrounded by friends and allies. Practically all of its neighbours are members of the EU or of NATO, or of both. This is the best geo-strategic position in which Germany has found itself for several centuries. The stabilis-ation of this situation is Germany's first foreign policy priority.

What once was called 'Ostpolitik' now has a different meaning. An important com-ponent of the relations with many of Germany's eastern neighbours has institutionally become part of what until the eastern enlargement of the EU and NATO used to be part of Germany's 'Westpolitik'. These new members are geographically close to Moscow but they very often hold a more negative view of Russia than the old members of the EU and NATO.

If you consider the deployment of Soviet troops in the GDR as a substitute for a direct neighbourhood, then Russia for several centuries – with the exception of few years – was a direct neighbour to Germany. This is no longer the case. For Germany, Russia nowadays is the most important country east of the EU and NATO. But the pol-icies, the security and the trade relations with Germany's eastern and Russia's western neighbours are as important as, and sometimes more important than, those with Russia. Germany's neighbours do not hold a veto power over Germany's bilateral relations with Russia. Germany's politicians will also in the future try to improve its relationship with Russia. But it will avoid deals with Russia over the heads of its neighbours. This is a change in the framework of Germany's foreign and security policy which in the US has not been seriously analysed and appreciated.

After the end of the Cold War, large-scale armed conflicts seemed to be a thing of the past for Europe. Unfortunately, this positive situation has changed. The armed con-flicts in Eastern Ukraine have caused a revision of previous assumptions. The actions of Russia have caused a deep schism in European politics. The goal of peaceful European arrangements that include Russia remains. However, realising this goal remains elusive for now. Instead, there are currently almost daily armed clashes, over 9000 deaths and over a million refugees within the Ukraine. This is the largest refugee movement within Europe since the end of World War II.

Who would have thought, only a few years ago, that German soldiers and airplanes would be used to provide a feeling of security for the Baltic States. Yet Germany plays a large role, together with France and the US, in trying to solve conflicts peacefully. We do not know how this conflict will end. Yet one thing is for certain, these developments have supported the view of those Europeans who see the US also in the future as an indispensable stabilising factor in Europe. The age of the Sleeping Beauty has ended for NATO. For the small neighbouring states of Russia, the security guarantee of NATO has again become more important than EU membership.

Although its priorities still remain predominantly within the EU, Germany is increasingly engaged as part of the EU, of NATO or other multilateral groups in the Middle East, Central Asia, Afghanistan, Iran, Africa and many more. It is also active when it comes to global questions, such as climate change, international terrorism, the drug trade and data security. In most of these issues the US is a welcome and indispensable partner. But in some issues, like climate change, the US government is part of the problem.

For the US – as a global power – Europe does not always play the most important role in the US's foreign and security policy. On the contrary. Obama's pivot to Asia was an expression of a longer term trend, which seems to be continuing during the administration of President Trump. As an economic player Germany is thinking globally. But Germany – unlike the US – is not a guarantor of security in East Asia. However, because we are impacted by developments in Asia and because we would not understand our US ally otherwise, we have to consider and deal not only with the economic but also with security challenges with which the US is confronted in Asia and through China.

Despite the increasing economic importance of China, Russia remains the most important strategic challenge for Germany, as well as a potential opportunity and sometimes a risk east of the borders of the EU and NATO. As long as economic or cultural problems dominate relations with Russia, the EU is at the forefront. As soon as security challenges increase, the role of the US and its relationship with Russian grows. Because of these different perspectives a transatlantic community of views and strategies cannot be taken as a given. It can only be the result of consultations and compromises.

This is even truer because the transatlantic relationship is by its nature asymmetric: the US is more important for Germany than Germany is for the US. In an asymmetric relationship the weaker partner is always asking themselves how they can influence the bigger partner. And the bigger partner is always asking for an increased relevance of the weaker partner. The growing role of the EU as a factor even in the bilateral relationship between the US and Germany is on the one hand an element which is making the management of the bilateral relationship more complicated. On the other hand, a stable and influential EU is a very important stabilising factor in the European–US relationship and also in the bilateral relationships between the US and all European countries.

The political cultures of Germany and the US have changed in recent years: The debates in the US have become more polarised, while Germany has developed a high degree of consensus on many societal and foreign policy issues (excluding the views of the extreme right and the extreme left). In the last decades Germany has become more liberal, while in the US after 9/11 the balance between security and freedom has shifted towards the former. Compared to its early years and despite legitimate

3

points of criticism, Germans now feel more assured in the stability of their democracy. They represent their interests with more self-confidence, and in individual cases unfortunately also with more arrogance.

In respect to immigration both societies have moved closer. Unlike the US, Germany is not a nation of immigrants. Yet we have become an immigration country, where the 'New Germans' influence and participate in the cultural, political, religious and economic discourse. In the previous century, many Germans fled their country. Now we have become a country that attempts to take in and to integrate a large number of refugees. This will change German society. It will also change our idea of what we see as being 'German'.

Due to their nature, these changes are being heatedly discussed – in the US as well as in Germany. My judgement might not be fair, but my impression is that the debate surrounding immigration and refugees is even shriller in the US than it is in Germany. If I compare the statements of presidential candidate and now President Trump with those of German politicians, I would be hard pressed to find something comparable even among the Christian Democrats, although some Bavarian voices might be an exception. When it comes to Trump, I am reminded less of the Christian Democrats than I am of the right-wing populist party 'Alternative für Deutschland'.

The experience of immigration connects Germany with the United States, even though the type of immigration differs. The overwhelming majority of immigrants to the US come from Latin America and Asia. And the overwhelming majority of Muslims migrating to the US come from Asia and belong to a large part to the American middle class. Unlike in Germany, a large proportion of Arab immigrants to the US are Christians. From personal experience I know that in the majority of mosques in the US the believers predominantly speak English with each other. That German becomes the language of communication in the majority of mosques in Germany is a goal for us, but it is not yet a reality. Our Muslim immigrants predominantly hail from Turkey and to a lesser degree from the Balkans, and recently in large numbers from the Middle East and Northern Africa.

Something that is often overlooked in the German debate is the fact that a large number – in some years around 50 per cent – of people immigrating to Germany come from other European countries. In the past that used to be Poland. Now, more and more immigrants stem from Romania and many from Bulgaria.

Compared to earlier decades the US may have lost some of its appeal. Yet as a society, it is still more appealing than the half-democratic or authoritarian societies of its rising competitors. Russian politics tries to promote the idea that Russian culture and values are superior to those of the US. But still, the children of the Russian elite are drawn to universities in the US or in the EU – far more than the other way around.

During the 1950s the American culture was a 'role model' for the majority of West Germans. Today, Germans feel more and more alienated when they read reports on political discussions in the US. Once, the political parties and debates in the US were regarded as pragmatic and characterised by the ability to find consensus. This has changed. Political debates in the US are being driven by more ideology and polarisation than previously. This polarisation is displayed in the media. Unlike in Germany with its primarily public TV and radio system, the different political orientations are reflected in different media, like Fox News and MSNBC, and not represented as a plurality of views in one TV or radio station. As a result of these structures in the media, the likelihood is reduced that an American is exposed to views which differ from their own views. This is another of many structural elements which support the growing polarisation in American political culture.

One can be rightfully sceptical whether it is possible to overcome this high level of polarisation in the political culture of the US. If not, the continuing polarisation in the US could radiate to Europe. There are already some indicators of a strong support for right-wing populist parties in Europe. They are very much homemade and their success oftentimes depends on different national causes. Yet victories for populism in the US would also negatively impact on the political culture in Europe.

The US and Europe do influence each other. They learn from each other – in good times and in bad. This will remain true for the future. In this process, we will make mistakes. We will argue with one another. We are not always good examples to each other. Yet I am certain that, just as in the last century, close transatlantic relations will have a positive impact on both sides of the Atlantic. They are a necessary, but not a sufficient precondition for a global order. I wish that these relations would continue to be a factor of peace, democracy and prosperity in a turbulent world.

INTRODUCTION

A Fragile Friendship: German–American Relations in the Twenty-First Century

KLAUS LARRES and RUTH WITTLINGER

INTRODUCTION

German–American relations are back in vogue. They have returned as an important relationship in international politics and have once again assumed their rightful place as a significant field of scholarship. And yet it was only a few years ago that German–American relations seemed to take second place to transatlantic relations in general and EU–US relations in particular. The advent of Donald Trump as US president in January 2017 has made all the difference. Trump's difficult personal relationship with German Chancellor Angela Merkel and his denigration of everything the western world, including the US itself, have stood for since 1949 have given a new significance to German–American relations in practice and theory. This special issue offers a much-needed analysis of empirical and conceptual aspects of German–American relations in the twenty-first century.

Throughout the cold war era, transatlantic relations were among the crucial pillars of global affairs. They provided long-term stability and reliability in a tumultuous and dangerous international environment. German–American relations, in turn, were an essential – if not the most essential – part of that complex relationship among the allies on both sides of the Atlantic. With hindsight it is obvious that the relative stability of global affairs in the years since World War II was caused by a number of factors such as the existence of the destructive potential of nuclear weapons and the bilateral nature of power politics, both of which contained any over-ambitious risk-taking in international politics. But there were also other less obvious factors that contributed to the maintenance of stability and calm. Mutually beneficial transatlantic and German–American relations were part and parcel of this.

Of course, there were still plenty of transatlantic crises. In fact one could argue that the history of transatlantic relations since the 1948 Marshall Plan and the creation of NATO a year later has been a succession of smaller and larger crises. But these manifold crises, we now know, were hardly ever of a fundamental or systemic nature. The departure of France from the military side of NATO in 1966 and the country's long-running battle with America for the soul of (western) Europe during President De Gaulle's long reign was the closest the alliance came to a possible break-up.

By contrast, German–American relations never looked into this kind of abyss. As no other European country, (West) Germany was fully aware of its utter dependence on the US. Initially this concerned both economic and security affairs, including the nuclear umbrella and political support offered by the US against the communist Soviet

Union. Throughout the cold war and beyond, with only the 1990s being an exception, Moscow was perceived as an aggressive, revanchist and anti-western power by almost all western countries. The era of détente in the 1970s, however, somewhat lessened the anxiety many in West Germany had about the Soviet Union. In particular since the *Ostpolitik* treaties of the early 1970s, the 1972 Berlin Four Power Agreement and the 1975 Helsinki conference, Europeans and in particular the Germans began to see the Soviet Union as a constructive and cooperative though still difficult economic and political partner. No longer was Moscow seen as posing a real risk to the European security set-up. This view was never shared on the other side of the Atlantic. Differing perceptions about the Soviet Union/Russia have consequently remained among the major bones of contention in German–American relations, well beyond the end of the cold war in 1989/90.

Naturally, the decreasing likelihood of a Soviet invasion of western Europe, at least as seen from Bonn, meant that West Germany's perceived dependence on the US receded from the early-to-mid 1970s. At the same time the US encountered its first significant economic problems. It was in 1971 that the now famously large US trade deficit commenced. In that year the US registered a small trade deficit for the first time in 100 years. It dramatically escalated in the following years and decades and undermined the standing of the US dollar as the provider of international monetary stability. Subsequently the US trade deficit with Europe's export champion Germany became particularly high and was only surpassed by the US deficits with China and Mexico.

Simultaneous European economic success as well as growing economic competition from countries such as Germany put transatlantic relations under stress during the final decades of the twentieth century. West Germany, the underling of the 1940s and 1950s, had become a serious economic competitor. On occasion the Bonn Republic even dared to challenge America's global wisdom in the security and political-economic sphere, as when sanctions imposed by the Reagan administration on the Soviet Union in the 1980s were much criticised. The famous shouting matches between US President Jimmy Carter and West German Chancellor Helmut Schmidt about both economic and military matters are also well known.

Still Germany and the US entered the new millennium in the glow of success regarding the intensified alliance between the two countries that had resulted from strong US support for German unification. President George H.W. Bush referred to Helmut Kohl's Germany as a 'partner in leadership' when addressing the German public in Mainz in May 1989. He thus called for a special German–American alliance even before the momentous events a few months later. Most analysts are agreed that Bush had not attempted to be merely polite. He was dead serious and saw Germany as Europe's only power with a possible future as an international player.

France, after all, had declined in international importance and its economic performance had begun to seriously lag behind Germany's. British Prime Minister Margaret Thatcher's nationalistic and less than visionary leadership in 1989/90 foreshadowed the increasing nationalisation and provincial small-mindedness of British foreign policy that ultimately culminated in the Brexit referendum of June 2016. This seemed to leave Germany as the only economically important European country with perhaps also a potential for global political if not military reach. While in this respect George H.W. Bush's expectation proved to be premature, his basic insight turned out to be right: without a strong and globally oriented Germany Europe would be unable to be an international player of significance.

Despite much encouragement from both the George W. Bush and the Obama administrations to become more involved in the world, by and large unified Germany has remained reluctant to act like a global power. Still, in particular in three areas, Berlin recently has begun to display a much greater international engagement than hitherto, often in cooperation with the US: (1) with regard to relations with China, a crucially important country for Germany's export industry, Berlin has assumed something approximating international leadership by, for instance, focusing on advancing German and EU investment relations and rule of law provisions with Beijing; (2) Germany has not shied away from contributing to western efforts to battle international terrorism: Berlin actively contributes to many global peace-keeping activities (Afghanistan, Sudan, Mali, for instance); (3) Germany has also grasped the mettle of international responsibility in terms of supporting and at times organising coordinated global environmental initiatives.

There is one more area in which Germany recently has begun to play a prominent role – but this time in opposition to the US. Since Donald Trump's inauguration and the implementation of some of his domestic and foreign policies that amount to undermining established western values, Germany's Chancellor Angela Merkel has become the spokesperson for defending and upholding the value system of the enlightenment. Berlin's political stance toward other countries that are also busily undermining democratic values, such as Turkey, Poland and Hungary, demonstrates that under Merkel's chancellorship, Germany does not shy away from defending core liberal values.

This has certainly given German–American relations a new and crucial importance and significance. Of course it has also led to a rather tense relationship with the Trump administration. The contributions to this special issue discuss a number of aspects of the current, much more fragile state of German–American relations from different perspectives.

The Preface to this special issue is provided by Dr Karsten Voigt, former Coordinator of German–North American Cooperation at the Foreign Office of Germany from 1999 to 2010. Voigt was a long-time senior SPD politician and member of the Bundestag from 1976 to 1998. Acknowledging that transatlantic relations are bound to change as the world around them changes, he points out that even though the two countries inspire each other, there is also a long history of the US criticising Europe and vice versa. Voigt also explains that the political cultures of Germany and the US have changed in recent years. Whereas the debates in the US have become more polarised, in Germany a high degree of consensus on many domestic and foreign policy issues has emerged, according to Voigt. The long-standing foreign policy expert concludes that whereas Germany has become more liberal over recent decades, in the US, after 9/11, the balance between security and freedom has shifted towards the former. Voigt, however, does not anticipate any lasting damage to German–American relations under Donald Trump's presidency. Whatever President Trump is saying and doing, argues Voigt, the societies on both sides of the Atlantic will remain connected through shared interests and values.

The schism that emerged between Germany and the US over the Iraq war is the subject of Dieter Dettke's contribution to this special issue. His article explores and explains Germany's pre-emptive 'No' to the war in Iraq and argues that this did not constitute a structural break of the relationship with the US, although for many its dramatic consequences appeared as a 'parting of ways' of two close allies. After the war in Kosovo and the German military contribution to the 'war on terror' in Afghanistan, there was no chance that the SPD/Green coalition would have been able to put together its own majority for an additional war effort in Iraq, according to Dettke. Opposing what was perceived as American unilateralism was popular and provided an opportunity to stand up to the Bush administration. It also offered Germany an opportunity to reclaim the right to national sovereignty in spite of its commitment to multilateralism. Dettke argues that this self-assertion was a new development in German foreign policy and that it is likely to characterise Germany's future actions. In Dettke's view, the arrival of the Trump administration in Washington and its challenge to the liberal world order America created after World War II could set the US and Germany on an even more profound collision course.

The article by Eric Langenbacher and Ruth Wittlinger examines recent dynamics of collective memory in German–American relations. After outlining the importance of history and memory for bilateral relations, they trace the evolution of collective memories of the two countries and identify the key filters through which they evaluate each other. The article then identifies the key characteristics of German–American relations since the advent of Donald Trump to the American presidency. This is followed by an analysis that examines Trump's use and abuse of history and memory and what that means for his foreign policy in general and German–American relations in particular. In view of the way Donald Trump has taken the subjective nature of collective memories to an extreme by largely disconnecting these memories from their historical context at the same time as extensively referencing his own history and experience, the authors conclude that we might be witnessing the end of memory, in particular the end of memory's direct impact on discourse and policy.

The contribution of Klaus Larres analyses the evolving relationship between Angela Merkel and Donald Trump since the latter moved into the Oval Office in January 2017. The article highlights both the more fundamental structural problems and the day-to-day political hurdles in German–American relations. It examines the way German Chancellor Merkel and US President Donald Trump did not get off to a good start, arguing that their relationship so far has been lukewarm at best. Trump's lack of support for democracy and the liberal world order as it was established by his predecessors in the mid-1940s deeply worries European politicians, according to Larres. In view of their own history and the expectation that Germany may have to step in and become the western world's leading defender of western values, most German policymakers, including the long-serving chancellor, are particularly annoyed and distraught about developments in the US.

Christian Schweiger's contribution to this special issue offers a comparative analysis of how the 2008–09 global financial crisis was perceived and how it has been addressed in Germany and the US. He argues that the financial crisis has significantly changed the parameters of the bilateral relations between Germany and the US in the context of wider EU–US transatlantic relations. In his view, the financial crisis has revealed systemic weaknesses in the governance of the euro zone and fundamental divisions between national governments in the EU on how these should be addressed.

In the context of German domestic politics the financial crisis has resulted in increasing scepticism towards US-style liberal market capitalism, according to Schweiger. He points out that Germany managed to maintain its strong economic standing under the adverse circumstances of the financial crisis. In his view, domestically the post-crisis political consensus has emphasised the strengths of Germany's coordinated market economy in contrast to the liberal model of the US.

Stephen Szabo's contribution examines the different approaches of Germany and the US towards Russia. According to him, Russia has been the focal point of the relationship since the end of World War II and has been both a wedge and a consolidator in German–American relations. The way the Soviet threat held Washington and Bonn together despite some important divergences in interests and policies during the cold war is remarkable, according to Szabo. He considers the close cooperation on Russia policy between President Obama and Chancellor Merkel over the Ukraine crisis a major achievement that was crucial in Germany's shaping of a unified EU sanctions regime. Despite this, however, the strategic glue which held the transatlantic relationship together weakened during the Obama years. Donald Trump's openly sympathetic attitude towards Putin and Russia poses an entirely new factor in the German–American approach towards Russia, according to Szabo. He expects the policy of sanctions and dialogue to continue to be at the centre of Germany's approach but questions whether this will be sustainable without American support. Most importantly, however, Szabo wonders whether Germany risks once again becoming the land between, this time not of its own volition but due to the policies of its closest allies.

Looking at immigration in particular, Joyce Mushaben examines to what degree the US and Germany have diverged in this policy area in recent years. Although both countries embraced restrictive practices during the 1980s, US law now concentrates on security first, relying heavily on exclusionary border control and 'national security' framing. Whereas the old FRG used complex, exclusionary laws to limit all forms of migration prior to 1998, united Germany has redefined itself as a 'welcoming culture', upholding human rights, open borders and pro-active resettlement policies. Focusing on the 'migration–security' nexus, the article compares fundamental changes in the admission and resettlement policies each now applies to persons seeking international protection. It reviews securitisation dynamics in the USA, followed by a treatment of developments at the European level that have conditioned reforms in Germany since 2005. The refusal of some EU member states to accept their fair share of the humanitarian burden arising from the 2015–16 refugee crisis has ironically contributed to Chancellor Angela Merkel's new image as Lady Liberty, according to Mushaben.

Dorle Hellmuth's contribution examines German and American responses to international terrorism from the end of the cold war to today. While terrorism was not a priority for much of the 1990s, the 9/11 attacks generated a long list of domestic counterterrorism measures in both countries. In the international realm, Germany and the United States did not agree on much, according to Hellmuth. The German government ended up participating in many US initiatives designed to hunt down al-Qaeda operatives and prevent them from launching another attack inside the United States, but German support was often secret and cooperation in the context of the 'war on terrorism' was considered controversial at home. When comparing German and US counterterrorism approaches, the article takes a unique approach by analysing how parliamentary and presidential government structures affected responses in terms of content and scope. Hellmuth's comparative analysis illustrates various similarities between German and US decision-making processes and argues that checks and balances continue to balance executive power gains in both countries.

Taken together, all the articles, as well as the introduction and Karsten Voigt's Preface, analyse the current state of German–American relations and highlight the serious and perhaps unprecedented challenges the two countries face at present.

DISCLOSURE STATEMENT

No potential conflict of interest was reported by the authors.

The 2003 Iraq War as a Turning Point in German–American Relations: Political Leadership and Alliance Cohesion[†]

DIETER DETTKE

The article explores and explains Germany's pre-emptive 'No' to the war in Iraq and argues that the 'No' was not a structural break in the relationship with the US, although for many its dramatic consequences appeared as a 'parting of ways' of two close allies. With the European Union deeply divided and the North Atlantic Treaty Organization split into two camps, the result was a profound disunity of the West. After the war in Kosovo and the German military contribution to the 'war on terror' in Afghanistan, there was no chance that the SPD/ Green coalition would have been able to put together its own majority for an additional war effort in Iraq. Opposing a perceived US unilateralism was popular and an opportunity to stand up to the Bush administration. On a more fundamental level, Germany reclaimed the right to national sovereignty in spite of its commitment to multilateralism. This self-assertion was a new development for German foreign policy and it will also characterise Germany's actions in the future. With the arrival of the Trump administration in Washington and its challenge to the liberal world order America created after World War II, the US and Germany could end up on an even more profound collision course.

INTRODUCTION

German opposition to the decision of the Bush administration to go to war in Iraq, disarm the country with military force and remove Saddam Hussein from power was a fundamental departure from the usually warm and close cooperation practised over the years in both countries. The consequences were dramatic. With the European Union deeply divided, the North Atlantic Treaty Organization (NATO) also ended up split into one group of member states supporting the war and another opposing the use of military force. A profound disunity of the West (see Habermas 2004) over the Iraq war dominated the public discourse. Large demonstrations against the war took place even in countries supporting it, such as Great Britain, Italy and Spain. The philosopher Jürgen Habermas and other German and European intellectuals saw the large European demonstrations on 15 February 2003 as the 'birth of a European public'

[†]The article draws on earlier works of the author on Germany's foreign and security policy in the context of the Iraq war. See in particular *Germany Says 'No'. The Iraq War and the Future of German Foreign and Security Policy* (Washington, DC: The Woodrow Wilson Center Press and Baltimore: The Johns Hopkins University Press, 2009).

(Habermas 2004)[1] and the manifestation of a European identity, emblematic of a Kantian peace against American unilateralism.

New for Germany and the United States was the bitterness accompanying the political disagreement. Mutual accusations and hard feelings were on public display on both sides and they appeared to amount to a 'parting of the ways' of two close allies (see Szabo 2004). The tensions boiled over in early 2003 after France and Germany in a highly public fashion declared their opposition to use military force in Iraq at a ceremony celebrating the 40th anniversary of the Franco-German Treaty at Versailles. The two countries agreed to establish common positions in the UN Security Council (UNSC) and to coordinate strategies vis-à-vis third countries.[2] Since France had veto power in the UN Security Council that signal was perceived as confrontational by the Bush administration. Secretary of Defense Donald Rumsfeld hit back only a day later, calling France and Germany representatives of 'old Europe' and singling out Germany as one of the few countries opposing the war in Iraq together with 'Cuba and Libya' (see Bernstein 2004). Former German foreign minister, Klaus Kinkel retorted that Rumsfeld had 'flipped out' (see Bernstein 2004). When Rumsfeld arrived in Munich for the annual Munich Security Conference from 7 to 9 February 2003, he was greeted with massive public protest. It was during that conference that German Foreign Minister Joschka Fischer famously remarked 'Excuse me, but I am not convinced' in response to the Rumsfeld speech trying to make the case for the use of force in Iraq (see Bernstein 2004).

While US public opinion was firmly behind the war, France and Germany were routinely ridiculed for their refusal to join the war effort against Saddam. The deep division of Europe over the war issue became obvious with the *Letter of the Eight* on 30 January 2003 in support of the US. It was signed by Jose Maria Aznar, Jose Manuel Barroso, Silvio Berlusconi, Tony Blair, Vaclav Havel, Peter Medgyessy, Leszek Miller and Anders Fogh Rasmussen.[3] The initiative was followed by the *Vilnius Letter* with a similar content and published on 5 February 2003 in conjunction with the presentation of Secretary of State Colin Powell at the UN Security Council making the case for war against Iraq. The letter was signed by the leaders of Albania, Bulgaria, Croatia, Czech Republic, Estonia, Latvia, Lithuania, Macedonia, Romania, Slovenia and Slovakia – all countries with aspirations to join NATO.[4] In the past, transatlantic differences of opinion on political, economic, security and defence policy issues were never entirely absent. The relationship was not conflict free, but leaders at the time, from John F. Kennedy and Willy Brandt to Helmut Kohl, Ronald Reagan, George H.W. Bush and Bill Clinton, were able to put common western security interests above personal reservations. Most importantly, the tone was different when disagreements were discussed publicly. The quality of leadership on both sides made it possible to overcome difficult moments in the relationship. Alliance cohesion prevailed over political differences.

A DEPARTURE FROM WESTERN SOLIDARITY

The Iraq crisis was different not only because the two leaders at the time, German Chancellor Gerhard Schröder and American President George W. Bush, were unable to establish a relationship of trust on a personal level. The war issue was more than a clash of personalities. In contrast to the persistent conviction of the

Bush administration that the German opposition to the war in Iraq was just electoral opportunism,[5] it is important to emphasise that much more profound and substantive differences dominated the decision-making process in Germany. It is true that in view of the 2002 federal elections, a pro-war position would have put the majority of the SPD/Green coalition in the Bundestag in jeopardy. Given the strong pacifist mood of the country, a pro-war position of the governing coalition would have given the far left PDS a good chance to take votes away from the SPD and the Green Party. Schröder and Fischer were certainly aware of the electoral risks involved in supporting the Bush administration. They decided to take a clear position of 'No' in the electoral campaign not only in the interest of seeking an electoral advantage.

Germany had a dual Iraq policy: one at home publicly opposing the war and another, in fact, supporting the war as part of the 'war on terror'. Such a policy does not reflect a structural break of German–US relations. German logistical support and the use of German and European infrastructure for American military operations were critical to the US military efforts. Intelligence cooperation continued uninterrupted and Germans even provided Saddam's secret defence plans of Baghdad, thereby facilitating the United States Central Command's (CENTCOM) invasion (see Dettke 2009, 11). The Bundeswehr took over the protection of American barracks and the equipment to detect weapons of mass destruction (WMD) remained in Kuwait throughout the war. As *New York Times* reporter Michael Gordon and General Bernard Trainor pointed out, 'Germans were safeguarding the waterways the United States was using to build up its forces in the Persian Gulf' (see Gordon and Trainor 2006, 123).

Any attempt at avoiding a clear position would have been unsustainable given the huge impact of the war on German public opinion. Schröder and Fischer came to the sober conclusion that after Kosovo and Afghanistan they would be unable to secure a majority for another war. They were convinced that in contrast to the cases of Kosovo and Afghanistan, opposition to the use of force in Iraq was the right political decision. With regard to the war in Iraq, a more fundamental conflict between different world order concepts in the US and Germany emerged. For Schröder and Fischer, the perceived unilateralism of the Bush administration was unacceptable.[6] The 'monopoly of force' of the United Nations was part of the 1998 Coalition Agreement of the SPD and the Green Party that served as a policy platform for the two parties, and it was binding. They had to defend this principle. But in the end, Schröder insisted on his 'No' to the war in Iraq even if the UN Security Council had supported the use of military force against Iraq.[7] This was not compatible with the commitment to multilateralism the coalition claimed to have adopted. In essence, Germany reclaimed the right to national sovereignty in spite of its commitment to multilateralism. Schröder's assertion on 13 September 2002 that 'on existential questions of the German nation, decisions are only made in Berlin and nowhere else' (see Schöllgen 2015, 668) confirms that, for Germany, the opposition to war was not primarily an issue for the 'power of peace' that Germany wanted to be. It was an issue of national interest and self-assertion. Former Chancellor Helmut Schmidt supported exactly that aspect of Schröder's Iraq policy, saying that with the decision to oppose a war in Iraq Germany liberated itself from American tutelage (see Schöllgen 2015, 668). The historian and biographer of Gerhard Schröder, Gregor Schöllgen concluded correctly that Germany's opposition to the Iraq war was precisely the moment when the country found its true self again (see Schöllgen 2004, 131–157).

More than any other chancellor of Germany in the past, Schröder moved Germany beyond multilateralism, a culture of restraint and reliance on the civilian power paradigm, towards a culture of realpolitik and the resolute pursuit of national interests. Germany was in the chair of the UN Security Council during the critical month of decision making on Iraq in February 2003. Actively working against the US government, which was seeking to obtain the support of the UN Security Council for invading Iraq, was unmistakably an act of balancing US power against a perceived American unilateralism. This can only be explained as a result of the turn to realpolitik in pursuit of German national interests. It was unexpected that a left-of-centre Red/Green coalition set the example of claiming the right to national sovereignty within an institution of multilateralism. Acting as a normal power and not only as a civilian power will also characterise German foreign policy in the future, including the use of force and the willingness to assert the country's national interest using its political, economic and military capabilities less reluctantly. This does not necessarily mean a rejection of multilateralism as a policy principle for Germany in general. It does mean, however, that the country will not accept multilateral decisions against its will. Given Germany's economic and political interdependence, the country will always put a premium on acting in the spirit of multilateralism, in particular on the basis of European integration. But there is also a pattern of bilateralism on the global level, in particular bilateralism with great powers.

With the arrival of the Trump administration in Washington, great power bilateralism will come into play more frequently and systematically. For German/American relations this can lead to close cooperation as well as conflict. Germany's behaviour in the case of Iraq shows that alliance cohesion of the kind both countries cultivated during the cold war will no longer remain the norm. Collision on the basis of common values is quite possible in the future. But collision is not the only future because there is still more that unites the two countries than divides them.

First and foremost, there is a common value basis. Today, Germany's identity as a nation is that of a modern society based on the universal values of democracy, freedom, human rights and the dignity of every individual. As long as this is shared with the United States, cooperation comes first, and national independence will only be stressed as necessary to preserve the country's identity. If America under the leadership of President Donald Trump moves in the direction of intrinsic nationalism and protectionism and opposes the liberal world order the US created after World War II, Germany, for reasons of its own identity as a nation based on universal values, will be on a collision course with an American government that no longer stands for universal values, free trade, openness and global markets.

For realists, it should not come as a surprise that once the most critical internal difficulties of uniting East and West Germany were overcome, the country would again reassert itself on the international level. Shortly after German unification Kenneth Waltz predicted that 'Germans may ultimately find that reunification and the renewed life of a great power are more invigorating than the struggles, complications and compromises that come during, and would come after, the uniting of Western Europe' (see Waltz 1993, 70). Even before unification one could observe a gradual evolution of

15

German foreign policy from putting multilateralism, European integration and alliance cohesion first to a more independent course of action. As a result of its growing economic weight in Europe and its export orientation, Germany, as a country on a non-military trajectory, grew into a role perception of greater freedom and room for political manoeuvre beyond European integration and alliances. Germany evolved into a geo-economic power (see Kundnani 2011). A dual nature of the pattern of foreign policy emerged. European integration, the Western alliance and multilateralism were no longer the only guiding principles of foreign policy. A distinct form of economic bilateralism and a focus on political great power partnerships also emerged, in particular with Russia and China. With more than 70 per cent of German exports going to European markets, Europe was certainly the crucial destination and will remain the lifeline for the German economy. Given the much faster growth rates of 'threshold countries', in particular the BRICS (Brazil, Russia, India, China and South Africa) a distinct political and economic bilateralism also became stronger (see Dettke 2009, 198). China and Russia are examples of a new pattern of bilateral partnerships.

A NEW GENERATION OF LEADERSHIP IN GERMANY

When the SPD and the Green Party won the 1998 national elections and Gerhard Schröder and Joschka Fischer took over power from Chancellor Kohl, the united Germany was a different country and the air was no longer filled with the aura of the 'end of history' (see Fukuyama 1989). Ethnic and religious conflict had returned in the Balkans throughout the 1990s, and the new German government, intent on economic reform and ecological renewal, was confronted with the looming war in Kosovo. Promising continuity of foreign policy in the electoral campaign, this included the possible use of force in the Kosovo conflict already anticipated by the Kohl government. For the new German government this could not have come at a more inconvenient time. Its primarily domestic reform programme was already overshadowed by war before it started. The SPD and the Green Party had strong pacifist wings in their rank and file and the use of military force in general was a delicate issue in German public opinion. Germany saw itself as a power of peace (*Friedensmacht*) and its constitution (Basic Law Article 26) banned wars of aggression and even actions designed to 'disturb the peaceful coexistence of countries'. Article 2 of the so called Two plus Four Treaty on Germany of 12 September 1990 also included the commitment of the two German states that 'from German soil only peace will emanate'.

The new generation of leadership in Germany was determined to begin a profound renewal of the country after 16 years under the leadership of Helmut Kohl. More self-confident than their parents, the 1968 generation felt quite comfortable standing up to America over issues such as the war in Vietnam, tolerating authoritarian regimes and undermining democratic governments of the left in Central and Latin America.[8] For the Red/Green coalition, moving the capital to Berlin thus also became the symbol of a departure into the future and an opportunity to set new twenty-first century benchmarks. In his first government declaration as chancellor on 10 November 1998,[9] Schröder interpreted the change of government also as a generational change and as the expression of the greater democratic self-confidence of a grown-up nation based on universal values. More importantly, the substance of the Red–Green policy programme

16

was formulated when Bill Clinton was still in power in the United States and from the beginning, Schröder emphasised the affinity of his economic and political reform programme with the Third Way initiative launched by Bill Clinton and Tony Blair.

Hardly any domestic or foreign policy programme of the Clinton administration remained unscathed when George W. Bush came to power in Washington. The Third Way initiative disappeared from the agenda as well as many foreign policy initiatives of the Clinton administration. Starting all over again with the Bush administration was difficult between two governments with very different policy agendas. Worse, given the new US administration's opposition to the Kyoto Climate Agreement, the two governments found themselves on a collision course on the issue of environmental policy which was the new leitmotif of German policy, a matter of identity and therefore untouchable. There was little or no room for compromise. The Bush administration made clear from the beginning that the US would officially withdraw from Kyoto.

When Chancellor Schröder visited Washington for his first meeting with President Bush, the two sides published a joint declaration called 'Vision for the 21st Century'.[10] The document emphasised continuity, but for the first time in the history of German–American relations, a disagreement about a major policy issue – climate protection – was put into the official text. There was no way to paper over political differences or simply not to mention the issue at all – the usual diplomatic way of handling controversial issues. The Red/Green coalition wanted the disagreement to be official, not only as a demonstration of its firm stand in all environmental matters, but also as an opportunity to show a new German assertiveness, courage and independence. Not doing so, Schröder and Fischer believed, would have created the impression of weakness at home. Compromising on a crucial issue for the new government would have undermined the legitimacy of the Red–Green programme. Red–Green would have lost its identity by siding or even compromising with the Bush administration on such a central issue of its policy platform. To stand firm in opposition to the US government, therefore, was a welcome opportunity to demonstrate strength of leadership to the domestic audience.

SCHRÖDER AND BUSH

The SPD and Greens had been in power for more than two years when George W. Bush became president of the United States. Schröder had already hosted European summits and a G-7 meeting and had demonstrated courage when faced with difficult decisions and opposition at home. He and Foreign Minister Joschka Fischer felt entitled to stand up for their record even in disagreement with the new US government. Schröder and Bush were different in almost every respect, but also had things in common, including their political experience on the state level before reaching the highest national office. Their strong willpower pushed them apart but also generated respect for each other. They were of the same baby boom generation but could not have been more different in their views about the meaning of 1968 and the tumultuous years of the Vietnam era. What Schröder and Fischer, who were actively involved in the revolutionary movement of the 1960s, perceived as liberating progress was seen as a dangerous aberration by George W. Bush and his cabinet members.

Schröder and Fischer came from very modest family backgrounds. Schröder experienced real poverty growing up. He had to fight his way to a university education and became a lawyer first before he entered politics. His self-made success story differs hugely from the privileged family background of George W. Bush, who floundered directionless for many years of his adult life. Only as a married man did he find his moorings as a born-again Christian (see in particular Smith (2016)). Both men were extremely strong-willed and saw compromising as a sign of weakness and lack of determination. Schröder's strong sense of being equal – or, as he often mentioned, able to 'interact on the same eye level' (see Dettke 2009, 151) – also gave him the backbone to say 'No' if he saw German national interests at risk. In spite of his left-wing past in the SPD youth movement, he was a pragmatist to the core and capable of showing flexibility. He was not afraid of changing his positions; and was free of fear in office as well as in his turbulent private life. His curriculum vita alone differed dramatically from that of George W. Bush and these differences inevitably showed up in their public roles and policies.

KOSOVO AND THE LIMITS OF CIVILIAN POWER

The difficulties of decision making in the war in Kosovo was the first lesson about the difference between running for office and being in office. They influenced Schröder's actions during the Iraq crisis in 2002 and 2003. He and Fischer saw Germany foremost as a civilian power and, in theory, one could interpret the 'No' to the Iraq war as an outflow of Germany's self-image as a *civilian power*.[11] The concept included primarily rules and principles designed to restrict the use of force de facto to self-defence and had strong backing among the general public. Its motto was 'never again, never alone and politics before force', and it reinforced the 'culture of restraint' that became a crucial characteristic of Germany's behaviour after World War II (see Maull 2014). The preference for civilian power also underlined that post-war Germany was not a 'normal power' in the sense that its primary goal as a nation was not only the 'pursuit of power' as posited by scholars in the tradition of realism (e.g. Mearsheimer 2001, 3). In fact, Chancellor Kohl's ultimate goal of unification was precisely this: to become a 'normal country' (see the article by Vinocur (1993)).

German actions during the Balkan wars demonstrate that step by step Germany began to act as a normal country and as a great power in Europe not only committed to the tradition of restraint. The commitment to multilateralism did not prevent the country from acting alone with regard to the recognition of Croatia and Slovenia as independent states. In the case of Kosovo, sticking with the rules and principles of the civilian power paradigm would have led the country into a morally untenable position of standing by while thousands were being raped and killed. The tragedy of Sebrenica[12] (Bosnia) in 1995, where up to 8000 boys and men were slain by Bosnian Serb forces, the worst mass murder in Europe since World War II, shook up the conscience of most Europeans.

Here and elsewhere an early use of force could have saved lives. Excluding the use of force a priori also weakened diplomacy. When diplomacy no longer generates results, the use of force cannot be excluded without encountering a moral dilemma: either just stand by while civilians are being killed by armed forces or use force to stop a potential genocide. Serbia's strategy of ethnic cleansing could have led to a bloodbath. More than 300,000 people had to flee when Serbian security forces used military force against the civilian population of Kosovo. When coercive diplomacy in the case of Kosovo did not generate results, the use of force became the last resort to stop the brutal ethnic cleansing by Serbian military forces. In spite of the fact that 90 per cent of the population of Kosovo were Albanian Muslims, Milosevic used a strategy of 'Serbianisation'.[13]

The SPD/Green coalition, in power from November 1998, less than six months later managed to obtain a majority in parliament for joining NATO in a military campaign in Kosovo. The predominantly anti-war public opinion turned out not to be unshakable. In fact, German public opinion, while opposing the use of ground forces, supported participation in NATO air strikes (see Friedrich 2000, 53). But it took an enormous amount of political capital to convince the public, and even more effort to obtain a majority for military action from a political party that, to a large part, grew out of the pacifist movement of the early 1980s. The SPD/Green coalition even acted in contrast to a condition almost edged in stone for the participation of German armed forces in NATO military operations: not to use force without the support of the UN Security Council. When diplomacy did not generate results, the country was able to join NATO in a military campaign beyond the boundaries of NATO, without a UN mandate and in spite of a strong opposition within the rank and file of the Green Party as well as the SPD.

9/11 AND THE CHALLENGE OF TERRORISM

Two years after Kosovo the terrorist attacks on the United States of 11 September 2001 shocked the entire world and the Red/Green coalition demonstrated again that a new realism was now guiding German foreign and security policy. On the day 9/11 happened the world was firmly on America's side and the French newspaper *Le Monde* said it best in its headline 'we are all Americans' now.[14] Chancellor Schröder interpreted 9/11 as a civilisational breach and promised 'unrestricted solidarity' with the United States.[15] At the time he and Prime Minister Blair as well as President Bush used similar language with regard to the 9/11 attacks as not only an attack on the US but the entire civilised world.

However, whereas Great Britain under the leadership of Blair stood also 'shoulder to shoulder' with the Bush administration when the invasion of Afghanistan began on 7 October 2001,[16] the German government needed time to secure the necessary majority in the Bundestag for any military engagement. The prospect of war in Iraq pushed the differences between Germany and Great Britain into the open. During his visit with President Bush in Crawford, Texas, in April 2002 Blair promised that 'Britain will be at America's side',[17] and on 28 July 2002, while suggesting to Bush that he needed to seek UN approval for any military action against Iraq, sent a note to President Bush saying that 'I will be with you, whatever'.[18] By siding completely with the Bush administration, Great Britain chose to try to influence the American decision-making process towards multilateralism, while in Germany opposition to the war in Afghanistan became stronger and stronger. Great Britain was 'bandwaggoning' in the language of realism whereas Germany began to 'balance' American power and a perceived US unilateralism.

When President Bush visited Berlin in May 2002, the issue of participating militarily in Iraq was still left open. George W. Bush declared that he had no war plans on his desk, but that the US had all the means at its disposal to deal with Saddam Hussein. He promised further consultations. In his statement Schröder said that 'should Iraq like Afghanistan harbour al-Qaeda fighters, we will be a reliable partner of the United States' (on the meeting see Schröder (2006, 198)). But hidden in these public pronouncements was a fundamental misperception. George W. Bush thought that Schröder would ultimately support the US war effort and he and Vice President Cheney were convinced that Iraq was part of a terrorist network (see Bush 2010, 234). Schröder meant that he would support military action against Iraq only if Iraq was involved in terrorism. But on the basis of his own intelligence and expert assessment, he had no evidence of an Iraqi terrorist connection. He was willing to support America in the fight against terrorism without any restriction and held that line against all opposition, including Defence Minister Peter Struck of his own party. But he was also determined not to go beyond the Afghanistan commitment by including other countries unrelated to terrorism.

As a result, German and American foreign and security policies diverged. Europe never accepted the notion that classical war could be an appropriate concept in the fight against terrorism. It was Blair who convinced George W. Bush to seek the approval of the UN Security Council before using military force. At first, decision making in the UN Security Council went smoothly. After the speech of the president at the UN in September 2002, the UN Security Council followed up with concrete action. UN Security Council Resolution 1441 of 8 November 2002 was adopted unanimously. Iraq was offered a final opportunity to comply with its disarmament obligations. Weapons inspectors returned and delivered several reports, the last before the war on 7 March 2003. At that point, Hans Blix and Mohamed ElBaradei, who were in charge of the inspection process, emphasised that the inspections needed more time, weeks or months, not years. However, the Bush administration argued that Iraq was in material breach of Resolution 1441 and demanded that the Security Council had to secure international peace and security. When President Chirac made clear that France and also Russia would veto any resolution implying military action, the US administration realised that there was no way to secure UNSC support. Instead, a meeting in the Azores on 16 March with Blair, Aznar and Barroso was convened to declare that diplomacy had run its course. Iraq was given an ultimatum for full compliance until 17 March. On 20 March, the war began.

THE GERMAN WAY

Schröder and Fischer were convinced that Germany had to be part of the fight against international terrorism in spite of the public's uneasiness about an additional military commitment. They came to the conclusion that not to follow up on Article 5 of the NATO treaty commitment and also not to respect UN Security Council decisions would amount to an 'organized lack of responsibility' (see Schröder 2006, 177). But resistance to the use of force in both parties was so massive that there was a real danger of failing to obtain a majority. In the end Schröder had to put his office on the line in order to secure a majority of the Red/Green coalition in the Bundestag for a German military contribution to the war in Afghanistan. He combined the German military aid package for Afghanistan with a vote of confidence according to Article 68 of the Basic Law and won the necessary majority for supporting the war. But it was by only one vote more than required that Schröder and Fischer managed to secure Germany's participation in Operation Enduring Freedom (OEF). One sentence in the text of the military mandate of the Bundestag suggested that Germany would not allow an enlargement of the mandate to include military action against any state other than Afghanistan: 'German military forces will participate in possible military deployments against international terrorism in other states than Afghanistan only with the consent of the respective government'.[19] Such a restriction of the mandate can only be explained as a reaction to the early debate about a possible military action against Iraq in the US. But enlarging the war on terror to include Iraq was exactly what Germany wanted to avoid when the Red/Green coalition decided to support the United States in Afghanistan.

Schröder did not hesitate to lend his full political and also – as much as he was able – military support to combating international terrorism. The use of force against Iraq was different. Germany never accepted the view that Iraq was involved in terrorism. The country had intelligence sources and information about the region for its own independent assessment. The 'German Way' that Schröder famously claimed for his programme of reform and renewal in his speech opening the 2002 electoral campaign on 5 August in Hannover was meant to be different from the American social and economic model. It was not the pattern of a new German 'Sonderweg' away from the West like after World War I. It was an independent 'German Way' within the West together with France against war.

The US determination to go to war against Iraq was already openly discussed from day one after 11 September 2001. The strongest arguments in favour of military action against Iraq immediately after 9/11 came from Vice President Cheney. He held the view that after 9/11, America had to worry about Iraq as a nexus between terrorism and weapons of mass destruction (see Cheney with Cheney 2011, 369). The Bush administration, Cheney wrote, firmly believed a state had to be behind the sophisticated 9/11 terrorist attacks. 'When we looked around the world in those first months after 9/11, there was no place more likely to be a nexus between terrorism and WMD capability than Saddam Hussein's Iraq' (see Cheney with Cheney 2011, 369). George W. Bush confirmed the view that the Iraq war had its roots in the 11 September 2001 terrorist attacks. In his memoir he wrote that the 'lesson of 9/11 was that if we waited for a danger to fully materialize, we would have waited too long. I reached a decision: We would confront the threat from Iraq, one way or another' (Bush 2010, 229).

The SPD/Green coalition learned from the visit of Foreign Minister Fischer to Washington on 18 and 19 September 2001 that the debate in Washington clearly went in the direction of an enlargement of the 'war on terror', possibly including Iraq as a target. He learned from his Pentagon interlocutors that there were up to 60 states supporting terrorism and that the United States would go after all of them (see Fischer 2007, 15). Fischer's impression after the visit alarmed the German government. He believed that the US reaction to 9/11 might lead to a 'new world war' (see Fischer 2007, 15). The result of his visit was that Chancellor Schröder began to add limits and a warning to his earlier commitment of 'unrestricted solidarity'. In his speech in the Bundestag on 19 September 2001 on his government's strategy against international terrorism, the chancellor already reflected the concern of his foreign minister when he repeated his commitment to 'unrestricted solidarity' with the United States but added that 'Germany is prepared to take risks, including military risks, but not to engage in adventures'.[20]

Germany never accepted the view that Iraq represented a case for the nexus between terrorism and weapons of mass destruction. With a majority of American public opinion in favour of taking military action, the Bush administration felt that in view of the mid-term elections in the US in November 2002, determination to go to war, if necessary, would help the White House to secure a Republican majority in the House and in the Senate. Most Democrats, too, supported a war if necessary. When President Bush sought congressional support for his plans against Iraq in October 2002, he received an overwhelming majority in the Senate of 77 to 23, including 29 Democratic senators in favour. On the House side 296 voted in favour and 133 against.[21]

In his interview with *The New York Times* on 5 September 2002 Schröder tried to push back against arguments for the war put forward by Vice President Cheney in his speech at the Veterans of Foreign Wars National Convention on 26 August 2002.[22] In essence, Cheney pointed out that relying on UN inspections would only provide false comfort. Regime change was in America's national interest and that could only be achieved by pre-emptive military action. Saddam would be able to acquire nuclear weapons within a year and 'Armed with weapons of mass destruction and sitting on top of 10% of the world's oil reserves' – he argued – 'Saddam could seek dominance of the entire Middle East and subject other countries, including the US, to nuclear blackmail' (see *The Iraq Papers* 2010). Schröder felt that Cheney's preference for pre-emptive action without relying on the UN inspection process would undermine the commitment of the governing coalition to strengthen the monopoly of the UN Security Council. So he warned against going to war irrespective of the results of the UN inspections. Without more progress in Afghanistan a military intervention would be counterproductive to the fight against al-Qaeda and international terrorism which was not finished. His arguments against a war with Iraq, he believed, were so strong that he would oppose one 'even if the Security Council approved' (see Erlanger 2002).

Many German observers who also opposed a war against Iraq felt that Schröder went too far by arguing that he would not even respect a Security Council decision in favour of war. In Schröder's logic, accepting a Security Council decision even before such a decision was made would undercut his anti-war policy and thus also his leadership. He felt that staying the course was necessary for him as chancellor and as party leader. But his position was not universally shared by the Green Party and Joschka Fischer. In contrast to Schröder, Fischer was willing to live with a majority of the Bundestag provided not only by the Red/Green coalition but also by votes from the CDU/CSU opposition. Schröder was convinced that a majority in parliament was indispensable for the survival of the coalition.

It is quite possible that the Red/Green coalition could have collapsed under the weight of the chancellor's position. Schröder wrote in his memoirs that he would have stepped down as chancellor rather than agree to an invasion (see Schröder 2006, 231). Fischer, on the other hand, maintained that he would have stepped down as foreign minister rather than risk the isolation of Germany in the Security Council.[23] According to Fischer, the potential French and Russian veto saved the Red/Green coalition from collapsing if the United States had been able to secure a majority in the UN Security Council for invading.

Now that more confidential information is accessible, one also has to conclude that the anticipated French and Russian veto in the UN Security Council saved the United Nations from losing credibility. Had the UNSC approved the use of force without being able to show the presence of weapons of mass destruction, the UN system would have been plunged into disrepute for a long time to come. The National Intelligence Estimate (NIE) of October 2002, on which the US decision to go to war was based, concluded that with regard to Saddam's pursuit of nuclear weapons 'we assess that Saddam does not *yet* have nuclear weapons or sufficient material to make any, he remains intent on acquiring them'.[24] The estimate of the State Department's intelligence arm (INR) was even more cautious than the NIE. In that same document INR concluded that 'The activities that we have detected do not, however, add up to a compelling case that Iraq is currently pursuing what INR would consider to be an integrated and comprehensive approach to acquire nuclear weapons'.[25] And yet Secretary of State Condoleezza Rice argued in the run-up to the war that 'we don't want the smoking gun to be a mushroom cloud',[26] as if a nuclear attack by Saddam was imminent. Based on its own documents, the US government must have known before 20 March 2003, when the war began, that there were no nuclear weapons.[27] The Bush administration obviously feared that the still ongoing UN inspection process in Iraq would lead to exactly that conclusion and that, therefore, the entire official rationale for going to war against Iraq would collapse. In legal terms, the best one could say about acting pre-emptively against Iraq is that it was a case of putative self-defence. It turned out that the need for pre-emption was fabricated along the line of arguments put forward by Vice President Cheney that 'the risks of inaction are far greater than the risk of action'.[28]

CONCLUSION

Most of those who supported the war in Iraq in 2003 would admit today that the decision to invade Iraq, occupy the country and remove Saddam Hussein from power was the wrong answer to the shaken confidence in America's security after the 2001 terrorist attacks. One important witness is Former Secretary of State Colin Powell, who admitted that his 5 February 2003 presentation at the United Nations making the case for war had been a mistake (see Powell with Koltz 2012, 217–224). The official rationale for the necessity to use military force against Iraq was alleged evidence that Saddam Hussein had WMD and was in the process of developing more, including nuclear weapons. This turned out to be without substance. There were no weapons of mass destruction and in particular no nuclear weapons, even after several US-led inspections and full access to potential weapon sites. Since the country was under occupation, US weapons inspectors had full access to any site at any time. Without weapons of mass destruction, former Secretary of State Colin Powell concluded, there would not have been war (see Powell with Koltz 2012, 217–224).

With US$1.4 trillion in long-term costs until 2017, according to the Congressional Budget Office,[29] and other estimates of up to more than $3 trillion, the war in Iraq was one of the costliest – second only to World War II – and together with Afghanistan the longest war in US history,[30] longer than the Vietnam War or World War II. America's reputation as a guarantor of international law was severely damaged and, as a result, America's normative authority is now compromised for a long time to come. Even eight years after the George W. Bush presidency, the Obama administration was not entirely successful undoing the damage caused by America's use of force in the Middle East. Concerns even increased after Donald Trump was elected president. The message of nationalism, protectionism and anti-multilateralism emanating from the White House today is a fundamental challenge for the liberal world order created by the US after World War II. More importantly, since the beginning of the wars in Afghanistan and Iraq a process of normalisation of war is unmistakable, and under the leadership of Donald Trump the use of force instead of diplomacy and conflict management appears to have increased, as the most recent air strikes in Yemen, Syria and Afghanistan have shown. As a result of efforts of the Trump administration to emphasise linkages between terrorism and Islam, visible in a more active and lethal role of the military against the Islamic State of Iraq and Syria (ISIS) as well as with measures such as a proposed travel ban exclusively for Islamic countries, the level of violence in the fight against terrorism can only increase and trigger even more hostility against the West.

While congratulating Donald Trump on his election,[31] Chancellor Merkel also indicated that future cooperation between Germany and the US should be based on shared values, in particular 'democracy, freedom, respect for the right and the dignity of the human being independent of origin, colour of skin, religion, gender, sexual orientation and political conviction'.[32] If America would indeed move away from the traditional support for European integration and NATO, opposing the principles of multilateralism and diplomacy first, Germany, for reasons of its identity as a modern society committed to universal values and a peaceful world order based on laws – not sheer power – would end up on a collision course with America. Trust in US leadership since Trump became president has declined dramatically.

More importantly, if Europe and America are on a collision course, the West will be greatly weakened economically and politically. The liberal world order shaped by the US after World War II has been extremely successful in creating economic growth, reducing poverty and improving the living standards of millions of people. The transatlantic marketplace is the largest and the wealthiest in the world, generating a total of $5.5 trillion in sales and employing 15 million people on both sides of the Atlantic (see Wayne and Hamilton 2017). Without Europe, America can hardly be first in any meaningful way. On a collision course, the US and Europe would lose their growth potential and their capacity to build peace would decline at a time when the world 'more than ever needs the liberal democratic values of Europe'.[33] EU Commission President Jean-Claude Juncker even warned that 'a break-up of the EU could trigger war in the western Balkans'.[34] It will take great leadership qualities to avoid such a development.

DISCLOSURE STATEMENT

No potential conflict of interest was reported by the author.

NOTES

1. See in particular in that volume the common appeal of Jürgen Habermas and Jacques Derrida, 'Der 15. Februar oder: Was die Europäer verbindet', pp.43–51.
2. See the text of the Joint Franco German Declaration, 22 Jan. 2003, available from http://www.leforum. de/de/de-traite-declcommune03.htm (accessed 8 June 2017).
3. See the text of the letter published by the BBC, available from http://news.bbc.co.uk/2/hi/europe/ 2708877.stm (accessed 8 June 2017).
4. See the *EU Observer*, 6 Feb. 2003, available from https://euobserver.com/enlargement/9269 (accessed 8 June 2017).
5. George W. Bush interpreted Schröder's position as driven by the 2002 German elections. See Bush (2010, 234).
6. See in particular the speech of Gerhard Schröder opening the final phase of the 2002 electoral campaign in Hannover, 5 Aug. 2002.
7. See the speech of Gerhard Schröder opening the 2002 electoral campaign in Hannover, 5 Aug. 2002.
8. Henry Kissinger delivered a strong criticism of the new political generation in Germany. See his article on 'The "Made in Berlin" Generation' in the *Washington Post*, 30 Oct. 2002, available from https:// www.washingtonpost.com/archive/opinions/2002/10/30/the-made-in-berlin-generation/09ea8c75-f82f-4139-ae60-9f5e665d131c/?utm_term=.087f67f90ad1 (accessed 8 June 2017).
9. See the text available from http://dip21.bundestag.de/dip21/btp/14/14003.pdf (accessed 8 June 2017).
10. See detailed information about the declaration in Dettke (2009, 148/149).
11. The most important pioneering contributions on civilian power came from François Duchéne, a former director of the International Institute for Strategic Studies in London. A comprehensive publication is Kohnstamm and Kohnstamm (1973). It includes an article by François Duchéne. In Germany Hanns Maull and his research colleagues at Trier University contributed the best studies on the role of civilian power for German foreign policy. See in particular Maull and Harnisch (2001).
12. See in particular the information provided by *Gendercide*, available at http://www.gendercide.org/case_ srebrenica.html (accessed 8 June 2017).
13. On the strategy of Serbianisation see Gow (2003, 57).
14. 'Nous sommes tous Americains' read the front page headline of *Le Monde*, 12 Sept. 2001.
15. Bundeskanzler Gerhard Schröder in his formal government declaration in the Bundestag on 12 Sept. 2001. See Deutscher Bundestag, 14. Wahlperiode, Plenarprotokoll 14/186, 12 Sept. 2001.
16. Prime Mister Blair on 12 Sept. 2001 as quoted in the *Report of the Iraq Inquiry* (Chilcot Report), Executive Summary (Crown Copyright, 2016) Number 48, p.10.
17. Text of the speech available from https://www.theguardian.com/politics/2002/apr/08/foreignpolicy.iraq (accessed 8 June 2017).
18. The note to President Bush of 28 July 2002 is mentioned in the Chilcot Report, number 94, p.15.
19. See the text of the mandate Deutscher Bundestag, Drucksache 14/7296, 14. Wahlperiode, 7 Nov. 2001, available from http://dip21.bundestag.de/dip21/btd/14/072/1407296.pdf (accessed 8 June 2017).
20. See the text of the speech of the Chancellor in the Bundestag, Deutscher Bundestag, Plenarprotokoll 14/ 187, 187. Sitzung, 19 Sept. 2001.
21. See Text of the Joint Resolution to Authorize the Use of United States Armed Forces Against Iraq Enacted and Signed by the President, 16 Oct. 2002, 107th Congress, Public Law 243. Vote results

available from http://usiraq.procon.org/view.additional-resource.php?resourceID=001987 (accessed 8 June 2017).
22. See the text of the vice president's speech at the Veterans of Foreign Wars 103rd National Convention, *The Iraq Papers* (2010).
23. See the interview with *Der Spiegel*, 1 Oct. 2007, pp.56–57.
24. See the full text of the National Intelligence Estimate of October 2002, released 2014/12/09 CO1030196.
25. Ibid.
26. Condoleezza Rice in an interview with Wolf Blitzer on CNN on 10 Jan. 2003, available from http://www.cnn.com/2003/US/01/10/wbr.smoking.gun/ (accessed 10 Feb. 2017).
27. This assessment is also shared by Bruce Riedel, a high-ranking former US intelligence official in an interview with the author on 22 March 2017 at the Brookings Institution in Washington, DC.
28. See the text of the speech by Vice President Cheney at Veterans of Foreign Wars 103rd National Convention.
29. As reported by Reuters, 24 Oct. 2007, available from http://www.reuters.com/article/us-iraq-usa-funding-idUSN2450753720071024 (accessed 8 June 2017).
30. For additional much higher estimates see *The Balance*, 17 Jan. 2017, available from https://www.thebalance.com/cost-of-iraq-war-timeline-economic-impact-3306301, and Qiu (2016).
31. See the text of Merkel's *Glueckwunsch Telegramm und Statement fuer die Presse*, 9 Nov. 2016, available from https://www.bundesregierung.de/Content/DE/Artikel/2016/11/2016-11-09-merkel-zu-us-wahl-trump.html (accessed 8 June 2017).
32. Ibid.
33. This is what Teresa May proclaimed when triggering the EU's Article 50 exit clause for Great Britain. See *Financial Times*, London, 30 March 2017, front page.
34. See Lionel Barber, 'Juncker Tells Trump to Stop "Annoying" Praise for Brexit', interview with EU Commission President Jean-Claude Juncker, *Financial Times*, 24 March 2017.

REFERENCES

Bernstein, Richard. 2004. "The German Question." *The New York Times Magazine*, May 2. Accessed March 12, 2018. http://www.nytimes.com/2004/05/02/magazine/the-german-question.html.

Bush, George W. 2010. *Decision Points*. New York: Crown Publishers.

Cheney, Dick, with Liz Cheney. 2011. *In My Time. A Personal and Political Memoir*. New York: Threshold Editions.

Dettke, Dieter. 2009. *Germany Says 'No'. The Iraq War and the Future of German Foreign and Security Policy*. Washington, DC: The Woodrow Wilson Center Press/Baltimore: The Johns Hopkins University Press.

Erlanger, Steven. 2002. "German Leader's Warning: War Plan Is a Huge Mistake." *The New York Times*, September 5. Accessed March 12, 2018. http://www.nytimes.com/2002/09/05/international/europe/german-leaders-warning-war-plan-is-a-huge-mistake.html.

Fischer, Joschka. 2007. "Between Kosovo and Iraq: The Process of Redefining the Transatlantic Relationship." *Bulletin of the German Historical Institute*, no. 41: 9–19.

Friedrich, Wolfgang, ed. 2000. *The Legacy of Kosovo: German Politics and Policies in the Balkans*. German Issues 22. Washington, DC: American Institute for Contemporary German Studies, The Johns Hopkins University.

Fukuyama, Francis. 1989. "The End of History?" *The National Interest* (summer 1989). Accessed March 12, 2018. https://www.embl.de/aboutus/science_society/discussion/discussion_2006/ref1-22june06.pdf.

Gordon, Michael R., and General Bernard E. Trainor. 2006. *Cobra II: The Inside Story of the Invasion and Occupation of Iraq*. New York: Pantheon Books.

Gow, James. 2003. *The Serbian Project and Its Adversaries: A Strategy of War Crimes.* Montreal: McGill-Queen's University Press.

Habermas, Jürgen. 2004. *Der Gespaltene Westen.* Frankfurt: edition Suhrkamp 2383.

The Iraq Papers. 2010. "Veterans of Foreign Wars 103rd National Convention." Edited by John Ehrenberg, J. Patrice McSherry, Jose Ramon Sanchez, and Caroleen Marjji Sayej. New York: Oxford University Press.

Kohnstamm, Max, and Wolfgang Hager, eds. 1973. *Zivilmacht Europa-Supermacht oder Partner.* Frankfurt/M: Suhrkamp.

Kundnani, Hans. 2011. "Germany as a Geo-economic Power." *The Washington Quarterly* 34 (3): 31–45.

Maull, Hanns W. 2014. "From 'Civilian Power' to 'Trading State'?" In *The Routledge Handbook of German Politics and Culture*, Online Publication, November 2014, Abstract. Accessed June 8, 2017. https://www.routledgehandbooks.com/doi/10.4324/9781315747040.ch25.

Maull, Hanns, and Sebastian Harnisch. 2001. *Germany as a Civilian Power? The Foreign Policy of the Berlin Republic.* Manchester: Manchester University Press.

Mearsheimer, John J. 2001. *The Tragedy of Great Power Politics.* New York: W.W. Norton and Company.

Powell, Colin, with Tony Koltz. 2012. *It Worked for Me In Life and Leadership.* New York: Harper Collins.

Qiu, Linda. 2016. "Did the US Spend $6 Trillion in Middle East Wars?" *Politifacts*, 27 October 2016. Accessed June 8, 2017. http://www.politifact.com/truth-o-meter/statements/2016/oct/27/donald-trump/did-us-spend-6-trillion-middle-east-wars/.

Schöllgen, Gregor. 2004. *Der Auftritt: Deutschlands Rückkehr auf die Weltbühne.* Berlin: Ullstein Buchverlag.

Schöllgen, Gregor. 2015. *Gerhard Schröder. Die Biographie.* München: Deutsche Verlagsanstalt.

Schröder, Gerhard. 2006. *Entscheidungen. Mein Leben in der Politik.* Hamburg: Hoffmann und Campe.

Smith, Jean Edward. 2016. *Bush.* New York: Simon and Schuster.

Szabo, Stephen F. 2004. *Parting Ways: The Crisis in German–American Relations.* Washington, DC: Brookings Institution Press.

Vinocur, John. 1993. "A Newly Excellent German Politics, Please." *The New York Times*, June 2. Accessed June 8, 2017. http://www.nytimes.com/1993/06/02/opinion/02iht-nuvi.html?pagewanted=2.

Waltz, Kenneth N. 1993. "The Emerging Structure of International Politics." *International Security* 18 (2): 44–79.

Wayne, Earl Anthony, and Daniel S. Hamilton. 2017. "America Can't Be First Without Europe." *The Conversation*, March 24, 2017. Accessed June 8, 2017. http://theconversation.com/america-cant-be-first-without-europe-75109.

The End of Memory? German-American Relations under Donald Trump

ERIC LANGENBACHER and RUTH WITTLINGER

This article examines recent dynamics of collective memory in German–American relations. After an introduction which outlines the importance of history and memory for bilateral relations, the article traces the evolution of collective memories of the two countries and identifies the key filters through which they evaluate each other. It then identifies the key characteristics of German–American relations since the advent of Donald Trump to the American presidency. This is followed by an analysis which examines Trump's use and abuse of history and memory and what that means for his foreign policy in general and German–American relations in particular. In view of the way Donald Trump has taken the subjective nature of collective memories to an extreme by largely disconnecting these memories from their historical context at the same time as extensively referencing his own history and experience, the article argues that we might be witnessing the end of memory, in particular the end of memory's direct impact on political discourse and policy.

All bilateral relationships are filtered through the lens of the past. This is certainly the case for the US–German relationship. Indeed, history and memory have been especially important for this relationship, particularly from the US side towards Germany, given the role of the US in militarily defeating Germany twice in the twentieth century and then defending the Federal Republic during the cold war. Moreover, the rise of Holocaust consciousness after the 1970s created another layer of memory through which Germany was perceived. But what about the present – almost 75 years since the end of World War II and with a very different president now in the White House?

First, what exactly do we mean when we speak of 'the past'? Most obviously, there is history, a narrative recording of the chronology of previous events with explanations provided for the forces or personalities propelling such events. Although the study of history clearly has its merits when examining bilateral relations, a focus on collective memory provides an important additional dimension for an understanding of the mindsets of political elites which provide the basis for their bilateral relationship. As Andrei Markovits and Simon Reich have pointed out, 'history is about cognition and knowledge, collective memory is about experience and feeling. If history is a matter of the past, collective memory is most definitely a phenomenon of the present'.[1] Or, to follow Pierre Nora, memory is emotionalised and motivating – the living past – whereas history encompasses the cold, dry facts with less influence on policy making.[2]

Collective memories – shared interpretations of a particularly poignant past filtered through the values and worldviews of the present – are important influences in a variety of political arenas including foreign policy and various bilateral relationships. Most generally, as constructivist IR scholars have argued, memories are ideas that affect the identities and values dominant in a political culture. Specifically, foreign policy makers are impacted by the memories and cultural environment that surround them. Memory helps to create the lens through which a problem or an actor is perceived. Indeed, since 'all consciousness is mediated through it',[3] collective memory plays a pivotal role in opinion and policy formation. It acts as a mechanism that provides orientation for groups, nations and states, helping to explain and make sense of the world and supplying standards for evaluating a range of moral issues.[4]

Memory also helps to prime what historical analogies a policy maker might utilise to respond to an issue in the present and the abiding lessons those historical experiences are said to teach.[5] For example, the strong western response to the Russian intervention in Crimea in 2014 was clearly affected by parallels drawn to aggressive German expansion in Europe in the 1930s, particularly the Sudetenland issue, and the lessons (such as the dangers of appeasement) drawn from them.[6] Likewise, US policy makers during the Vietnam War were deeply influenced by the memory of the Korean War, which, in turn, was impacted by the memory of 'Munich' in the 1930s.[7] More generally, the widespread post-nationalism on the European continent and the strong Franco-German relationship are deeply conditioned by the memory of what happened when nationalism was rampant a century ago and the lessons derived from it.

Furthermore, there has always been a difference between official policies and diplomatic ties and the attitudes of people towards the other side. Sometimes the two dimensions are in sync and sometimes the tendencies evolve differently. For example, there has been positive sentiment and a pool of goodwill of (West) Germans vis-à-vis Americans over the post-war period, even though relations were sometimes better and sometimes worse (depending on the chemistry between leaders or specific policy disputes). At times, anti-American sentiment has surfaced – but sometimes this did not align with official policy (the NATO 'double-track' decision) and sometimes it did (opposition to the 2003 invasion of Iraq when Germans and their government said no[8]) Alternatively, despite the continuing animosity of many Americans towards Germans after World War II – a critical frame that was strengthened as the country was increasingly seen through the Holocaust prism after the 1970s – US policy was consistently supportive of (West) German interests. Yet since the turn of the millennium there seems to have been a trend towards warmer attitudes at least at the level of public opinion,[9] even though policy disagreements have occurred over Germany's lack of support for the invasion of Iraq, for example, leading Condoleezza Rice to suggest to 'Punish France, Ignore Germany and Forgive Russia'.[10]

THE EVOLUTION OF COLLECTIVE MEMORIES

This article looks at the impact of collective memories on the German–American relationship. As with any bilateral relationship, history and memory matter – but here the relationship is rather complex and asymmetric. Germany, with its by now well-developed culture of contrition, operates in a very high memory context. There is overwhelming evidence over the 70+ years of the Federal Republic that the concerns of memory and the lessons from the past have conditioned virtually every major international decision – from rearmament in the mid-1950s, to reunification, the expansion of the European Union and to the establishment of the euro.[11] For example, former Chancellor Helmut Kohl repeatedly stated that the EU and the euro were necessary to forever overcome a negative historical inheritance. In a famous interview from 2002, he noted: 'Nations with a common currency never went to war against each other. A common currency is more than the money you pay with.' Moreover: 'I wanted to bring the euro [sic] because to me it meant the irreversibility of European development ... for me the euro was a synonym for Europe going further.'[12]

The United States and especially policy makers, by contrast, have appeared much less influenced by such concerns. Instead, explanations of American policy decisions approximate what realist IR scholars have asserted – calculated self-interest in the context of international anarchy and hegemonic US power. Nevertheless, memory does matter even in the ever future-oriented USA, but in less conditioning ways than in Germany – the filter of memory is more general and modified by other (realist) considerations. This has been increasingly apparent since the turn of the millennium and appears particularly to be the case with the current Trump administration.

The US Memory Filters towards Germany

Although we are primarily concerned about the German–American relationship in recent decades and the present, in light of the deeply conditioning and lingering impact of history and memory, more remote periods should be considered. In the nineteenth century, there was almost no bilateral relationship to speak of (Germany only unified in 1871). Perhaps one could better describe a variety of multilateral relationships between various German states (like Prussia or Austria-Hungary), but certainly without the unified impact of a France or Britain. A big exception was immigration. For many in the German lands, America, with its vast, unsettled frontier, represented the new world, a land of opportunity. Already at the time of the founding there were significant German communities and there were even discussions about making German an official language – something early leaders like Benjamin Franklin resisted.[13] A surge of immigration after the failed revolutions of 1848 attested to this strong draw. Over the nineteenth century 7 million Germans emigrated to the US.

Even today, there is a sizeable proportion of the US population that claims German ancestry. In 2014 this was still the largest group at about 14 per cent of the population (a quarter of whites).[14] In 1980, they were 23 per cent of the total population but 28 per cent of whites. In 1900, 9 per cent of Americans were first or second generation German immigrants, the largest group by far.[15] Of course, immigrants had very different reasons for coming to the US and had varying attitudes towards their home country. But at many points in time, this group has been a factor in US policy and the bilateral relationship. The German–American community was a reason for the late entry of the US into World War I, for the lengthy period of isolationism and even appeasement in the 1930s, and then arguably it was a force behind the staunch defence of the Federal Republic during the cold war.

It is an open question what (if any) influence these individuals exert over the bilateral relationship today. One might speculate that this is a moderating force (because of lingering positive sentiments towards one's ancestors' homeland) when policy makers contemplate a harsher stance toward contemporary Germany. Another moderating force is German investment and related jobs in the US today. By some estimates 672,000 US jobs are supported by German affiliates, making Germany the third largest foreign employer.[16] Moreover, about half of these jobs are in the manufacturing sector – a major rhetorical focus of the Trump administration – and also largely situated in the deep red states of the South.[17] Despite the current $68 billion trade deficit that the US has with Germany, and which Trump has repeatedly criticised, these commercial ties are broad, deep, and mutually beneficial. Merkel certainly tried to convey this point by bringing numerous CEOs of German companies to her first meeting with Trump at the White House in March 2017.

Germany also impacted on higher education in the US, and thus influenced elites. The Humboldtian research university (first adopted at Johns Hopkins University) became the model for the modern American university. German influence in various disciplines was strong until World War II – an influence that continued with the numerous emigrés from the 1930s onwards. Today, strong investments by the German government (through the DAAD [Deutscher Akademischer Austauschdienst] – the centres of excellence) and generous opportunities for exchanges and research have solidified the relationship and created not just venues but a reservoir of intercultural understanding, if not goodwill, influencing US elites. For example, Obama's last chief of staff, Denis McDonough, spent a year in Germany on a Bosch Fellowship. The more general cultural and political infrastructure especially in the US capital – German Marshall Fund of the United States, German Historical Institute, Atlantic Council, Bertelsmann and the political foundations – are active players in many policy discussions. There are Goethe Institutes in six cities and DAAD offices in two.

From the American side, the Federal Republic has long been viewed through the lens of Nazism, World War II and the Holocaust. In a 2015 Pew Survey, 47 per cent (51 per cent in the 18–29 age group) of Americans, but only 20 per cent of Germans thought World War II and the Holocaust were the most important events in US–German relations; 20 per cent of Germans but only 3 per cent of Americans said the Marshall Plan. Meanwhile, 35 per cent of Germans and 28 per cent of Americans said the fall of the Berlin Wall was the most important historical event.[18]

Interestingly, this framing was less pronounced during the (earlier) decades of the cold war. During that time, the FRG was often seen as a front-line state, the last free bulwark against the communist menace, and most likely the first victim of an invasion from the East (the Fulda Gap). West Germany was weak and vulnerable and needed US protection. Brian Etheridge calls this the cold war narrative, in contrast to the world war/Holocaust version.[19] It was also true that 10 million US servicemen were stationed in Germany over these decades, creating a familiarity with the country.[20] One could even point to relatively benign depictions of World War II-era German and Nazi soldiers (*Hogan's Heroes*, *The Great Escape*). There was more focus on the battles and conventional military history (the Rommel/Desert Fox fetish) and less on the anti-Semitic, racist and genocidal core of the Nazi project. There appeared to be official and popular-culture support for the (long) Adenauer-era differentiation of Germans from Nazis with the assertion that the criminals were in fact dead or imprisoned. The myth of the 'clean' Wehrmacht lasted on both sides of the Atlantic until well into the 1990s.[21]

Certainly, there was a degree of mistrust, particularly at first, in light of several hundred thousand US battle deaths in the two world wars. Even if the draconian Morgenthau Plan did not come to pass, many policy makers and citizens agreed with Lord Ismay, the first NATO secretary general, who described the intent of the Atlantic alliance as 'to keep the Russians out, the Americans in and the Germans down'. Indeed, US policy makers pursued a strategy of 'dual containment', worried not just about the communist threat from the USSR, but also a resurgent or even neutral Germany.[22] US policy makers also insisted that the Basic Law of the Federal Republic contain certain institutional and policy safeguards that would preclude a repetition of the past, namely strong federalism and a decentralised fiscal system.[23] The renunciation of chemical and nuclear weapons and severe constraints on the deployment of the Bundeswehr (after 1955) were also strongly supported by US policy makers. Nevertheless, such concerns were not filtered through the lens of the Holocaust, but rather more traditional realist concerns about power, resources and war-making capacity.

The Nazi and Holocaust framing of Germany and the US–German relationship really came to the fore towards the end of the cold war and the reunification of Germany. Part of this was due to the rise of Holocaust consciousness and the Americanisation of the Holocaust, dating to the 1970s.[24] Popular culture was crucial in this process, exemplified by the airing of the NBC miniseries *Holocaust* in 1978. The Bitburg Affair in 1985, where Helmut Kohl and Ronald Reagan attempted to celebrate the 40th anniversary of the end of World War II at a military cemetery containing the graves of members of the SS became an international incident, condemned by a vote of the US Congress.[25] The movement to establish a Holocaust Memorial Museum started with Jimmy Carter and the museum was opened in 1993 by Bill Clinton – the 'year of the Holocaust', when *Schindler's List* also was released. Memorials and museums are found across the country today and the Holocaust has also become a mandatory part of secondary school curricula in the various states.[26] Increased attention over the 1990s towards debates in Germany about this memory were push and pull factors in the greater salience of the Holocaust filter utilised towards Germany.

More recently, there is evidence that a more positive filter, less encumbered by the past, has arisen among Americans. This is marked by a respect for recent German achievements – the culture of contrition, Germany's soft power, soccer, the strong economy and export prowess. Certain aspects of the German model have been especially lauded – vocational training (even by Trump), the ability to maintain a vibrant manufacturing sector, low inflation, sound public finances and relatively little debt. Especially after Merkel's shift in policy regarding the refugee crisis in 2015 and then after Trump's victory in November 2016, there was much praise at least from the centre and left for Germany and Merkel being the last bastion of liberal, western values. Some even tout her as 'the leader of the free world'.[27]

Another development over the last few years is that beyond a bipartisan consensus on some issues, e.g. both Democrats and Republicans have criticised German trade surpluses and other related policies (artificially low value of the euro to boost German exports), the most vehement criticism now appears to come from the right. Previously, criticism of Germany came from the left, i.e. criticism of inadequate coming to terms with the past, the perceived lack of sensitivity towards any xenophobic attack or politician, allegations of political-cultural continuity with the Nazi past. With the image of Germany transformed, now into a liberal icon, a lot of the most vehement criticism has come from the right – especially the so-called alt-right, which promotes 'America First' via Breitbart, for example.[28]

German Filters towards the US

Such distinct phases of perception are not as evident on the German side. Throughout the post-war period, Germans have had divided, even contradictory attitudes towards the US. For example, the adult generations of the 1950s and 1960s were fairly pro-American and Atlanticist and there was much goodwill towards the US – thanks to the Berlin Airlift (with the raisin or candy bombers), the nuclear/security guarantee, the Marshall Plan and more general US support for rehabilitating the FRG as quickly as possible and integrating it into NATO and other organisations. JFK was treated as a hero during his trip to the FRG and West Berlin in 1963, when he gave his famous 'Ich bin ein Berliner' speech. Reagan at least partially rehabilitated his war-mongering image in Germany with his famous 'Mr. Gorbachev, tear down this wall' speech just over 30 years ago, while also reaffirming western solidarity.[29]

Another high point of goodwill surrounded the process of German reunification. US policy makers, especially President George H.W. Bush and Secretary of State James Baker, were steadfast supporters. They helped to assuage the concerns of other allies like France, Britain and the USSR. Right before formal unification on 2 October 1990, Bush stated:

> The United States is proud to have built with you the foundations of freedom; proud to have been a steady partner in the quest for one Germany, whole and free. America is proud to count itself among the friends and allies of free Germany, now and in the future. Our peoples are united by the common bonds of culture, by a shared heritage in history. Never before have these common bonds been more evident than in this past year as we worked in common cause toward the goal of German unity. Today, together, we share the fruits of our friendship.[30]

Helmut Kohl, speaking for many Germans, returned the admiration, stating that 'George Bush was for me the most important ally on the road to German unity',[31]

But there was always an underbelly of criticism – and not just from Frankfurt School intellectuals who disdained 'Americanisation' as crass, standard-less, consumerist drivel.[32] After all, the US was a victorious and occupying army with bases around the country. The US Air Force had helped to destroy many German cities not too long before. The generation that experienced this remembered it. And of course the late 1960s – just 20 years after the founding of the FRG – saw much leftist criticism of US 'imperialism' – in Vietnam, Iran and the 'Third World' more generally. The peace movement of the 1970s and early 1980s was often explicitly anti-American, for example in its opposition to the NATO 'double-track' decision. Similar opposition occurred in the early 2000s over the Bush administration's decision to invade Saddam Hussein's Iraq.[33]

Despite Barack Obama's high level of personal popularity, there were many tensions in the US–German relationship during his presidency. German and European policy makers understood that the so-called 'pivot to Asia' would decrease American security assets in and attention to Europe.

US policy makers also disagreed with German policy responses to the financial and especially the Euro crisis.[34] Paul Krugman spoke for many US policy makers in 2013 when he pointed out Germany's contribution to the crisis: 'Yet Germany has failed to deliver on its side of the bargain: To avoid a European depression, it needed to spend more as its neighbors were forced to spend less, and it hasn't done that … Germany's trade surplus is damaging.'[35] Tensions persisted when the German government broke with allies and failed to join the action against Libya in 2011. Then, in 2013, news broke that the US National Security Agency (NSA) had been spying on German leaders like Angela Merkel. This reminded many Germans of their totalitarian history, with attitudes to secret service wiretapping being very much influenced by the collective memory of this history. By 2014, only 35 per cent of Germans expressed trust in the US, compared to 74 per cent when Barack Obama took over.[36]

The last years of the Obama era became a high point of comity – indeed at times Obama was (much) more popular in Germany than at home. Merkel and Obama developed a particularly close collaboration and friendship, forged in the joint effort to manage and solve various crises, such as post-2014 Russian aggression, the Euro crisis, the Paris Climate Agreement and the Iranian nuclear deal. During one of his last trips to Europe in April 2016, President Obama described the bilateral relationship with particularly warm words:

> On behalf of the American people, I want to thank Angela for being a champion of our alliance. And on behalf of all of us, I want to thank you for your commitment to freedom, and equality, and human rights, which is a reflection of your inspiring life … I have to admit that I have developed a special place in my heart for the German people … And as always, I bring the friendship of the American people. We consider the German people, and all of our European allies, to be among our closest friends in the world.[37]

GERMAN–AMERICAN RELATIONS IN THE TRUMP ERA

German-American relations under the 45th president have entered, at the best, a phase of uncertainty, and, at the worst, a nadir. As David Frum, former speech-writer to George W. Bush opined: 'The spinal column of the Western alliance is the U.S.-Germany relationship, and Trump has undermined it since Day One.'[38] Given the wild swings in policies and tweets from Donald Trump, assessments of the state of relations change rather frequently. Early in the campaign in October 2015, Trump was very critical of Merkel: 'They're going to have riots in Germany … I always thought Merkel was, like, this great leader. What she's done in Germany is insane.'[39] In December 2015, he said she was 'ruining' Germany with her refugee policy.[40] Then in August 2016 he stated:

> In short, Hillary Clinton wants to be America's Angela Merkel, and you know what a disaster this massive immigration has been to Germany and the people

of Germany. Crime has risen to levels that no one thought they would ever, ever see. It is a catastrophe.[41]

This came after he expressed great respect – albeit with a degree of bitterness – for her: 'Germany's like sitting back silent collecting money and making a fortune with probably the greatest leader in the world today, Merkel ... She's fantastic ... highly respected.'[42] During their first meeting at the White House in March 2017, the tensions were palpable. There were allegations that Trump did not shake Merkel's hand when asked and that he presented her with a 'bill' for what Germany owed the US for providing security.[43] But then, not much later, Trump was talking about the excellent chemistry he had with her. In May 2017, Trump criticised Germany again at the NATO meeting and G7 Summit and then in a variety of tweets. Germany was 'bad, really bad', German automobile exports were unfair (singling out BMW) and Trump asserted once again that the country owed the US money for security. Newspaper headlines spoke of Merkel and Trump 'hating' each other.[44]

Trump has also made unsettling comments about the European Union, probably the most important German foreign policy precept. He supported Brexit and asked publicly which member state will be next to leave. Yet at other times he has said: 'The EU, I'm totally in favour of it. I think it's wonderful, if they're happy. If they're happy – I'm in favour of it.' But then he went on: 'You look at the European Union and it's Germany. Basically a vehicle for Germany. That's why I thought the UK was so smart in getting out.'[45]

Before the G20 Summit in July 2017, he pointedly visited Poland, where he was feted by the ruling national-conservative Law and Justice Party. He reiterated the dominant narrative of Polish history: 'What great spirit. We salute your noble sacrifice and we pledge to always remember your fight for Poland and for freedom ... Your oppressors tried to break you, but Poland could not be broken.' Although he did finally affirm the Article 5 guarantee and committed to western values such as freedom of speech, gender equality and the rule of law, he also conceived of the West in terms that do not align themselves easily with the more universalist or post-national manner dominant in Germany:

> Americans, Poles, and the nations of Europe value individual freedom and sovereignty. We must work together to confront forces, whether they come from inside or out, from the South or the East, that threaten over time to undermine these values and to erase the bonds of culture, faith and tradition that make us who we are. If left unchecked, these forces will undermine our courage, sap our spirit, and weaken our will to defend ourselves and our societies ... The world has never known anything like our community of nations. We write symphonies. We pursue innovation. We celebrate our ancient heroes, embrace our timeless traditions and customs, and always seek to explore and discover brand-new frontiers.[46]

Finally, most explicitly, he points out the central role of history and memory, even though he does not elaborate on the specifics:

> Our own fight for the West does not begin on the battlefield – it begins with our minds, our wills, and our souls. Today, the ties that unite our civilization are no

less vital, and demand no less defense, than that bare shred of land on which the hope of Poland once totally rested. Our freedom, our civilization, and our survival depend on these bonds of history, culture, and memory,[47]

The views of Trump's former advisor and chief strategist Stephen Bannon also matter, even though he was forced to resign from these formal roles in August 2017. Overall, Bannon thinks the European Union is a threatening example of 'globalism' and he was thus a strong supporter of Brexit. In his widely quoted 2014 Vatican speech he noted:

I think strong countries and strong nationalist movements in countries make strong neighbors ... That is really the building blocks that built Western Europe and the United States, and I think it's what can see us forward ... the world, and particularly the Judeo-Christian West, is in a crisis ... [Europeans want] sovereignty for their country, they want to see nationalism ... They don't believe in this kind of pan-European Union.[48]

Merkel responded to Trump's election victory with her usual aplomb, although a sharper edge was evident in the message:

Germany and America are bound by common values – democracy, freedom, as well as respect for the rule of law and the dignity of each and every person, regardless of their origin, skin color, creed, gender, sexual orientation, or political views. It is based on these values that I wish to offer close cooperation, both with me personally and between our countries' governments.[49]

Her then vice-chancellor and current foreign minister Sigmar Gabriel was harsher:

Trump is the trailblazer of a new authoritarian and chauvinist international movement. ... They want a rollback to the bad old times in which women belonged by the stove or in bed, gays in jail and unions at best at the side table. And he who doesn't keep his mouth shut gets publicly bashed.[50]

Months and several awkward meetings later – including the NATO Summit when Trump would not formally support Article 5 or the G7 Summit in Italy in May 2017 where he pushed another leader out of the way and expressed misgivings about the Paris Climate Agreement, Merkel stated at a campaign rally:

The time in which we could fully rely on others is a bit in the past ... I have experienced that in the past several days. And, because of that, I can say now that we Europeans truly have to take our fate into our own hands.[51]

Although it is difficult to predict how the situation will develop, the negativity and equivocations from the White House have had a deleterious impact in Germany. A Harvard University study of media coverage of Trump's first 100 days showed that Germany's public television channel was the most critical, with 98 per cent of stories coded as negative.[52] Germans have also had a more unfavourable view of the US compared to other Europeans in 2016: 57 per cent of Germans had a favourable view, versus 63 per cent of the French or 61 per cent of British people.[53]

Trump's negative comments about NATO, the European Union and Germany's trade surplus have created much consternation. In February 2017, 78 per cent of

Germans viewed Trump with concern, whereas only 58 per cent took the same position towards Putin's policies.[54] By late June 2017, confidence that the US president would do the right thing regarding world affairs had plummeted to 11 per cent of Germans versus 86 per cent at the end of Obama's presidency. There were similar declines in many other countries, and only increases in Israel (slight) and Russia.[55] Representatives of the Trump administration have also been met with public ridicule – such as when Ivanka Trump tried to defend her father's treatment of women in Berlin in April 2017, when Commerce Secretary Wilbur Ross was allegedly cut off for going over his allotted time when addressing a CDU group in June 2017, and during protests in conjunction with the G20 Summit in Hamburg in July 2017.[56]

UNDERSTANDING TRUMP?

There does not seem to be a foreign policy area that is important to the Germans that has not been unsettled or discredited by the Trump administration – the European Union, the euro, NATO, the UN (Trump deemed it an 'underperformer' and wants to eviscerate US funding[57]), policy towards Russia,[58] Iran, the Middle East more generally, climate/ environment, trade and TTIP (Transatlantic Trade and Investment Partnership).[59] But how can we understand Trump and the policies of his administration? And how does he view history; which historical periods, events and phenomena does he invoke to formulate and substantiate 'his message'? And, of course, what collective memory strands do politicians and the press resort to in order to evaluate President Trump and what he stands for? What key collective memory strands is Trump tapping into, promoting or even creating?

The key text (of 12 books on business and politics) here is *The America We Deserve*, published in 2000 when Trump contemplated running for the presidency for the Reform Party.[60] As is the case with many texts allegedly authored by politicians, we do not know, of course, how much or how little of the content can actually be attributed to Trump himself. We have to assume, however, that the texts reflect his views at least to a degree. Much of what he wrote in this book – for instance on immigration, tax policy or a dystopian view of contemporary America – has also been expressed since he became president. For instance, he lauds his family: 'I haven't been as successful in my marriages as my parents were, but marriage is not the only family value that matters. The importance you give to your relationship with your kids is a family value' (p.25). His political self-image and basis of his appeal is also evident: 'But I'm also bringing a perspective to politics that most politicians don't have. I've built a multi-billion dollar empire by using my intuition' (p.35).

Trump has little to say about the past and what he does say is couched in his life history. He does seem to be particularly drawn to the Great Depression (character-building), the 1950s (the golden age) and the 1970s (decadent decline): 'I will never forget the 1970s, when reckless regulators were running the show – make that horror show' (p.45). In a section called 'Our Next Comeback' he lauds the American dream and his father and grandfather: 'In those days you didn't hoof it down to the welfare line when hard times hit, you hit the bricks looking for work' (p.42). All of this prefigures his 2016 campaign slogan 'Make America Great Again', harkening back to the mythical golden age of the 1950s,[61] or even Theodore Roosevelt in the early twentieth century – a time of rapid industrialisation and growth and great fortunes (the robber barons).[62]

Regarding German history, at various points, he expressed disagreement with positive comments Pat Buchanan made about Hitler around that time: 'Hitler was a monster and it was essential for the allies to crush Nazism ... My grandfather was German. But I am proud of the vital role the United States played in defeating the Third Reich' (p.17). Trump subsequently reconciled with Buchanan, who has actually said that his ideas (economic nationalism) have finally triumphed with the 45th president.[63]

His thinking on foreign policy is also outlined. He notes: 'In the modern world you can't very easily draw up a simple, general foreign policy ... We deal with all the other nations of the world on a case-by-case basis. And a lot of those bystanders don't look so innocent' (p.111). He also articulated criticism of NATO:

> Pulling back from Europe would save this country millions of dollars annually. The cost of stationing NATO troops in Europe is enormous, and these are clearly funds that can be put to better use. Our allies don't seem to appreciate our presence anyway. We pay for the defense of France, yet they vote against us at the United Nations and choose the side of the North Koreans, the Libyans, and other rogue nations. (pp.142–3)

His policy flip-flops as president are also prefigured and grounded in at least a vague conception of history:

> But, ultimately, I don't think that we should abandon Europe completely ... His [Buchanan's] recommendations of appeasement toward the Nazi regime sounds exactly like what liberals said about Hitler in the '30s and what liberals today are saying about rogue states like North Korea. If you applied the same doctrine of appeasement to domestic criminals, you'd be giving murderers and armed robbers stern reprimands and setting them free. (p.143)

His views on trade have also barely changed. He sees the world in martial, zero-sum terms. Everything is deal-making and he proclaims a unique skill set in this regard: 'Frankly, there are many aspects of trade where my negotiating skills could be useful' (p.147).[64] Moreover:

> It's become cliché to say that business, especially trade, is like war ... But cliché or not, it's true. Germany and Japan were our enemies in World War II, and for decades afterward each was a powerful competitor in trade – tough in peacetime as each had been in war. (Though both have fallen on lean times recently, they will become worthy adversaries again.) We didn't make the best possible trade deals with them. We're not making smart deals now ... the core of these problems is that we don't know how to negotiate. We don't know how to get what we want out of the people we're sitting across the table from. (p.146)

There is a constant tendency to define the world in Manichean terms. Americans are always the good guys and there is a constant need to have bad guys, some 'worthy adversary', opponent, enemy, or 'other' – illegal Mexican immigrants, North Korea, China, the European Union, or perhaps now Germany. Trump also seems always to require a dramatically staged 'feud' – previously with Rosie O'Donnell, during the campaign with a gold star family and with 'Morning Joe' journalists Mika Brzezinski and Joe Scarborough. He also seems to have problems with facts, for instance that trade deals are negotiated with the EU and not individual member states like Germany, and he has flirted with conspiracy theories (birtherism) and conspiracy theorists (Alex Jones).[65]

One of the references most frequently used by Donald Trump has been 'America First', which relates to the isolationist, anti-Semitic group which pushed for America to stay out of World War II. It had also been used as a slogan by Woodrow Wilson and more recently by Pat Buchanan. Trump has used the phrase extensively during his election campaign but also during his first few months in office.

Just like America's other allies, German politicians reacted with concern at the suggestion that the United States wanted to withdraw from its international role. As Robert Kagan has pointed out, the phrase gained more prominence after the Iraq and Afghan wars and the financial crisis to the point that it became a 'national phenomenon'. According to Kagan, there was a transition away from considering the United States as an 'indispensable nation', as Bill Clinton had phrased it, already under President Obama, with Trump's election representing a 'decisive break' from this internationalist tradition.[66] As one commentator put it, '[t]he history that haunts them [the Europeans] is that of the 1930s, when a self-absorbed America stood by as Europe fell to fascism and war'.[67] It was the lessons learnt from the 1930s, however, that led Washington to design 'a new, US-led global order' after World War II.[68]

In a press statement on the outcome of the US presidential elections – and presumably in response to Trump's use of the slogan 'America First' during the election campaign – Merkel pointed out that the importance of the outcome of presidential elections went far beyond the United States. She emphasised that those who govern this large country carry responsibility which can be felt nearly everywhere in the world. Addressing concerns that had been raised during the campaign about Trump's lack of democratic credentials, Merkel asserted that the bond between Germany and America was based on common values – the appreciation of which can clearly be seen to have arisen out of the experience of Germany's totalitarian pasts. It was only on the basis of these values that Merkel offered the new president close cooperation.[69]

As it turns out, Trump has shifted his position in the meantime considerably from describing NATO as obsolete to confirming its significance for transatlantic relations and peace and stability (for example during British Prime Minister Theresa May's visit to Washington in January 2017, in a telephone conversation with Merkel on 28 January 2017, and in his 6 July 2017 speech in Warsaw[70]). He also explicitly dismissed the idea of being an isolationist in a press conference with Angela Merkel.[71]

Trump thus seems to have used references to 'America First' only as soundbites to mobilise his followers rather than actually evoking a particular memory or message. Without paying much attention to the historical context of the slogan, he thus seems to have disconnected memory from history altogether, giving it a life of its own in the process.

The past that does seem to play a role in President Trump's understanding of the world is the one that goes right up to his inauguration as president, that is the bad past from which he wants to 'liberate' the American people. With his slogan 'Make America great again', he has frequently also referred back to a better past, being quite nostalgic about this past, without ever really pinpointing to when this past was. Particularly in his inaugural address, President Trump evokes images of a liberation from an oppressive past of the American people, some kind of oligarchy, which he describes as an 'American carnage' which 'stops right here and stops right now'. He speaks of a 'great national effort to rebuild our country and to restore its promise for all of our people', promising to transfer power from Washington and 'giving it back to you, the American people'. In his view, 'January 20th 2017, will be remembered as the day the people became the rulers of this nation again' and American will be made 'great again'.[72]

References to a better past seem to have persuaded some Americans. According to Anne Applebaum, Trump's appeal to the working class was cultural since he promised to bring back the kinds of jobs their fathers had and, 'by implication, the whiter, simpler, post-war world when America had no real economic competition'.[73]

But how has the Trump administration handled America's traditional collective memory strands? On 27 January 2017, Holocaust Memorial Day, Trump managed to make a widely criticised statement in which he omitted to mention the millions of Jews that were killed in the Holocaust.[74] Trump in his usual outspoken manner criticised Germany and Angela Merkel for her refugee policy, Germany's trade surplus and for using the EU as a vehicle to advance Germany's economic interests and Germany (also more widely, Europe) for a lack of burden-sharing in terms of defence. However, although it would have been very easy, he has not made use of German history, in particular the Nazi past, to underline his views. Besides the Warsaw speech discussed above, the one memorable time that former press secretary Sean Spicer referred to the Nazi past was a very unfortunate one when – after the poison gas attack in Syria – he claimed that not even somebody as despicable as Hitler had sunk to using chemical weapons during World War II and referred to concentration camps as 'Holocaust centres' (for which he later apologised).

In the bilateral relationship, Trump also does not allude to a common history. In the joint press conference with Angela Merkel during her visit to Washington in March 2017, he emphasised that the two countries share the 'desire for security, prosperity and peace'.[75] Angela Merkel, however, right at the beginning, undertook an excursion into the past:

> Let me look back into the past. We, the Germans, owe a lot to the United States of America, particularly as regards the economic rise of Germany. This was primarily due to the help through the Marshall Plan. We were also able to regain German unity after decades of the United States standing up for this, together with other allies, and standing by our side during the period of the Cold War. And we are gratified to know that today we can live in peace and freedom as a unified country due to that.[76]

In order to get a fuller picture, it is also important to consider the references to history the world around Trump has used to assess him and his policies. There is no doubt that his election victory has very much been assessed with references to totalitarianism. His advent to power has been described as 'the end of the west', 'the end of the liberal era' and 'a new fascism coming to power', and Trump himself has been described as 'not a democrat' but a 'fascist' with parallels being drawn to Mussolini and Hitler. His advent to power has also been described as the beginning of a new 'authoritarian era'.[77]

In his column in the *Washington Post*, Robert Kagan, in a piece called 'This is how fascism comes to America', on 18 May 2016 issued the following warning:

This is how fascism comes to America, not with jackboots and salutes (although there have been salutes, and a whiff of violence) but with a television huckster, a phony billionaire, a textbook egomaniac 'tapping into' popular resentments and insecurities, and with an entire national political party – out of ambition or blind party loyalty, or simply out of fear – falling into line behind him.[78]

When Barack Obama made his last phone call as American president to Angela Merkel, this was interpreted as not just a goodbye but described as him 'handing over his baton. The German Chancellor isn't just the leader of Europe, she is now the de-facto leader of the free world'.[79] Trump's travel ban, the attempt to stop people arriving from countries with a predominantly Muslim population, confirmed his illiberal stance and the concern that America was turning into an inward-looking country which discriminated against people based on their religion. A title page of the news magazine *Der Spiegel* in early February 2017, which showed the American president beheading the Statue of Liberty, expressed this criticism. The cartoonist himself said that the image represented 'the beheading of democracy' and that he wanted to compare Islamic State and Donald Trump, saying 'both sides are extremists'.[80]

Also drawing on this dichotomy, when Angela Merkel visited the American president in March 2017, the *New York Times* described it as 'an awkward encounter that was the most closely watched of his young presidency' which took on 'an outsize symbolism': 'the great disrupter confronts the last defender of the liberal world order'.[81]

A lot of Trump's views go against everything Merkel stands for considering that she grew up in a totalitarian regime: his dismissive views of the press, his plans to build a wall, his illiberal stance that does not accommodate diversity. As one commentator put it, 'Trump is no doubt Merkel's idea of a nightmare US president. Growing up in the communist bloc, she always saw America as a key repository of western values'.[82] Particularly Trump's plan to build a wall between the US and Mexico is clearly unlikely to evoke pleasant memories for the German chancellor who grew up in the GDR.

Trump's attack on the media (or in his words, 'the fake news media') as the 'enemy of the American people' reminds observers of a phrase commonly used by authoritarian and totalitarian regimes to discredit its critics. The term 'enemy of the people' (*Volksfeinde*) has been used by dictatorships throughout history to describe and discredit political opposition as 'the enemy within' and to justify its fights against these 'internal enemies'.

Trump's attack on the press as 'the fake news media' also brings to mind the term *Lügenpresse* ('lying press'). It is probably best known for the way the Nazi regime dismissed the free press as using their outlets to spread lies. The term *Lügenpresse* has more recently also been resurrected by the Islamophobic Pegida movement and the AfD in Germany to discredit the critical press.[83]

Whether Trump is actually aware of the historical connotations is unsure. In either case, it is worrying. His appointment of Stephen Bannon – even though he was not part of the administration for long – who is widely known as right-wing and anti-Semitic, as his advisor and chief strategist, who even initially became a member of the Principals Committee of the National Security Council (he was removed from it in April 2017), was certainly of concern and supported the evocation of references to totalitarianism and fascism.

According to the BBC correspondent Jenny Hill, the anniversary of the *Reichskristallnacht* ('Night of the Broken Glass') and the fall of the Berlin Wall – 'and all that they represent of this country's past explain, partially at least, why Germans were so repulsed by Donald Trump's election rhetoric and why so few (4 per cent by one poll's reckoning) wanted him in the White House.[84]

THE END OF MEMORY?

Trump does not appear to have the standard provision of references to history available to him as other politicians do. He seems to use historical references at face value – for example, 'America First' – probably not realising that the isolationist stance associated with the term did not work well in the past. But overall, there are not many references to history at all. Trump and his team do not seem to have much awareness of history and of the present as having evolved from history. Maybe he does not need to use collective memory (or maybe he cannot because his historical knowledge is very restricted) because he is not afraid to use blunt messages. Whereas other politicians use collective memories to make their case and substantiate their arguments, he just says directly what he thinks and does not seem to see the need for making a case by evoking particular memories or historical parallels.

Maybe Trump has simply taken the use of collective memory to an extreme. He uses references to history as soundbites which help him mobilise his followers. This is also what other politicians do, albeit in a more sophisticated way. They use collective memory strands in a kind of 'pick'n'mix' or 'bricolage' way to make their points. Trump has taken this further by disconnecting it pretty much altogether from the historical context – in a rather postmodern, 'floating signifier' fashion. (It has been pointed out that Trumpism is appropriating and inverting the identity politics and concepts of the left.)[85]

Rather than employing collective memory strands to make his point, he seems to reference his own history and experience in his politics. As one source told the *Guardian* in the context of the ill-fated G7 summit on Sicily in May 2017:

> Every time we talked about a country, he remembered the things he had done. ... Scotland? He said he had opened a club. Ireland? He said it took him two and a half years to get a licence and that did not give him a very good image of the EU.[86]

Maybe the use of personal rather than collective memory is to be expected from somebody with a personality that has frequently been described as narcissistic.[87]

Perhaps there is more going on here, though. Perhaps we are witnessing the end of memory – specifically, the end of memory's direct impact. Germans may no longer actively remember the support of the US against the communist threat. And perhaps Americans, Trumpistas in particular, are no longer seeing Germany through a cold war or Holocaust lens. Perhaps this is the ultimate moment of normalisation – cold, hard reason; self-interest; deals. Indeed, much has been made of Trump's ahistorical, deal-based leadership style. This was perhaps best summed up by two advisors, stating that Trump has

> a clear-eyed outlook that the world is not a 'global community' but an arena where nations, nongovernmental actors and businesses engage and compete for

advantage. We bring to this forum unmatched military, political, economic, cultural and moral strength. Rather than deny this elemental nature of international affairs, we embrace it ... we delivered a clear message to our friends and partners: Where our interests align, we are open to working together to solve problems and explore opportunities ... In short, those societies that share our interests will find no friend more steadfast than the United States. Those that choose to challenge our interests will encounter the firmest resolve.[88]

The contrast with Merkel and other European leaders could not be stronger. This is a rather Nietzschean moment – *Umwertung aller Werte* – where what has been said or thought about the other is now inverted. It was not that long ago that observers fretted deeply about parallels to Weimar in Germany – during the wave of xenophobic violence in 1992 for instance, or when the unemployment rate spiked in the 1990s first in eastern Germany and then in the western regions as well (sick man of the euro). Now there is a small library full of such analyses of the US and Trump.

DISCLOSURE STATEMENT

No potential conflict of interest was reported by the authors.

NOTES

1. Andrei S. Markovits and Simon Reich, 'The Contemporary Power of Memory: The Dilemmas for German Foreign Policy', in John S. Brady, Beverly Crawford and Sarah Elise Williarty (eds), *The Postwar Transformation of Germany: Democracy, Prosperity, and Nationhood* (Ann Arbor: University of Michigan Press, 1999), p.445.
2. Pierre Nora, 'Between Memory and History: Les Lieux de Mémoire', *Representations* 26 (1989), pp.7–24.

3. Jarnes Fentress and Chris Wickham quoted in Jan Werner Miiller, 'Introduction: The Power of Memory, the Memory of Power and the Power over Memory', in Jan Werner Miiller (ed.), *Memory and Power in Post-War Europe* (Cambridge: Cambridge University Press, 2002), p.1.
4. Ruth Wittlinger, 'British–German Relations and Collective Memory', *German Politics and Society* 25/3 (2007), p.44.
5. Ernest May, *'Lessons' of the Past: The Use and Misuse of History in American Foreign Policy* (Oxford: Oxford University Press, 1975).
6. http://www.bbc.com/news/world-europe-26488652 (accessed 6 July 2017).
7. Yuen Foong Khong, *Analogies at War: Korea, Munich, Dien Bien Phu, and the Vietnam Decision of 1965* (Princeton, NJ: Princeton University Press, 1992).
8. Dieter Dettke, *Germany Says 'No': The Iraq War and the Future of German Foreign and Security Policy* (Baltimore, MD: Johns Hopkins University Press, 2009).
9. https://www.deutschland.de/en/topic/politics/germany-europe/americans-praise-germany (accessed 28 Aug. 2017).
10. https://www.brookings.edu/opinions/punish-france-ignore-germany-forgive-russia-no-longer-fits/ (accessed 28 June 2017).
11. Eric Langenbacher, 'From an Unmasterable to a Mastered Past: The Impact of History and Memory in the Federal Republic of Germany', The Federal Republic at 60, Special Issue of *German Politics* 19/1 (2010), pp.24–40.
12. https://euobserver.com/political/119735 (accessed 31 July 2017).
13. https://www.theatlantic.com/politics/archive/2008/02/swarthy-germans/48324/ (accessed 28 June 2017).
14. https://factfinder.census.gov/faces/tableservices/jsf/pages/productview.xhtml?src=bkmk (accessed 28 June 2017).
15. https://usa.usembassy.de/etexts/ga-asn0983Luebke.htm; https://www.census.gov/newsroom/cspan/1940census/CSPAN_1940slides.pdf (accessed 28 June 2017).
16. http://www.rgit-usa.com/german-business-matters/ (accessed 30 June 2017).
17. http://www.justaddgerman.org/career-portal/career-opportunities-in-the-us/; https://www.nytimes.com/2017/05/31/us/south-carolina-bmw-us-german-trade.html (accessed 30 June 2017).
18. http://www.pewglobal.org/2015/05/07/2015-u-s-germany-survey-presentation/ (accessed 28 June 2017).
19. Brian C. Etheridge, *Enemies to Allies: Cold War Germany and American Memory* (Lexington, KY: University Press of Kentucky, 2016), p.279.
20. http://www.heritage.org/defense/report/global-us-troop-deployment-1950-2003 (accessed 28 June 2017).
21. Ronald Smelser and Edward J. Davies, *The Myth of the Eastern Front: The Nazi–Soviet War in American Popular Culture* (New York: Cambridge University Press, 2008).
22. Ruud van Dijk, 'Winning the Peace: The United States, Western Germany and the Ambiguity of "Dual Containment", 1945–50', in Detlef Junker et al. (eds), *The United States and Germany in the Era of the Cold War, 1945–1968*, Vol. 1 (Cambridge: Cambridge University Press, 2004), p.93.
23. Michael H. Bernhard, *Institutions and the Fate of Democracy: Germany and Poland in the Twentieth Century* (Pittsburgh, PA: University of Pittsburgh Press, 2005).
24. Peter Novick, *The Holocaust in American Life* (Boston: Houghton Mifflin, 1999).
25. Geoffrey H. Hartman, *Bitburg in Moral and Political Perspective* (Bloomington, IN: Indiana University Press, 1986).
26. Oren Baruch Stier, *Holocaust Icons: Symbolizing the Shoah in History and Memory* (New Brunswick, NJ: Rutgers University Press, 2015).
27. http://www.politico.com/magazine/story/2017/03/the-leader-of-the-free-world-meets-donald-trump-214924 (accessed 28 June 2017).
28. http://www.nationalreview.com/article/448150/germanys-negative-attitude-toward-us-isnt-new (accessed 28 June 2017).
29. https://www.the-american-interest.com/2017/06/11/tear-down-this-wall-at-thirty/ (accessed 6 July 2017).
30. https://usa.usembassy.de/etexts/ga6-901002.htm (accessed 28 June 2017).
31. http://coed.com/2017/06/16/helmut-kohl-quotes-best-sayings-german-chancellor-rip-cold-war-germany/ (accessed 28 June 2017).
32. Dan Diner, *America in the Eyes of the Germans: An Essay on Anti-Americanism* (Princeton, NJ: Markus Wiener Publishers, 1996).
33. http://www.economist.com/news/europe/21642211-anti-americanism-always-strong-german-left-growing-right-ami-go-home (accessed 28 June 2017).
34. http://www.politico.com/agenda/story/2017/05/26/trump-right-about-germany-trade-000445 (accessed 28 June 2017).

35. http://www.nytimes.com/2013/11/04/opinion/krugman-those-depressing-germans.html (accessed 28 June 2017).
36. https://www.theatlantic.com/international/archive/2017/05/trump-nato-germany/528429/ (accessed 28 June 2017).
37. https://obamawhitehouse.archives.gov/the-press-office/2016/04/25/remarks-president-obama-address-people-europe (accessed 28 June 2017).
38. https://www.theatlantic.com/international/archive/2017/07/trump-warsaw-speech/532917/ (accessed 1 August 2017).
39. http://abcnews.go.com/Politics/trump-merkel/story?id=46198767 (accessed 28 June 2017).
40. http://www.dw.com/en/things-donald-trump-said-about-angela-merkel-and-vice-versa/a-37889332 (accessed 28 June 2017).
41. https://www.washingtonpost.com/news/the-fix/wp/2016/09/29/donald-trumps-flip-flop-on-angela-merkel-is-mind-boggling/?utm_term=.757985efe6f8 (accessed 28 June 2017).
42. Ibid.
43. http://www.independent.co.uk/news/world/americas/us-politics/donald-trump-angela-merkel-nato-bill-defence-ignore-usa-germany-spending-a7650636.html (accessed 28 June 2017).
44. https://www.nytimes.com/2017/06/01/opinion/donald-trump-angela-merkel-nato.html?_r=0 (accessed 28 June 2017).
45. http://www.independent.co.uk/news/world/americas/us-politics/donald-trump-european-union-eu-us-president-totally-in-favour-wonderful-steve-bannon-mike-pence-a7596731.html (accessed 28 June 2017).
46. http://www.cnn.com/2017/07/06/politics/trump-speech-poland-transcript/index.html (accessed 1 Aug. 2017).
47. Ibid.
48. http://www.politico.com/magazine/story/2017/03/trump-steve-bannon-destroy-eu-european-union-214889 (accessed 28 June 2017).
49. https://www.washingtonpost.com/news/worldviews/wp/2016/11/09/angela-merkel-congratulates-donald-trump-kind-of/?utm_term=.ba8a2251154c (accessed 28 June 2017).
50. ibid.
51. http://www.newyorker.com/news/amy-davidson/angela-merkel-and-the-insult-of-trumps-paris-climate-accord-withdrawal (accessed 28 June 2017).
52. https://shorensteincenter.org/news-coverage-donald-trumps-first-100-days/ (accessed 28 June 2017).
53. http://www.pewglobal.org/2016/06/29/as-obama-years-draw-to-close-president-and-u-s-seen-favorably-in-europe-and-asia/ (accessed 28 June 2017).
54. https://www.bloomberg.com/news/articles/2017-02-17/trump-worries-germans-more-than-putin-in-poll-of-election-mood (accessed 28 June 2017).
55. http://www.pewglobal.org/2017/06/26/u-s-image-suffers-as-publics-around-world-question-trumps-leadership/ (accessed 30 June 2017)
56. https://www.nytimes.com/2017/04/25/world/europe/ivanka-trump-is-jeered-in-berlin-after-defending-her-father.html?_r=0;   https://www.washingtonpost.com/news/politics/wp/2017/06/28/trumps-pledge-to-keep-the-world-from-laughing-at-us-hits-another-setback/?hpid=hp_hp-top-table-main_trump-world-325pm%3Ahomepage%2Fstory&utm_term=.20ae41f9c9d3 (accessed 6 June 2017).
57. http://www.bbc.com/news/world-us-canada-40035837 (accessed 29 June 2017).
58. See also Stephen Szabo's contribution to this special issue.
59. http://www.ecfr.eu/article/commentary_trumps_poisoned_ttip_chalice (accessed 29 June 2017).
60. Donald J. Trump with Dave Shiflett, *The America We Deserve* (Los Angeles: Renaissance Books, 2000).
61. https://www.theatlantic.com/business/archive/2015/09/when-america-was-great-taxes-were-high-unions-were-strong-and-government-was-big/407284/ (accessed 5 June 2017).
62. https://www.nytimes.com/2016/03/27/us/politics/donald-trump-foreign-policy.html?action=Click&contentCollection=BreakingNews&contentID=61307450&pgtype=Homepage&_r=0 (accessed 5 June 2017).
63. http://www.politico.com/magazine/story/2017/04/22/pat-buchanan-trump-president-history-profile-215042 (accessed 5 July 2017).
64. https://www.vox.com/a/donald-trump-books (accessed 30 June 2017).
65. http://www.newyorker.com/news/daily-comment/donald-trump-and-the-amazing-alex-jones (accessed 6 July 2017).
66. https://www.ft.com/content/782381b6-ad91-11e6-ba7d-76378e4fef24 (accessed 23 May 2017).
67. https://www.ft.com/content/ae092214-d36f-11e6-b06b-680c49b4b4c0 (accessed 23 May 2017).
68. Ibid.
69. https://www.bundesregierung.de/Content/DE/Mitschrift/Pressekonferenzen/2016/11/2016-11-09-statement-merkel-us-wahlen.html (accessed 29 June 2017).

70. https://www.whitehouse.gov/the-press-office/2017/01/28/readout-presidents-call-chancellor-angela-merkel-germany (accessed 29 June 2017).
71. https://www.whitehouse.gov/the-press-office/2017/03/17/joint-press-conference-president-trump-and-german-chancellor-merkel (accessed 29 June 2017)
72. https://www.whitehouse.gov/inaugural-address (accessed 27 June 2017).
73. http://www.spiegel.de/international/world/anne-applebaum-interview-about-president-donald-trump-a-1130988.html (accessed 29 June 2017).
74. https://www.whitehouse.gov/the-press-office/2017/01/27/statement-president-international-holocaust-remembrance-day (accessed 29 June 2017).
75. https://www.whitehouse.gov/the-press-office/2017/03/17/joint-press-conference-president-trump-and-german-chancellor-merkel (accessed 29 June 2017).
76. Ibid.
77. http://www.spiegel.de/politik/ausland/us-wahl-donald-trumps-wahl-ist-das-ende-des-westens-a-1120608.html (accessed 29 June 2017).
78. https://www.washingtonpost.com/opinions/this-is-how-fascism-comes-to-america/2016/05/17/c4e32c58-1c47-11e6-8c7b-6931e66333e7_story.html?utm_term=.ef29cbcb09da (accessed 29 June 2017).
79. http://www.independent.co.uk/voices/angela-merkel-donald-trump-democracy-freedom-of-press-a7556986.html (accessed 27 June 2017).
80. http://www.bbc.co.uk/news/world-us-canada-3886796 (accessed 27 June 2017).
81. https://www.nytimes.com/2017/03/17/world/europe/angela-merkel-donald-trump.html?_r=0 (accessed 29 June 2017).
82. https://www.theguardian.com/commentisfree/2017/mar/17/angela-merkel-donald-trump-threat-europe-white-house-meeting (accessed 27 June 2017).
83. In fact, Lügenpresse was voted the Unwort des Jahres 2014, see http://www.spiegel.de/kultur/gesellschaft/luegenpresse-ist-unwort-des-jahres-a-1012678.html (accessed 29 June 2017).
84. http://www.bbc.co.uk/news/election-us-2016-37936207 (accessed 29 June 2017).
85. www.huffingtonpost.ca/lauryn-oates/identity-politics-alt-right_b_14481006.html (accessed 29 June 2017).
86. https://www.pressreader.com/uk/the-guardian/20170527/281986082505538 (accessed 29 June 2017); https://www.theguardian.com/us-news/2017/may/26/donald-trump-complained-belgian-pm-difficulty-golf-resorts-eu (accessed 29 June 2017).
87. http://www.rollingstone.com/politics/features/trump-and-the-pathology-of-narcissism-w474896 (accessed 6 June 2017).
88. https://www.wsj.com/articles/america-first-doesnt-mean-america-alone-1496187426 (accessed 29 June 2017).

Angela Merkel and Donald Trump – Values, Interests, and the Future of the West

KLAUS LARRES

German Chancellor Merkel and US President Donald Trump did not get off to a good start. Their relationship so far has been lukewarm at best. Trump's deficits in understanding and lack of support for democracy and the liberal world order as it was established by Trump's predecessors in the mid-1940s deeply worries European politicians. In view of their own past history and the expectation that Germany may have to step in and become the western world's leading defender of western values, most German policy makers, including the long-serving chancellor, are particularly annoyed and distraught about the developments in the US. This article will analyse the evolving relationship between Angela Merkel and Donald Trump since the latter moved into the Oval Office in January 2017. The article will highlight both the more fundamental structural problems and the day-to-day political hurdles in German–American relations.

Chancellor Merkel has been in office since October 2005.[1] During that comparatively long period of time she has had to deal with three American presidents. None of her relations with the self-confident but prickly leaders were easy. The current incumbent, however, appears to present a particular challenge. Within days of Donald Trump's election victory in early November 2016 German–American relations plummeted. Subsequent phone calls and meetings between Merkel and Trump, either in a bilateral or a multilateral context, could not overcome the coldness between the two leaders. In fact, relations seem to have become worse over time. In this article, I wish to trace German–American relations under Merkel and Trump and analyse the deeper reasons for the growing estrangement between the two governments which, after all, have been close allies and partners for almost 70 years. In fact, despite the deep divisions over the Iraq war of 2003 and various other smaller crises, until very recently Germany could be regarded as one of America's closest and most reliable global allies.

BUSH, OBAMA, AND ANGELA MERKEL

Germany's relationship with George W. Bush's America was burdened by the legacy of the invasion of Iraq that was much opposed by the German public and the Schröder government, though not by Angela Merkel herself.[2] Chancellor Schröder deeply angered the US when he pronounced that 'this country under my leadership is not available for adventures'.[3] Not much was left of the idea expressed by the older President

Bush during a speech in Mainz in May 1989 that Germany ought to be a 'partner in leadership' with the US.[4] Opposition leader Merkel actually supported America's war in Iraq half-heartedly. This attitude helped her when she attempted, successfully as it turned out, to overcome frosty German–American relations and develop a good working relationship with President George W. Bush. This was perhaps best symbolised by the friendly and unusually personal shoulder rub Bush gave the chancellor when passing by her seat during the G8 meeting in St. Petersburg in early 2006.[5] In his memoirs Bush referred to Merkel as 'trustworthy, engaging and warm'; she quickly became one of 'my closest friends on the world stage'.[6] By the time he wrote his memoirs shortly after leaving office in 2009 the initial tension between him and the German chancellor had long since been forgotten.

Merkel's relations with the succeeding Obama administration also proved contentious at first. Not least this was due to the global financial and economic crisis and the Euro crisis that resulted. Washington put forward a number of prescriptions of how to tackle the dire situation by means of deficit spending and a huge stimulus programme that found very little favour in Berlin and Brussels.[7] Eventually, however, Obama largely came round to the German view. As early as 5 June 2009, during a joint press conference with Merkel in Dresden, he indicated somewhat reluctantly that the growth of the US economy (and by implication global growth) 'can't be based on overheated financial markets or overheated housing markets or U.S. consumers maxing out on their credit cards or us sustaining non-stop deficit spending as far as the eye can see'.[8] Yet Obama never wavered in his criticism of Germany's export surpluses, which in his view were not put to good use. Instead of the revenues being utilised to bolster German saving accounts and the coffers of the finance minister, they ought to be invested to spur growth and demand. The Germans should spend and consume more, he advised.[9]

Edward Snowden's revelations of US espionage activities in Germany during Obama's second term caused much resentment and for a time led to a significant cooling of German–American relations.[10] Yet, on the whole, Merkel managed to sustain good relations with the administration. Not least, both politicians liked to intellectually spar with each other and shared a deep belief in the importance of upholding western values and democratic institutions. Being invited to address a joint session of Congress in 2010, the first German chancellor to do so for 52 years,[11] and the award of the Presidential Medal of Freedom less than two years later were the outward high points of her excellent relationship with Obama.[12] In fact, despite tense beginnings with Presidents Bush and Obama, Merkel succeeded in developing relations with both that approximated genuine friendships, in particular with Obama. Fostering a personal relationship with President Trump, however, has proven to be much more challenging.

Trump's Election Campaign

It is doubtful if Merkel had ever heard of Trump before he began running for president in 2015. The notorious prominence he had established in the US since the 1970s as a ruthless New York property baron and then, from 2003, as the TV host of *The Apprentice* did not make much headway in Europe. The TV series was shown in the UK, however, and was equally popular. It featured British entrepreneur Alan Sugar as host, who, like Trump, seemed to get a thrill out of firing people who in his view did not make the cut. The adoption of the show in Germany in 2004 with a local host proved to be a flop, however.[13]

It was during the Republican primary elections that Trump came to general attention in Germany. His strident rhetoric and his skilful and frequently vulgar outmanoeuvring of his Republican rivals such as Jeb Bush, Marco Rubio and many others made him a household name among those interested in American politics. This included the German chancellor and the country's foreign policy establishment. Trump had no hesitation to refer to the chancellor in many of his campaign speeches and interviews – usually in a less than complimentary manner. Certainly, his German ancestry did not seem to influence him in a pro-German way. Trump's grandfather grew up in the village of Kallstadt less than 50 miles from Frankfurt and in 1885 aged 16 he emigrated to the US to escape poverty.[14]

It appears that Trump had genuine respect for Merkel's long-standing skilful leadership qualities but was deeply upset by her immigration and refugee policies.[15] In October 2015, for instance, he said in an interview: 'What she's done in Germany is insane'. He predicted that 'They're going to have riots in Germany'.[16] He talked about Merkel having made a 'catastrophic mistake' and called her refugee policy a 'total disaster'. He indicated to Germany's mass circulation newspaper *Bild* in January that opening the door to refugees was allowing potential terrorists in. 'I like her but I think it was a mistake. And people make mistakes, but I think it was a very big mistake.'[17] Ever competitive and keen on the limelight, he was upset when *Time Magazine* did not choose him as the Person of the Year. Trump complained via Twitter in late 2015 that the magazine had preferred instead to pick the woman who was 'ruining Germany'.[18]

Commenting on the New Year's Eve assaults on women in Cologne at a campaign event in Iowa, Trump once again predicted unrest in Germany and also attacked Merkel personally. He declared that 'The German people are going to riot. The German people are going to end up overthrowing this woman. I don't know what the hell she is thinking'.[19] In the same month he returned to the issue. 'What Merkel did to Germany is a shame, it's a sad, sad shame', he pronounced.[20] A few months later he referred to Germans leaving their country in droves. 'These are people', he explained, 'that were very proud Germans that were beyond belief, they thought the greatest that there ever was [sic!] and now they're talking about leaving Germany.'[21]

These sharp criticisms, however, did not stop him from changing his mind when it pleased him. In September 2016 Trump explained in an interview that he thought 'Merkel is a really great world leader'. Yet he could not get over her refugee policy. 'I was very disappointed', he said, about 'the whole thing on immigration. It's a big problem and really, you know, to look at what she's done in the last year and a half. I was always a Merkel person. I thought really fantastic. But I think she made a very tragic mistake a year and a half ago'.[22]

Trump's Electoral Victory and the Reaction in Germany

When Trump won the election on 8 November 2016, the German foreign policy establishment was profoundly shocked. Like most foreigners, the Germans had confidently expected Hillary Clinton to move into the Oval Office.[23] Yet, although Clinton won the popular vote by a majority of almost 3 million, Trump managed to win more states and thus a greater number of electoral college votes.[24] As is customary, Merkel, like other international leaders, congratulated the new president-elect on his victory. The chancellor used the opportunity, however, to remind him of the importance of upholding western values.

Merkel's remarkable and unprecedented statement did not go down well with the president-elect. Extraordinarily, she not only congratulated him on his election victory but also indicated that Germany's relations with her European partners were 'deeper' than those with the United States. 'Germany's ties with the United States of America are deeper than with any country outside of the European Union', she put it diplomatically. Getting into her stride in the very next sentence, she issued a set of conditions for cooperating with Trump's government, conditions than ran counter to many of the ugly and nationalistic pronouncements the president-to-be had made during the election campaign.[25] Her statement said:

> Germany and America are bound by common values – democracy, freedom as well as respect for the rule of law and the dignity of each and every person, regardless of their origin, skin color, religion, gender, sexual orientation or political views

'It is based on these values', the chancellor continued, 'that I wish to offer close cooperation, both with me personally and between our countries' governments.' It seemed that no cooperation was possible if these values were not respected by the 45th president. Still, she continued more tactfully, 'partnership with the United States is and will remain a keystone of German foreign policy so that we can tackle the great challenges of our time'.[26]

Other German politicians were less polite. Defence Minister von der Leyen referred to Trump's victory as a 'heavy shock' and the German justice minister thought that 'the world won't end, it just keeps getting crazier'. Sigmar Gabriel, the outspoken economics minister, who in late January 2017 was appointed Germany's foreign minister, said at the time that Trump was 'the trailblazer of a new authoritarian and chauvinist international movement … They want a rollback to the bad old times'. Gregor Gysi, the formidable former leader of the Left party, put it particularly succinctly when he told German radio that Trump was 'a simple soul, not particularly well-educated, he's coarse'. Gysi feared that 'this will give right-wing populism a new boost in Europe'.[27] Foreign Minister Steinmeier, who was elevated to the German presidency in March 2017, uttered in exasperation that 'nothing will be easier, a lot will be more difficult. We don't know how Donald Trump will govern America'. One thing is certain, he presciently told the German news agency DPA, 'U.S. foreign policy will be less predictable'.[28]

UNEASE ABOUT THE VALUES OF THE NEW PRESIDENT

German policy makers, including the chancellor, felt that they were called upon to educate the new nationalist American president, who was inaugurated on 20 January 2017 and did not seem to have much sympathy for or understanding of western democratic values. For the German public and German politicians, it was difficult not to look back to January 1933 when Hitler took power in Berlin. He charmed and bullied the electorate with outrageous nationalist and racist promises to make Germany great again and put Germany and the Germans first.[29] Trump did not refer to the at least 6 million Jews who perished at the hand of the Nazis when he issued a statement to commemorate Holocaust Remembrance Day on 27 January 2017.[30] This confirmed a rather uneasy feeling among most Germans regarding the strange convictions and worldviews held by Donald Trump and the people around him.

This unease and concern was confirmed by Trump's executive order 13769 of 27 January that limited immigration from seven Muslim countries, suspended all refugee admissions for four months and barred all refugees from Syria indefinitely.[31] Before a court order temporarily halted the president's executive order two days later, apparently at least 60,000 visas were revoked that had been issued to citizens of these countries.[32] Trump's second, somewhat watered down, travel ban, dated 6 March, fared no better. It excluded Iraqi travellers, made no explicit reference to religion and removed a complete ban on Syrian refugees. Yet it was also struck down by the courts, as were the subsequent appeals.[33] In late June the Supreme Court, however, overturned these decisions and allowed a partial travel ban to come into effect. It also provided for a great number of exceptions when travellers from the affected six Muslim countries had family and institutional links to the US. The court announced that it would hear the whole case in full in October.

Obviously, Trump is no Hitler and America's democratic institutions are much more formidable than the weakened democratic set-up of the Weimar Republic. Tension and mutual incomprehension between the US president and the German chancellor are rather unfortunate, however.[34] They may well have serious consequences for the western world and perhaps even for global stability and peace. For better or worse, the US remains the world's leading economic power. The country also has by far the globe's most formidable military, both in terms of its conventional and nuclear arsenal and Washington's warfighting expertise and experience. Despite Germany having the world's fourth strongest economy, by comparison the German chancellor and her much smaller country are much less important.

Nevertheless, due to recent developments in the context of the Euro crisis and the renewed rise of populist nationalism and racism in many EU countries, Angela Merkel has been catapulted to being perhaps the last hope for the survival of liberal democracy and democratic stability on the European continent.[35] The Greek state and many Italian banks continue to be highly overleveraged and could collapse any time soon. Both Spain and post-Brexit UK are faced with serious threats to their national unity, if respectively Catalonia and Scotland succeed in their strivings for independence. The UK was further destabilised by an unnecessary snap general election in June 2017. The election outcome led to a new unstable Conservative government that was dependent on the Northern Irish unionists for its narrow majority.[36]

There are also frequent disconcerting flashes of violence and unrest in the Balkans. Russian pressure and intimidation in much of eastern Europe – and not just in Ukraine – is meant to encourage the countries in the region to re-consider their links with NATO and the western world. Increasingly autocratic governments in Hungary, Poland and also in the Czech Republic are making determined efforts to restrict the rights to free speech, free assembly and other democratic rights. They are undermining the values

Europe has been based on for the last 70 years. Similarly, the autocratic developments and multiplying human rights violations in Turkey, a NATO member and still formally an aspirant for EU membership, are viewed with great suspicion by most European countries.

Bilateral relations between the US president and the German chancellor thus matter a lot, perhaps much more than at any time since the end of World War II. For Trump is a 'people person', he told the visiting British prime minister in late January 2017.[37] Good relations with a particular government appear to depend on whether or not Trump hits it off with the leader of that country. Trump is clearly fond of strong autocratic men and has repeatedly praised leaders such as Russia's Putin, Turkey's Erdogan, El-Sisi of Egypt, Chinese President Xi Jinping, the Saudi monarch, Philippine President Duterte and similar figures. He admires their ability to issue commands without having to be too concerned about public opinion, political criticism and messy deliberations of democratically elected parliaments. The world in the Trump era is witnessing the return of personal power politics. And in this context Angela Merkel and the Germans, as well as the other members of the western alliance, of course, face an uphill task to make their voices and the voice of liberal democracy heard in Washington, DC.

The First Phone Call and the First Visit

It was more than two months after Merkel congratulated Trump on his election victory and a week after his inauguration that the two politicians touched base for the first time by talking on the phone on 28 January. American and Russian officials needed two hours to release a joint press statement after the first phone conversation between Donald Trump and Vladimir Putin on the same day. It took American and German officials more than twice this time to work out a statement after the phone communication between the US president and the German chancellor.[38] This was one of several indications that the 45-minute talk between Trump and Merkel was actually much more challenging for Trump than his talk with the Russian autocrat. It may also have been much less pleasant and flattering.

The phone conversation between Trump and Merkel, however, was amiable enough at first. The tension and mutual recriminations built up during the US election campaign appeared to be forgotten. Trump, after all, has a certain rough-and-ready charm if he puts his mind to it and Merkel is also quite capable of employing well-honed social skills. The long-serving German chancellor and the new president were able to agree on some matters, such as the importance of further deepening 'the already excellent bilateral relations in the coming years'. Trump was happy to accept an invitation to attend the G20 summit in Hamburg in July. He expressed the hope that he would 'soon' have the pleasure of welcoming the German leader in Washington. Despite Trump referring to NATO as 'obsolete' only a few weeks prior during the election campaign, both politicians emphasised the 'fundamental significance' of the NATO alliance for transatlantic relations and the fight against international terrorism.[39] Already in his press conference with the British prime minister Theresa May in late January, the president had confirmed that he was '100% behind NATO'.[40]

Merkel was ready to compromise on some issues, as she had indicated in the last few weeks. Much to Trump's delight, the two of them agreed on the necessity of making new 'investments in the military capabilities' of the alliance. They also emphasised the importance of 'a fair contribution of all allies to collective security'. Trump's push to get all NATO members to actually dedicate 2 per cent of their GNP to their defence spending found Merkel's approval. This is a self-mandated commitment that has long been accepted in principle by all NATO members. It was first drawn up as a guideline at the 2006 NATO meeting in Riga, though it was not even mentioned in the summit communique. In 2014, at the Cardiff summit, a few months after Russia had annexed Crimea and invaded eastern Ukraine, NATO members agreed that all members should 'move toward' the 2 per cent goal by 2024.[41] This was not a binding commitment either; rather it was a serious aspiration. Trump's treatment of the 2 per cent defence contribution of NATO members as a binding and non-negotiable target which needs to be met immediately does not reflect what was actually agreed upon. Despite raising its contribution recently, Berlin itself only manages to dedicate just about 1.2 per cent of the country's GNP to defence but the Germans intend to invest more in the future.[42]

Trump has also consistently misunderstood the contributions NATO member states make. The 2 per cent refer to an increase in the defence expenditure of each member state; how they then spend their defence budget is left entirely up to them. It is not a contribution to a common and shared NATO budget. Such a budget does not exist. While all member states make a small contribution to NATO headquarters for the running and administrative management of the headquarters, this is a tiny sum and none of the NATO members are in arrears regarding this contribution.[43]

Apart from security matters, during their phone conversation Merkel and Trump also talked about the situation in the Middle East and in North Africa. They also discussed relations with Russia and the Ukraine question.[44] Whether or not the lifting of the sanctions on Russia was talked about remained unclear initially. Yet a day later Merkel's spokesman, Steffen Seibert, said that EU sanctions on Russia had indeed been discussed. Soon he also made clear that Merkel had talked to Trump about his executive order of 27 January restricting travel from seven Muslim-majority countries. 'The chancellor regrets the U.S. government's entry ban against refugees and the citizens of certain countries', her spokesman announced.[45]

It appears that Merkel lectured Trump in no uncertain terms about her firm conviction 'that the necessary decisive battle against terrorism does not justify a general suspicion against people of a certain origin or a certain religion'. Merkel explained to the freshman president that 'the Geneva refugee convention requires the international community to take in war refugees on humanitarian grounds. All signatory states have this obligation'. This seemed to be quite new to Trump, who had only vaguely heard about the Geneva Convention.[46] Not unexpectedly, the new president, who has a rather delicate ego and is used to giving commands at Trump Tower, his business headquarters, was not impressed by Merkel's admonition. In fact, Trump appeared to view Merkel with increasing suspicion, if not disdain.

Only a few days later, before her press conference with Ukrainian President Poroshenko on 30 January, the German chancellor once again referred to Trump's executive order on mostly Muslim immigration to the US as unacceptable.[47] The day after, during a visit to Stockholm, Merkel sharply rejected Trump economic adviser Peter Navarro's accusation in the *Financial Times* that Germany was unfairly benefiting from a 'grossly undervalued' euro. He claimed that Germany kept the euro artificially weak in order to obtain an export advantage and thus exploit both its EU partners and the US. He also said that this German policy had been the main hurdle during the TTIP (Transatlantic Trade and Investment Partnership) negotiations between the EU and the US during the Obama years. They were now effectively dead, he said.[48] Already during the election campaign Trump had accused China of manipulating its currency to obtain trade advantages. The administration was now making similar accusations against Germany (and also Japan), though the phrase 'currency manipulation' was not used, possibly because it would have certain legal implications. But soon the president called the EU a 'vehicle for Germany', much antagonising the German government in the process.[49]

These were worrying developments. Already the Trump administration's withdrawal from the Asian TPP (the Trans-Pacific Partnership), Washington's desire to re-open the negotiations for a North Atlantic Free Trade Agreement (NAFTA) with Mexico and Canada and various other hostile remarks by the new president indicated that Trump had turned against multilateral free trade arrangements. He was in favour of bilateral deals where US power and influence can dominate more easily. Speaking in Stockholm, Merkel defended Germany by saying that the European Central Bank was totally independent and did not take instructions from national governments. Indeed, the German government has been very critical of the European Central Bank's bond buying programme that has weakened the common currency.[50] However, the large German trade surplus with the US and much of the euro zone has been controversial for some time. Berlin, some analysts have concluded, as had President Obama in 2009, ought to rebalance its economy by stimulating domestic consumption and embarking on a domestic investment programme. There is indeed some wisdom in these calls.[51]

Still, Navarro's attempt to drive a wedge between the EU countries was a disconcerting development. This used to be just Russia's and China's policy; the Trump administration seemed to have jumped on board for purely nationalist economic reasons. Trump intended to dismantle multilateral economic globalisation in favour of bilateralism. Navarro approved of a 20 per cent import tax plan that he believed would pay for Trump's pet project, the building of a wall along the border with Mexico. In his *FT* article, he explained that the new US administration thought it best to unwind and repatriate the international supply chains that all global multinational companies require. 'We need to manufacture those components in a robust domestic supply chain that will spur job and wage growth' in the US, he outlined.[52] For Germany, one of the world's most globally integrated economies, and its strong export industry such a nationalist and protectionist American approach would be disastrous.

A few weeks after her phone conversation with Trump Merkel attended the Munich Security Conference. Her meetings with Vice-President Pence and other members of the administration, such as Secretary of State Tillerson and Defence Secretary Mattis, went very well. Merkel hoped that a personal talk with the new president himself would also make a positive difference. 'Face-to-face talks are always much better than talking about each other',[53] she told journalists.

On 17 March 2017 Merkel came for a flying one-day visit to Washington, DC. She brought chief executives from Siemens and BMW along as both companies have large factories in the US and provide employment for thousands of American workers. But the main reason for her visit was to set up a decent working relationship with the new administration.

The talks with the new president did not go too well, however. The body language of both politicians indicated no real warmth between them. And in the Oval Office Trump even seemed to ignore Merkel's suggestion to shake hands again when a reporter asked them to do so again for the sake of the cameras (they did shake hands when they first met). He looked straight ahead and did not seem to have heard her, or pretended not to have heard her. Over lunch Trump reportedly even handed Merkel a fake invoice for over $300 billion, the amount, according to the calculation of the White House, the Germans had not spent on defence since the late 1990s. The chancellor was not impressed; a German minister called it 'outrageous'.[54]

The substantive talks between Trump and Merkel went fairly well, however, though they remained quite superficial. Both leaders believed that sanctions on Russia should only be lifted if Moscow implemented the Mink II agreement fully to resolve the Ukrainian situation. Merkel agreed with Trump that NATO members should increase their defence spending. She also emphasised the value of free trade and the inadvisability of protectionism. Several times Trump proposed a bilateral trade agreement between the US and Germany, in order to reduce the high German export surplus with the US. The president, however, did not understand that the chancellor was neither ready, nor able to respond to this, as already many years ago the individual EU member states had delegated the task of negotiating trade deals to the EU Commission. Since then they have not been entitled to negotiate bilateral national deals.

When Trump eventually grasped this, he said that in that case the US and the EU needed to embark on trade negotiations. It remained an open question whether he was serious. Did this mean that the administration would be interested in reviving the TTIP negotiations that have been on halt since Obama left the White House? Altogether the first Trump–Merkel meeting did not result in a new closeness in German–American relations. The *Washington Post* talked of a 'frosty' event.[55]

Moreover, only a day later, during the G20 meeting of finance ministers and central bankers in the German Baden-Baden, the US Treasury Secretary Mnuchin refused to sign the customary G20 declaration that expressed strong support for free trade and condemned trade protectionism. While the meeting was friendly and non-combative, apparently, the White House had not given him the authority to do so. A reference to the expectation of the G20 to finance measures against climate change was also dropped from the final communiqué that is meant to be unanimous. Both the US and Saudi Arabia had opposed its inclusion, though this had not been a problem during the previous year's G20 finance meeting.[56]

THE NATO AND G7 MEETINGS – MAY/JUNE 2017

An open clash between Trump and America's allies occurred during the president's visit to NATO headquarters outside Brussels on 30 May 2017 and the subsequent G7 meeting on Sicily in which he participated. In particular Angela Merkel was incensed. It was Trump's first presidential trip abroad and before coming to Europe he had visited Saudi Arabia and Israel. Both countries feted him in a grand way which he greatly enjoyed. They certainly spared him any critical questions. This was rather different in

Europe. The other leaders of the G7 countries (Canada, Germany, France, Japan, Italy, the UK) regarded Trump with great scepticism. They wished to persuade him to express his wholehearted support for NATO. They also urged him to commit his administration to continued membership in the Paris Climate Pact that after difficult and complex negotiations President Obama had signed together with his Chinese, Russian and European counterparts in December 2015. In the meantime, virtually all other countries on earth have joined and mostly ratified the pact (only Syria and Nigeria are not on board).

Yet both endeavours failed. Instead Trump persistently refused to announce his support for Article 5 of the NATO Treaty – the crucial mutual defence clause in case of an attack on any member state. Effectively, the entire NATO alliance is based on this Article. The US president only spoke in very vague words of the American approval of the alliance, but avoided any more concrete commitment. In fact, a few days later it emerged that Trump's advisers had given him a speech which contained strong positive words that endorsed Article 5. But Trump had deliberately ignored these words and taken out the relevant line when giving his speech. He clearly seemed to still doubt the value of NATO and continued to be deeply annoyed that the European allies in his view spend too little on defence. In fact, his speech contained angry words of admonition for the Europeans to increase their defence spending significantly.[57]

Trump puts up his own country as a role model in this context. The first draft budget the Trump administration submitted to Congress included a 10 per cent increase in US military spending (the draft budget is unlikely to pass without major congressional revisions, however). In fact, the Trump administration wishes to add $54 billion to the US defence budget. This increase is almost as much as the entire Russian defence budget. If this is granted, the navy will receive most of the additional money. A large portion of it will be dedicated to a strengthened US engagement in the Pacific. This means in effect that Obama's never properly implemented 'Pivot to Asia' for better or worse may well be realised by the Trump administration.[58]

The dinner that followed Trump's 'public tongue lashing' of his NATO allies appears to have been even worse. NATO leaders were 'appalled' according to sources who were at the dinner. Trump gave an improvised speech, once again complaining that the NATO allies did not contribute enough to defence. They should not only spend 2 per cent of their GDP but it would be best if they spent 3 per cent of GDP. He seems to have threatened to cut US defence spending unless NATO allies made up the shortfall of not having spent at least 2 per cent during the last two decades. The president talked about 'back pay' due to NATO. And Trump does not seem to have wanted to discuss Russia's activities in Ukraine and eastern Europe at all. 'Oh, it was a total shitshow', one participant of the dinner said later. 'The dinner was far worse than the speech', a former US official said, who was informed about the dinner. 'It was a train wreck. It was awful.'[59]

No wonder that a few days after Trump's European visit German Chancellor Merkel gave a much-noticed speech in Munich: 'The era in which we could fully rely on others is over to some extent', she said, before adding: 'That's what I experienced over the past several days.' She explained that 'we Europeans truly have to take our fate into our own hands – naturally in friendship with the United States of America, in friendship with Great Britain, as good neighbours with whoever, also with Russia and other countries'. For Merkel, it was clear however that 'we have to know that we must fight for our future on our own, for our destiny as Europeans'.[60] Although Merkel was in the middle of her re-election campaign to gain a fourth term as chancellor, her words were meant very seriously.

Subsequently, immediately after the NATO meeting in Brussels, the G7 meeting on Sicily took place. Here, however, the allies were no more successful in obtaining a commitment from Trump. This time they urged the president to adhere to the December 2015 Paris Climate Pact. Much to the consternation of the assembled western leaders the president explained that he had not yet made up his mind whether or not the US would leave the pact. He would announce his decision within the next few days on his return to the US.

This announcement occurred on 1 June when Trump assembled a large number of people in the White House Rose Garden and dramatically proclaimed that the US would leave the climate pact. Most of the world was shocked. Especially America's European allies, in particular Germany, were greatly dismayed. Soon the Europeans decided to attempt to circumvent the White House and work with environmentally conscious American cities and states to continue implementing the climate pact.[61] Perhaps even more important was the agreement between the EU and China to establish an alliance to cooperate in fighting climate change.[62]

Thus, instead of improving transatlantic relations Trump's journey to Europe contributed to a worsening of alliance relations. His journey did not help to clarify the traditionally strong American commitment to NATO and European integration. Instead, Trump's rather lukewarm words on Article 5 and his strong criticism of the insufficient defence expenditure of most NATO countries undermined further the belief in US support for the western alliance.

On 9 June 2017, when answering a question about the US commitment to NATO at a press conference with visiting Romanian President Klaus Iohannis, Trump said, out of the blue, 'Absolutely, I'd be committed to Article 5 ... certainly we are there to protect'. While all NATO members were relieved to hear him say this, it was a little late. Why had Trump not said so during the NATO summit in May? It did not go unnoticed either that Trump did not volunteer this information but gave it in response to a reporter's question.[63]

Within only a short period of time Trump has indeed managed to make all NATO members wonder whether America has become a liability with regard to stability and reliability in global affairs. It also remains an open question whether or not the Trump administration has a genuine interest in the continuation of the transatlantic partnership. Canada, for instance, announced shortly after Trump's NATO visit the expansion of its defence budget as the US could no longer be relied upon to provide global leadership.[64]

Trump, his Advisers, and Germany's Foreign Policy Establishment

The Trump presidency clearly continues to deeply worry the German foreign policy establishment. At first it was hoped in Berlin that once inaugurated the new president would stop his rather simplistic pronouncements and move away from his divisive election campaign toward the political centre. Trump, it was expected, would use the transition period and the early days of his presidency to transform himself into a much more mature and respected statesman (and perhaps even delete his twitter account). Yet this did not happen. By now German politicians have given up hope that Trump will ever develop into a responsible politician. It seems that the world will have to come to terms with a rather impulsive, irrational, vain and frequently ill-informed and ill-advised president.[65] Trump, many are convinced, is an embarrassment to America and the western world but it is unlikely that he will be forced to leave office early.[66]

German foreign policy experts are deeply upset about Trump's inner circle. After all, a predilection for constant change, turmoil and self-promotion is the one enduring and reliable factor that characterises the administration and the president himself. This state of affairs reflects a deeper split within the Trump White House. A battle is being waged between the ideological Steve Bannon faction and a more pragmatic faction. Bannon himself, however, was dismissed as the President's Chief Strategist in August 2017. While the former faction wishes to bring down the modern bureaucratic (or administrative) state and go back to the America of Andrew Jackson and the supremacy of the white 'common man', the latter camp sees itself in the tradition of the conservative Reagan administration when the US was the undisputed global leader. As Andrew Sullivan argues persuasively, Bannon and company have a 'passionate loathing of the status quo' and a strong desire to return to America's golden self-contained past 'in one emotionally cathartic revolt'.[67] This applies to domestic but also to foreign affairs.

The more pragmatic faction is no less hard-line, but attempts to push the administration toward a more engaged and cooperative foreign policy that is, however, still based on rather nationalistic 'America First' sentiments. The president is frequently uncertain where to position himself and plays it by ear, allowing himself to be influenced by the situation at hand and the people he happens to encounter at any one time.

The administration, it seems, is still in transition regarding the personalities that shape the Trump era. With the exception of the 'Decisive Three' – the president himself and his two closest advisers, who happen to be married to each other and are drawn from his immediate family[68] – a closely knit network of Trump policy makers is only very gradually emerging. Berlin was greatly concerned about Trump's first national security adviser, General Michael Flynn. German diplomats regarded him as seriously 'durchgeknallt' (off the wall) and considered him to be rather a loose cannon.[69] His dismissal after only 24 days in office confirmed Berlin's assessment. But Germany remains deeply worried about some of Trump's advisers who also have a strong ideological bent.

Right-wing ideologues and inflexible economic nationalists such as Steve Bannon, Steve Miller, Sebastian Gorka, Kellyanne Conway, Peter Navarro and Kathleen McFarland are less important than they were in the very early days of the administration but most of them remain influential, even after some of them have left the White House such as Gorka, McFarland and, of course, Bannon himself. In particular, Miller and Conway are still important members of Trump's inner circle. Bannon and Miller authored Trump's gloomy inauguration speech which talked about the 'carnage' which allegedly dominated life in America. Both men are obsessed with the dangers accruing from Islamic jihad.[70] And Conway, who coined the silly phrase 'alternative facts', cannot even remotely be considered a serious foreign policy thinker either.[71]

Jared Kushner, the president's inexperienced 36-year-old son-in-law, an orthodox Jew, has been given responsibility for focusing on foreign policy toward Israel, China and Russia. While he travels the world on behalf of Trump, he seldom says anything in public. There are no speeches or press statements that outline his views. He has remained a rather dark horse. After the election but prior to Trump's inauguration Kushner proposed to Russian ambassador Kislyak to set up a backchannel using the equipment of the Russian embassy in Washington while keeping it secret from US authorities.[72] This bizarre and possibly illegal episode, as well as Trump's firing of FBI director Comey and the alleged contacts between his campaign team and Russia, are now being investigated by at least three congressional committees, including the Senate Intelligence Committee, as well as by a special counsel (former FBI director Robert Mueller).

Lately more competent experts with a greater grasp on reality, such as National Economic Council chairman Gary Cohn, a former Goldman Sachs banker, have seen their influence grow. Not least, the advice given by defence experts such as General H.R. McMasters, the national security adviser, and Secretary of Defence General James Mattis as well as Secretary of State Rex Tillerson are being taken more seriously by the White House – at least on occasion – than was the case initially.[73]

Yet this situation is in flux and there is no guarantee that the 'grown-ups' in the administration will continue to increase their influence. In fact, Tillerson has turned out to be a rather ineffective secretary of state. He is also in the process of downgrading staff numbers and thus the available expertise in the State Department to a significant extent.[74] McMaster is credited with having 'professionalised' the National Security Council, but lately Trump appears to have become 'disillusioned' with him. He has complained that his policy is being undermined and the president has openly clashed with the formidable general several times. McMaster's attempt to appoint Brigadier General Rick Waddell as his deputy was blocked by the White House.[75] For the time being McMaster remains in office; this may ensure that together with the skilful work of Defence Secretary Mattis a dose of reality continues to influence US foreign policy. Mattis is the administration's only formidable foreign and defense policy thinker. Tillerson has been rather disappointing in this as well as in many other respects. Furthermore, former four star General John Kelly has turned out to be a controversial and only semi-effective Chief of Staff.

Still, since the *Wall Street Journal* published an article co-authored by General McMasters and Gary Cohn one has to wonder whether there really are such big differences between the two foreign policy factions in the White House. The two authors explained, after all, that Trump had recognised with 'clear view' that there is no 'global community' and both friends and enemies compete vigorously with each other in the jungle of international relations. Instead of denying this elementary fact of international relations, the article emphasised, the Trump administration welcomed this fact.[76] Life was 'the naked, selfish struggle for money and power', a commentary in the *New York Times* summed up the foreign policy philosophy of the Trump government. Idealistic notions such as altruism, cooperation and fairness remained completely ignored. These convictions, according to the newspaper, were shared by all the important foreign policy experts in the Trump White House. This also explained the sympathy of the president for autocrats like Erdogan, Putin and similar undemocratic rulers, as they were all thinking along similar lines.[77]

While the Obama White House was proud of coming across as a reliable, trustworthy and predictable government,[78] Trump aspires to the opposite. He is mightily proud of his 'flexibility' which, he believes, enables him to change course quickly whenever it seems appropriate to him.[79] 'We must, as a nation, be more unpredictable', he declared in April 2016 during a major campaign speech [80] To many observers at home and abroad, however, this unpredictability comes close to incoherence and confusion, as the *Washington Post* has argued.[81]

The German foreign policy establishment is scared of the possible disastrous consequences of Trump's presidency regarding intra-western relations and global stability and peace. In particular Trump's trade policy, his attitude toward the EU and transatlantic relations and in this context also his ambiguous relationship with Russia deeply worry Berlin (as well as many other EU states).[82] EU Council President Donald Tusk, a former Polish prime minister, even said in January 2017 that for him a newly aggressive China, Putin's Russia, ISIS and Donald Trump were the greatest external threats to the survival of the EU.[83]

Trade policy. In Berlin there is a great deal of concern regarding the new president's protectionist trade policy which envisages the imposition of import tariffs as high as 35 per cent on, for instance, car manufacturers who do not produce their cars in the US but in cheap-labour countries. While all of Germany's luxury car manufacturers such as BMW and Mercedes Benz as well as Volkswagen have factories on American soil, they also produce a great number of their vehicles in Mexico for export to the US. BMW and Daimler are in the process of building new factories in Mexico and Audi completed a brand new one last year. Although China has become a much more important market for German car companies, the US market remains vital. It is Germany's second largest car market. In 2016 approximately 1.3 million German cars were sold in the US. The threatened imposition of high tariffs on German cars imported from Mexico would probably make them rather uncompetitive in the US.[84]

The growing German–American rift regarding Germany's export surplus with the US was on prominent display when Trump visited Brussels in March 2017. Just before he lambasted his NATO allies for not meeting NATO's 2 per cent defence spending target, he had a meeting with EU officials. According to several press reports Trump said: 'The Germans are bad, very bad.' 'See the millions of cars they are selling in the U. S.? Terrible. We will stop this.' EU Commission President Juncker, who participated in the meeting, attempted to calm down the row. Juncker explained to journalists that Trump said 'we have a problem, as others do, with the German surplus. So he was not aggressive at all.

Yet the damage had been done. It had become obvious that for the first time since the Iraq war of 2003 the Germans and Americans were on a serious collision course. The chairman of the foreign affairs committee of the German parliament did not hide his anger. 'U.S. President Trump isn't capable of leading the Western alliance. In any case', Norbert Röttgen fumed; 'he isn't interested in it at the moment'.[85]

European integration. 'Brexit is going to be a wonderful thing for your country', the US president told British Prime Minister May when she visited him in late January 2017.[86] Trump's public support of Brexit, which he referred to as 'fantastic', his repeated public praise about Britain re-gaining its independence and its borders as well as his expectation that other countries will follow the British example has also profoundly upset German policy makers.[87] Transatlantic relations were often influenced by economic rivalry and political difficulties. Yet from Truman and Eisenhower to Obama, all US administrations have strongly supported the European integration process. The only exception was the lukewarm attitude, for economic reasons, of the Nixon administration. But even Nixon fully realised how important for stability and peace (and economic well-being) on the continent the European project was.[88]

Despite some changes in the Trump administration's attitude, great enthusiasm or even strong support for the EU and the European integration process cannot be detected in Trump's Washington. Essentially Trump and his entourage believe in bilateralism, not in multilateralism. For a strong power such as the US it is of course easier to conduct talks and negotiations in a bilateral setting than in a multilateral one where the input of many smaller countries make it much more difficult for any power, strong or weak, to dominate the talks. Such a bilateral approach, for example, is also China's preferred course of action when discussing the problems in the South China Sea with the other nations that have sovereignty claims in the disputed waters.

Trump also has a very traditional understanding of the role of sovereign nation-states. It is essentially based on the concept of the concert of nations that dominated international politics in the nineteenth and the first half of the twentieth century. The president would certainly have no difficulty in agreeing with the well-known real political testimony given by British Prime Minister Palmerston. In 1848 Palmerston explained that his country had no eternal allies but that its interests were eternal and that it would be a duty to follow these interests. Palmerston – not unlike Trump – never referred to a country's values and the benefits of international cooperation. Clearly, this belief in a narrowly defined national interest also explains Trump's scepticism of NATO.

Russia.   The new president's praise for Russian autocrat Putin has also led to much anger and anxiety in Europe. Moscow clearly meddled to a significant extent in the American election process and the connection between the Trump campaign and Russia remains a source of confusion.[89] Trump's strange fascination for the strongman in the Kremlin is greatly resented in Berlin and in eastern Europe. No one really understands it. In March 2014 Moscow, after all, violently annexed Crimea, an integral part of sovereign Ukraine, and Russian soldiers clandestinely invaded eastern Ukraine, thus attempting to destabilise the entire country. Putin's threatening behaviour toward the Baltic states and occasionally Finland and Sweden is also disconcerting.[90] In the final days of the Obama administration it led to the stationing of NATO troops in Poland, close to the Russian border.

In the last couple of years the barbaric bombing campaigns of the Russian air force on Aleppo and elsewhere in war-torn Syria on the side of Iran and Syrian President Assad has turned the German public and the German establishment abruptly against Putin, despite long-standing economic and cultural links between the two countries.[91] While Trump reacted forcefully when Assad's air force used chemical weapons on civilians in Syria in early April, Moscow claimed that it was not Assad but the rebel forces or perhaps the inadvertent explosion of a warehouse with chemicals that had led to the incident. On the whole, the Trump administration's policy toward Russia remains ambiguous. No clear policy line has yet emerged. This is despite the fact that economic sanctions on Russia have not been lifted. Trump was even forced by Congress to strengthen sanctions in certain respects. Although he reluctantly went along with Congress, he made it clear that he considered the move counter-productive. The western alliance had first imposed sanctions on Russia after Moscow's annexation of Crimea in March 2014. This is a confusing state of affairs which the Europeans find highly disconcerting and unnerving.

CONCLUSION: WHERE DO WE GO FROM HERE?

German–American relations remain crucial for the stability, security and well-being of Europe. They also remain vital for America. Both within the EU and NATO, Germany is one of America's most important, economically strongest and most stable allies. It is crucial therefore that the US president, after all still the leader of the 'free world', and the German chancellor get their act together. Trump needs to overcome his suspicion and mistrust of Angela Merkel. The German chancellor is already well aware of the fact that despite all his many political and personal flaws and nationalistic beliefs, engagement with Donald Trump and his administration is essential.

The US and united Germany are the leaders of the West. Essentially there is no one else with the capability to take over in an ever more complex, intertwined and dangerous world. Both leaders should live up to that awesome responsibility and try to get on with each other. Multilateral international cooperation, including European integration, are actually advantageous to the US and greatly beneficial to American well-being and security. Like it or not, in a tumultuous and volatile world, the US and Germany need each other and ought once again to cooperate closely with each other. Let's hope the Trump White House will become aware of this soon.

DISCLOSURE STATEMENT

No potential conflict of interest was reported by the author.

NOTES

1. See Alan Crawford and Tony Czuczka, *Angela Merkel: A Chancellorship Forged in Crisis* (Chichester, West Sussex: John Wiley/Bloomberg, 2013); Stefan Kornelius, *Angela Merkel und ihre Welt* (Hamburg: Hoffmann und Campe, 2013); Gerd Langguth, *Angela Merkel: Rise to Power* (Munich: dtv, 2005).
2. See the article by Dieter Dettke in this issue.
3. Quote: Hans-Peter Schwarz, 'Outlook: America, Germany, and the Atlantic Community after the Cold War', in Detlef Juncker (ed.), *The United States and Germany in the Era of the Cold War, 1945–1990. A Handbook, Vol.2: 1968–1990* (Cambridge: Cambridge University Press, 2004), p.561.
4. See Klaus Larres and Peter Eltsov, 'How Adolf Hitler haunts Angela Merkel,' *Politico*, 26 May 2015: http://www.politico.com/magazine/story/2015/05/angela-merkel-hitler-118287 (accessed 30 June 2017).
5. While Merkel did no't like it, Bush clearly meant it as a sign of affection. See Luke Harding, 'Bush Rubs Merkel the Wrong Way', *The Guardian*, 28 July 2006, available from https://www.theguardian.com/news/blog/2006/jul/28/bushrubsmerkel; for the video, see: https://www.youtube.com/watch?v=tUTwaSPcGno (accessed 30 June 2017).
6. George W. Bush, *Decisions Points* (New York: Random House, 2010), pp.412–13.
7. See George K. Zestos, *The Global Financial Crisis: From U.S. Subprime Mortgages to European Sovereign Debt* (London: Routledge, 2016).
8. Quoted in Crawford and Czuczka, *Angela Merkel*, p.109.
9. Ibid., p.108.
10. See for example, 'U.S. Spy Scandal Triggers Outrage, Paranoia in Germany', *NBC News*, 2 Aug. 2014, available from http://www.nbcnews.com/storyline/nsa-snooping/u-s-spy-scandal-triggers-outrage-paranoia-germany-n170366 (accessed 30 June 2017)
11. In 1957 Konrad Adenauer had also addressed both Houses of Congress (but in two separate sessions).
12. For the video clips of both occasions, see: https://www.c-span.org/video/?289781-1/german-chancellor-address-joint-meeting-congress (3 Nov. 2009); https://www.youtube.com/watch?v=EZ5qOTEC93g (7 June 2011) (accessed 30 June 2017).
13. See Alan Sugar, *What You See is What You Get: My Autobiography* (London: Macmillan, 2008).
14. At the age of 16 Donald Trump's grandfather Friedrich Trump emigrated to the US in order to escape poverty. He followed in the footsteps of his sister Katherine who had gone to the US two years earlier. Friedrich (now called Frederick) soon moved to British Columbia and opened a hotel and restaurant near the Klondike Gold Rush. He was stripped of his German citizenship in 1889 (when he left Bavaria he had not de-registered, and he had not fulfilled his mandatory military service). He became a US citizen three years later.In the same year, in 1892, he returned to Kallstadt to attend the wedding of his sister. Five years later, in 1897, Trump's grandfather visited Kallstadt again, where he met and became engaged to 20-year-old Elisabeth Christ, also from Kallstadt. In 1902 Friedrich Trump returned for a third time to Kallstadt to get married to Elisabeth; they moved to New York.But he had promised his wife that they would eventually settle in Kallstadt and in 1904 they returned there. Although he told the US authorities he would come back to the US, he took all his savings with him. However, he was unable to re-obtain his German citizenship; instead he was asked to leave within eight weeks, otherwise he would be deported, as he had left Germany without permission and before having fulfilled his military service. Thus in July 1905 Friedrich and his wife had no choice but to return to New York.Soon afterwards, in October 1905, Trump's father Fred was born. Just over 40 years later, in June 1946, Donald Trump was born in the same city. Incidentally, John Henry Heinz, the grandfather of the founder of the Heinz Ketchup empire (Henry J. Heinz), was also born in Kallstadt; he had immigrated to the US in 1840 aged 19. Henry J. Heinz was a second cousin of Donald Trump's grandfather, Frederick Trump.See Janosch Delcker, 'Donald Trump, Germany's Disfavoured Son', *Politico*, 23 and 28 Sept. 2017, available from http://www.politico.eu/article/donald-trump-ancestry-forefathers-kallstadt/For a detailed account, see Gwenda Blair, *The Trumps: Three Generations of Builders and a President, with a New Foreword* (New York: Simon & Schuster, 2001); and the documentary movie by Simone Wendel, 'Kings of Kallstadt' (2014), available from https://www.youtube.com/watch?v=1dSq6Sc35bY (all accessed 30 June 2017).
15. See Robin Alexander, *Die Getriebenen: Merkel und die Fluechtlingspolitik. Report aus dem Inneren der Macht* (Hamburg: Siedler, 2017).
16. 'Things Donald Trump Said About Angela Merkel – and Vice Versa', *Deutsche Welle*, 13 March 2017, available from http://www.dw.com/en/things-donald-trump-said-about-angela-merkel-and-vice-versa/a-37889332 (accessed 30 June 2017).
17. See Kevin Liptak, 'Trump Welcomes Merkel after Bashing her on Campaign Trail', *CNN*, 17 March 2017, available from http://www.cnn.com/2017/03/16/politics/angela-merkel-donald-trump-washington-visit/index.html (accessed 30 June 2017).

18. 'Things Donald Trump Said About Angela Merkel – and Vice Versa', *Deutsche Welle*, 13 March 2017. See also Meghan Keneally, 'What Trump and Merkel Have Said About Each Other', *ABC News*, 17 March 2017, available from http://abcnews.go.com/Politics/trump-merkel/story?id=46198767 (accessed 30 June 2017).

19. Ibid.

20. For a good overview see NBC News, 'Trump to Speak with Merkel after a Campaign's Worth of Criticism', 27 Jan. 2017, available from http://www.newsjs.com/url.php?p=http://www.nbcnews.com/politics/white-house/trump-phone-merkel-after-campaign-s-worth-criticism-n713376; See also James P. Rubin, 'Why is Trump Picking on Merkel?', 16 Jan. 2017, available from http://www.politico.com/magazine/story/2017/01/why-is-trump-picking-on-merkel-214641 (all accessed 30 June 2017).

21. See 'Things Donald Trump Said About Angela Merkel – and Vice Versa', *Deutsche Welle*, 13 March 2017.

22. Ibid.

23. See Klaus Larres, 'Donald Trump's Foreign Policy: what do we know, what can we expect?' In *Depth Newsletter*, University of Nicosia, Cyprus, Vol.13/6 (December 2016): (Accessed 30 June 2017): http://www.cceia.unic.ac.cy/index.php?option=com_content&task=view&id=538&Itemid=538n.

24. See Jonathan Allen and Amie Parnes, *Shattered: Inside Hillary Clinton's Doomed Campaign* (New York: Crown, 2017).

25. For the video tape of her congratulatory statement, see: https://www.youtube.com/watch?v=VnA0RtmzYBM (accessed 30 June 2017).

26. Carol Giacomo, 'Angela Merkel's Message to Donald Trump', *New York Times*, 9 Nov. 2017, available from https://www.nytimes.com/interactive/projects/cp/opinion/election-night-2016/angela-merkels-warning-to-trump (accessed 30 June 2017).

27. For all quotes, see 'Merkel Congratulates Trump as Politicians Express Shock', *Deutsche Welle*, 9 Nov. 2017, available from http://www.dw.com/en/merkel-congratulates-trump-as-politicians-express-shock/a-36318866 (accessed 30 June 2017).

28. For the video of Steinmeier's short statement on 9 Nov. 2016, see https://www.youtube.com/watch?v=SIGffrTUuD8 (accessed 30 June 2017).

29. This section has been guided by my article 'Hitler's Long Shadow: Donald Trump and Angela Merkel', *E-International Relations*, 8 Feb. 2017, available from http://www.e-ir.info/2017/02/08/hitlers-long-shadow-donald-trump-and-angela-merkel/ (accessed 30 June 2017).

30. 'Statement by the President on International Holocaust Remembrance Day', 27 Jan. 2017, available from https://www.whitehouse.gov/the-press-office/2017/01/27/statement-president-international-holocaust-remembrance-day (accessed 30 June 2017).

31. 'Executive Order: Protecting the Nation from Foreign Terrorist Entry into the United States', 27 Jan. 2017, available from https://www.whitehouse.gov/the-press-office/2017/01/27/executive-order-protecting-nation-foreign-terrorist-entry-united-states (accessed 30 June 2017).

32. '"Justice Department lawyer says ... "', 3 Feb. 2017, *Washington Post*, available from https://www.washingtonpost.com/local/public-safety/government-reveals-over-100000-visas-revoked-due-to-travel-ban/2017/02/03/7d529eec-ea2c-11e6-b82f-687d6e6a3e7c_story.html?utm_term=.4e3df60446c5 (accessed 30 June 2017).

33. See Adam Liptak, 'Trump Loses Travel Ban Ruling in Appeals Court', *New York Times*, 12 June 2017, available from https://www.nytimes.com/2017/06/12/us/politics/trump-travel-ban-court-of-appeals.html?hp&action=click&pgtype=Homepage&clickSource=story-heading&module=first-column-region&region=top-news&WT.nav=top-news. See for a timeline of Trump's executive orders on immigration and the consequences and reactions: http://abcnews.go.com/Politics/timeline-president-trumps-immigration-executive-order-legal-challenges/story?id=45332741 (all accessed 30 June 2017).

34. For an article on the 'mutual incomprehension' between the U.S. and Germany over the Iraq war of 2002, see Klaus Larres, 'Mutual Incomprehension? U.S.-German Value Gaps over Iraq and Beyond', Washington Quarterly, Vol. 26, No.2 (spring, 2003), 23–42. http://digirep.rhul.ac.uk/file/ca2b7c4c-45f3-0764-7ab3-b4354346f0d7/1/Larres–Washingon%20Quarterly%20as%20publ.pdf (accessed 30 June 2017).

35. See 'Angela Merkel is Now the Leader of the Free World, Not Donald Trump', *The Independent*, UK, available from http://www.independent.co.uk/voices/angela-merkel-donald-trump-democracy-freedom-of-press-a7556986.html (accessed 30 June 2017). For two interesting recent short books on right-wing populism, see Jan-Werner Mueller, *What is Populism?* (Philadelphia, PA: University of Pennsylvania Press, 2016); John Judis, *The Populist Explosion: How the Great Recession Transformed American and European Politics* (New York: Columbia Global Reports, 2016).

36. Theresa May's government had a majority of 17 seats but she wished to strengthen her position with a much larger majority in parliament and thus called a snap election that took place on 8 June 2017. The

opinion polls gave her a huge lead and Labour leader Jeremy Corbyn seemed to be a weak opponent. Yet she badly miscalculated and lost her majority in parliament, thus greatly weakening her position.

37. 'PM Press Conference with U.S. President Donald Trump: 27 January 2017', available from https://www.gov.uk/government/speeches/pm-press-conference-with-us-president-donald-trump-27-january-2017 (accessed 30 June 2017).

38. 'Trump laedt Merkel ins Weisse Haus ein', available from http://www.bild.de/politik/ausland/donald-trump/telefonat-mit-merkel-50001996.bild.html (accessed 30 June 2017).

39. 'Readout of the President's Call with Chancellor Angela Merkel, of Germany', 27 Jan. 2017, available from https://www.whitehouse.gov/the-press-office/2017/01/28/readout-presidents-call-chancellor-angela-merkel-germany (accessed 30 June 2017).

40. 'PM Press Conference with U.S. President Donald Trump: 27 January 2017'.

41. Peter Baker, 'Trump says NATO Allies don't pay their Share. Is that true?' New York Times, May 26, 2017: https://www.nytimes.com/2017/05/26/world/europe/nato-trump-spending.html; David Adesnik, 'NATO's European Members Should Increase Defense Spending,' National Review, July 8, 2016: http://www.nationalreview.com/article/437598/nato-members-defense-spending-must-meet-target (accessed 30 June 2017).

42. See 'Germany Mulls a Real, But Unrealistic, Pledge on Defence Spending', Deutsche Welle, 24 Feb. 2017, available from http://www.dw.com/en/germany-mulls-a-real-but-unrealistic-pledge-on-defense-spending/a-37709485; for a discussion of European defence efforts, see Klaus Larres, 'Europe Démilitarisé? Un Regard Américain', Politique étrangère 79/1 (2014), pp.39–52. English version 'The United States and the "Demilitarization" of Europe: Myth or Reality?' (spring 2014), available from http://www.cairn.info/resume.php?ID_ARTICLE=PE_141_0117 (accessed 30 June 2017).

43. See Baker, 'Trump Says NATO Allies Don't Pay their Share. Is that True?'.

44. 'Readout of the President's Call with Chancellor Angela Merkel, of Germany', 27 Jan. 2017.

45. See for example, The Guardian, UK, 29 Jan. 2017, available from https://www.theguardian.com/world/2017/jan/29/merkel-explains-geneva-refugee-convention-to-trump-in-phone-call (accessed 30 June 2017).

46. 'Angela Merkel "Explains" to Donald Trump … ', The Independent, UK, 30 Jan. 2017, available from http://www.independent.co.uk/news/world/europe/anglea-merkel-explains-donald-trump-geneva-refugee-convention-obligations-muslim-immigration-ban-us-a7552506.html (accessed 30 June 2017).

47. German main evening news, 30 January 2017, 8 pm, available from http://www.tagesschau.de/multimedia/sendung/ts-18145.html (accessed 30 June 2017).

48. 'US Trade Chief Seeks to Reshore Supply Chain', Financial Times, 31 Jan. 2017, available from https://www.ft.com/content/8dc63502-e7c7-11e6-893c-082c54a7f539 (accessed 30 June 2017).

49. 'Trump Takes Swipe at EU as "Vehicle for Germany"', Financial Times, 15 Jan. 2017, available from https://www.ft.com/content/1f7c6746-db75-11e6-9d7c-be108f1c1dce (accessed 30 June 2017).

50. 'Transatlantic Mood Sours as Merkel Refutes Trump on Euro', Bloomberg News, 31 Jan. 2017, available from https://www.bloomberg.com/politics/articles/2017-01-31/trump-adviser-blasts-germany-for-exploiting-undervalued-euro (accessed 30 June 2017).

51. See ibid.; and Wolfgang Muenchau, 'Navarro has a Point When it Comes to Germany and the Euro', Financial Times, 5 Feb. 2017.

52. 'US Trade Chief Seeks to Reshore Supply Chain', Financial Times, 31 Jan. 2017.

53. See Kevin Liptak, 'Trump Welcomes Merkel after Bashing her on Campaign Trail', CNN, 17 March 2017, available from http://www.cnn.com/2017/03/16/politics/angela-merkel-donald-trump-washington-visit/index.html (accessed 30 June 2017).

54. Rebecca Flood, 'Trump Printed Out Fake 300 bn NATO Invoice … ', The Independent, 26 March 2017, available from http://www.independent.co.uk/news/world/americas/us-politics/donald-trump-angela-merkel-nato-bill-defence-ignore-usa-germany-spending-a7650636.html (accessed 30 June 2017).

55. See Anthony Faiola, '"The Germans are Bad, Very Bad": Trump's Alleged Slight Generates Confusion, Backlash', Washington Post, 26 May 2017, available from https://www.washingtonpost.com/world/trumps-alleged-slight-against-germans-generates-confusion-backlash/2017/05/26/0325255a-4219-11e7-b29f-f40ffced2ddb_story.html?utm_term=.63afdc6e0107 (accessed 30 June 2017).

56. See Balazs Koranyi and Gernot Heller, 'G20 Financial Leaders Acquiesce to U.S., Drop Free Trade Pledge', Reuters, 18 March 2017, available from http://www.reuters.com/article/us-g20-germany-trade-idUSKBN16P0FN (accessed 30 June 2017).

57. For Trump's full speech at the NATO summit on 25 May 2017, see: https://www.youtube.com/watch?v=_L3JuowHGKs (accessed 30 June 2017),

58. For the enormous planned increase of the defence budget to a total of $603 billion (including an increase from c. 285 to 355 battleships), see an article focusing on the congressional hearing with Defence Secretary Mattis on 12 June 2017: Joe Gould, 'Mattis: Trump Military Build-up Begins in 2019', DefenseNews, 12 June 2017, available from http://www.defensenews.com/articles/mattis-trump-military-buildup-begins-in-

2019 (accessed 30 June 2017). See the book by the Obama official who claims to have invented the 'Asian pivot', Kurt M. Campbell, *The Pivot: The Future of American Statecraft in Asia* (New York: Twelve, 2016).

59. Robert Gramer, 'Trump Discovers Article 5 After Disastrous NATO Visit', *Foreign Policy*, 9 June 2017, available from http://foreignpolicy.com/2017/06/09/trump-discovers-article-5-after-disastrous-nato-visit-brussels-visit-transatlantic-relationship-europe/ (accessed 30 June 2017).

60. Guilia Paravicini, 'Angela Merkel: Europe Must Take "Our Fate" into Own Hands', *Politico*, 28 May 2017, available from http://www.politico.eu/article/angela-merkel-europe-cdu-must-take-its-fate-into-its-own-hands-elections-2017/ (accessed 30 June 2017).

61. See 'EU Seeks Climate Allies among U.S. Cities, States, EU's Sefcovic Says', *Reuters*, 5 June 2017, available from http://www.businessinsider.com/r-eu-seeks-climate-allies-among-us-cities-states-eus-sefcovic-says-2017-6 (accessed 30 June 2017)

62. See Daniel Boffey and Arthur Neslen, 'China and EU Strengthen Promise to Paris Deal with US Poised to Step Away', *The Guardian*, 1 June 2017, available from https://www.theguardian.com/environment/2017/may/31/china-eu-climate-lead-paris-agreement (accessed 30 June 2017).

63. Gramer, 'Trump Discovers Article 5 After Disastrous NATO Visit'.

64. Ibid.

65. 'Germany Gives Up On President Trump … ', *Salon*, 26 Jan. 2017 (based on a story in the German newspaper *Handelsblatt*), available from http://www.salon.com/2017/01/26/germany-gives-up-on-president-trump-angela-merkels-advisors-dont-believe-hell-act-presidential/ (accessed 30 June 2017).

66. See Erick Erickson, 'The Fantasy of Impeachment', *New York Times*, 12 May 2017, available from https://www.nytimes.com/2017/05/12/opinion/erick-erickson-the-fantasy-of-impeachment.html (accessed 30 June 2017).

67. Andrew Sullivan, 'The Reactionary Temptation', *New York Magazine*, 2 May 2017. See also Joshua Green, *Devil's Bargain: Steve Bannon, Donald Trump, and the Storming of the Presidency* (New York: Penguin Press, 2017).

68. This is of course a rather unusual and probably highly ill-advised situation. I am referring to Jared Kushner, Trump's son-in-law, and Ivanka Trump, his oldest daughter. See Peter Baker, Glenn Thrush and Maggie Haberman, 'Jared Kushner and Ivanka Trump: Pillars of Family-Driven West Wing', *New York Times*, 15 April 2017, available from https://www.nytimes.com/2017/04/15/us/politics/jared-kushner-ivanka-trump-white-house.html (accessed 30 June 2017).

69. Confidential information.

70. For an enlightening video on the career and political view of Steve Bannon and some of his associates, see PBS/Frontline video 'Bannon's War', 23 May 2017 (54 minutes), available from http://www.pbs.org/wgbh/frontline/film/bannons-war/ (accessed 30 June 2017).

71. Eric Bradner, "Conway: Trump White House offered 'alternative facts' on crowd size," (Jan. 23, 2017): https://www.cnn.com/2017/01/22/politics/kellyanne-conway-alternative-facts/index.html

72. Matthew Nussbaum et al., 'Kushner's Alleged Russia Back-channel Attempt Would be Serious Break From Protocol', *Politico*, 27 May 2017, available from http://www.politico.com/story/2017/05/27/jared-kushner-russia-backchannel-protocol-238888 (accessed 30 June 2017).

73. See Klaus Larres, 'Reality Check: Donald Trump shies away from isolationism during his first meeting with Chinese president,' *International Politics and Society* (April, 2017): http://www.ips-journal.eu/topics/international-relations/article/show/reality-check-1976/ (accessed 30 June 2017).

74. See Max Bergmann, 'Present at the Destruction: How Tillerson is Wrecking the State Department', *Politico*, 29 June 2017, available from http://www.politico.com/magazine/story/2017/06/29/how-rex-tillerson-destroying-state-department-215319 (accessed 30 June 2017).

75. See Elli Lake, 'Washington Loves General McMaster, But Trump Doesn't', *Bloomberg News*, 8 May 2017, available from https://www.bloomberg.com/view/articles/2017-05-08/washington-loves-general-mcmaster-but-trump-doesn-t (accessed 30 June 2017).

76. H.R. McMaster and Gary D. Cohn, 'America First Doesn't Mean America Alone', *Wall Street Journal*, 30 May 2017, available from https://www.wsj.com/articles/america-first-doesnt-mean-america-alone-1496187426 (accessed 30 June 2017).

77. David Brooks, 'Donald Trump Poisons the World', *New York Times*, 2 June 2017, available from https://www.nytimes.com/2017/06/02/opinion/donald-trump-poisons-the-world.html?_r=0. See also David Frum, 'The Death Knell for America's Global Leadership', *The Atlantic*, 31 May 2017, available from https://www.theatlantic.com/international/archive/2017/05/mcmaster-cohn-trump/528609/; Jeet Heer, 'H.R. McMaster and the Foolish Trust in Trump's "Generals"', *New Republic*, 2 June 2017, available from https://newrepublic.com/article/143040/hr-mcmaster-foolish-trust-trumps-generals (accessed 30 June 2017).

78. See Klaus Larres, 'Obamas Mixed Foreign Policy Balance Sheet,' *The National Interest* (Oct.18, 2016): http://nationalinterest.org/feature/obamas-mixed-foreign-policy-balance-sheet-18089 (accessed 30 June 2017).

79. Lisa Hagen, 'Trump: "You Have to be Flexible"', *The Hill*, 3 March 2016, available from http://thehill.com/blogs/ballot-box/presidential-races/271751-trump-you-have-to-be-flexible (accessed 30 June 2017).

80. Noah Bierman, 'Trump is Delivering on his Promise … to be Unpredictable on Foreign Affairs', *LA Times*, 16 Dec. 2016, available from http://www.latimes.com/politics/la-na-pol-trump-unpredictable-20161218-story.html (accessed 30 June 2017).

81. Kevin Sullivan and Karen Tumulty, 'Trump Promised an "Unpredictable" Foreign Policy. To Allies, it Looks Incoherent', *Washington Post*, 11 April 2017, available from https://www.washingtonpost.com/politics/trump-promised-an-unpredictable-foreign-policy-to-allies-it-looks-incoherent/2017/04/11/21acde5e-1a3d-11e7-9887-1a5314b56a08_story.html?utm_term=.2c2b18c5ccd5 (accessed 30 June 2017). Plenty of evidence for this was then presented convincingly in Michael Wolff's book *Fire and Fury: Inside the Trump White House* (New York: Henry Holt, 2018).

82. See also Klaus Larres, 'Donald Trump's Foreign Policy: What Do We Know, What Can We Expect?', *In Depth Newsletter*, University of Nicosia, Cyprus, 13/6 (Dec. 2016), available from http://www.cceia.unic.ac.cy/index.php?option=com_content&task=view&id=538&Itemid=538 (accessed 30 June 2017).

83. 'Donald Tusk says Donald Trump Poses Existential Threat to EU', *The Independent*, UK, 31 Jan. 2017, available from http://www.independent.co.uk/news/world/europe/donald-tusk-donald-trump-existential-threat-europe-brexit-eu-theresa-may-a7555061.html (accessed 30 June 2017).

84. See for example, 'Trump Attacks BMW and Mercedes, but Auto Industry is a Complex Target', *New York Times*, 16 Jan. 2017; 'Trump: German Automakers Will Pay Tariff on Cars Built Outside U.S.', *Washington Post*, 16 Jan. 2017, available from https://www.washingtonpost.com/news/innovations/wp/2017/01/16/trump-german-automakers-will-pay-tariff-on-cars-built-outside-u-s/?utm_term=.0a20401dc8ca (accessed 30 June 2017).

85. See for the quotes Faiola, '"The Germans are Bad, Very Bad"'. See also Markus Becker and Peter Mueller, 'Dieser Besuch verlief nicht ganz so "amazing"', *Spiegel online*, 25 May 2017, available from http://www.spiegel.de/politik/ausland/donald-trump-trifft-jean-claude-juncker-und-donald-tusk-in-bruessel-a-1149256.html (accessed 30 June 2017).

86. See *The Telegraph*, 28 Jan. 2017, available from http://www.telegraph.co.uk/news/2017/01/27/theresa-may-meets-donald-trump-white-house-live/ (accessed 30 June 2017).

87. 'Trump Gives Backing for Brexit … ', 28 Jan. 2017, available from http://www.dailymail.co.uk/wires/pa/article-4165034/Trump-hails-special-relationship-Britain-United-States.html (accessed 30 June 2017). For an excellent recent overview of the European integration process, see Winfried Loth, *Building Europe: A History of European Unification* (Berlin/Boston: De Gruyter/Oldenbourg, 2015).

88. For a good short overview, see Geir Lundestad, *'Empire by Integration'. The United States and European Integration, 1945–1997* (Oxford: Oxford University Press, 1998).

89. See for instance: 'Russian Hacking Looms Over Germany's Election', *Politico*, 19 Dec. 2017, available from http://www.politico.eu/article/russian-influence-german-election-hacking-cyberattack-news-merkel-putin/ (accessed 30 June 2017)

90. See Peter Eltsov and Klaus Larres, 'Putin's Targets: Will Eastern Ukraine and Northern Kazakhstan be next?' *New Republic*, online, 10 March 2014, available from http://www.newrepublic.com/article/116965/putins-next-targets-eastern-ukraine-and-northern-kazakhstan (accessed 30 June 2017).

91. 'Fool me Once: Germany Turns Sour on Russia', *The Economist*, 23 April 2016, available from http://www.economist.com/news/europe/21697236-germanys-establishment-once-believed-conciliation-russia-no-longer-fool-me-once (accessed 30 June 2017).

The Global Financial Crisis and the Euro Crisis as Contentious Issues in German-American Relations

CHRISTIAN SCHWEIGER

This article examines the impact of the 2008–09 global financial crisis on the dynamics of transatlantic relations. The financial crisis has revealed systemic weaknesses in the governance of the eurozone and fundamental divisions between national governments in the EU on how these should be addressed. In the context of German domestic politics the financial crisis has resulted in increasing scepticism towards US-style liberal market capitalism. Germany managed to maintain its strong economic standing under the adverse circumstances of the financial crisis. Domestically the post-crisis political consensus has hence emphasised the strengths of Germany's coordinated market economy in contrast to the liberal model of the US. This article offers a comparative analysis of how the crisis was perceived and how it has been addressed in Germany and the US. It argues that the financial crisis has significantly changed the parameters of the bilateral relations between Germany and the US in the context of wider EU–US transatlantic relations.

THE DUAL CRISIS IN US–GERMAN RELATIONS

The Long Shadows of Iraq

The traditionally close relations between Berlin and Washington have been significantly strained during the past 15 years. The fundamental and outspoken opposition of the red–green coalition under Chancellor Gerhard Schröder in 2009 pushed Germany to the side-lines of Defense Secretary Donald Rumsfeld's dichotomy of old versus new Europe.[1] Rumsfeld had assumed that the Schröder government's opposition to the military intervention in Iraq, which he branded as irresponsible, would ultimately weaken Germany's standing in the enlarging new EU. Germany was supposed to be isolated in this new Europe, where the acceding East-Central European member states sympathised with the Anglo-American war on terror approach of preventive military intervention against states that were deemed to be a threat to European security. The attempts made by the administration of Republican President George W. Bush to divide the Europeans over Iraq ultimately however resulted predominantly in the marginalisation of the United Kingdom's influence. Between 1997 and 2002 Blair managed to significantly shape the EU's political agenda on the reform of the Single Market, as well as on defence and security, through a principally constructive cooperative approach. Blair's ultimate ambition to exercise leadership in the EU was however significantly undermined as his political credibility faded away in the aftermath of Iraq. As a result, France and Germany, which had started to drift apart in the late 1990s, regrouped and revitalised their bilateral partnership.[2] Even under difficult external circumstances Germany was therefore able to maintain the leading role in the EU which Bush's predecessor Bill Clinton had envisaged after the end of the cold war. Clinton considered Germany as Washington's main partner in post-cold war Europe, which was an acknowledgement of the growing economic and political power of the reunified country.[3] Even the subsequent Bush administration had to accept that Germany remained a key player in the EU. The old Europe category consequently clashed with the reality of Germany's importance as the key strategic economic and political partner for the new member states in East-Central Europe that had joined the EU in 2004.[4]

The election of Barack Obama as US president in 2008 seemed to open up the opportunity for recalibration of the strained transatlantic relations and in particular the bilateral relations between Berlin and Washington. After the deepening divide in transatlantic relations under the administration of President George W. Bush, the German public overwhelmingly welcomed the election of Democrat President Barack Obama in November 2008. Obama had already gained public sympathy during his triumphant campaign visit to Germany on 24 July 2008, when he rallied the crowds during his speech in front of the Brandenburg Gate. In the speech, Obama called on Europe to stand closely with America and to 'forge trade that truly rewards the work that creates wealth, with meaningful protections for our people and our planet'.[5] At the time of his inauguration, support for Obama in Europe was most pronounced in Germany, where 92 per cent approved his leadership in the White House in comparison with the 12 per cent approval ratings his predecessor George W. Bush had received.[6] By 2014 this had changed substantially, with approval ratings for Obama's presidency in Germany having dropped down to 56 per cent.[7] Five years into the Obama presidency a majority of Germans (57 per cent) were also again in favour of a European approach which aspired to be more independent from the US.[8]

Obama had decisively rejected his predecessor's unilateral approach. Instead he offered partners in Europe a new pragmatic and at its core realist multilateralism as the fundament for a revitalised and strengthened transatlantic partnership.[9] Obama's realist multilateralism posed both opportunities and challenges for Germany. On the one hand, Obama showed little interest in limiting himself to America's traditional cultural ties, such as the special relationship with the United Kingdom. Here he obviously lacked the 'sentimental attachment to Britain' previous presidents like Bush and Reagan had displayed.[10] On the other hand, he openly demanded the acceptance of a realist assessment of military burden-sharing within NATO on the part of the Europeans, most of all Germany. During his campaign visit in Berlin he also told the German public that it was his belief that both the US and Europe were facing the growing 'burdens of global citizenship' and would have to shoulder it jointly: 'In this new century, Americans and Europeans alike will be required to do more – not less'.[11] This was the reflection of the fact that under the growing financial constraints which resulted from America's domestic economic challenges, investment in NATO would increasingly be assessed rationally rather than emotionally.[12]

Obama's defence secretary, Robert Gates, who had also been in the post during the second administration of George W. Bush, repeatedly warned the European allies that their aversion 'to military force and the risks that go with it' would no longer be acceptable.[13] These demands clashed with the culture of German foreign and security policy, which is strongly focused on the preference for soft power diplomacy. All German government coalitions led by Angela Merkel since she became chancellor in 2005 have tried to circumvent these demands by concentrating on the development of the EU's defence and security policy, which is obviously more in line with the '"civilian power" foreign policy narrative'.[14] The preoccupation with the global financial crisis and the eurozone sovereign debt crisis has to a certain extent made it easier for the German government to ignore Washington's demands. These events however only offered a short-term cover for Germany's civilian power approach and would later resurface as a major stumbling block for German–US bilateral relations.

The Global Financial Crisis

The financial crisis, which spread like a tidal wave across the world in 2008, had its origins in the irresponsible lending culture of the US financial industry. The subprime loan crisis emerged on the basis of the subprime loans American mortgage providers and banks issued to customers who were clearly incapable of paying back the levels of debt they were allowed to acquire. The housing bubble started to burst in the late summer of 2007 as record numbers of private borrowers defaulted and the full extent of the subprime lending practices became obvious. The sudden shortfall in capital resulted in a domino effect which saw an increasing number of financial services companies default and culminated in the collapse of global financial services company Lehman Brothers on 15 September 2008. The speed and gravity of events caused alarm bells to ring in Washington and forced the Bush administration, which was very reluctant to interfere in market activity, to take over the Fannie May and Freddie Mac mortgage providers and to initiate a US$700 billion economic stimulus package on 3 October 2008.

Contention between Germany and the US quickly resurfaced as the ripple effects of the financial crisis in the US swept in and caused the triple effect of a profound and widespread recession in the EU, a banking crisis and a subsequent profound sovereign debt crisis in some member states. The German public discourse singled out the irresponsible and greed-fuelled culture of unregulated US liberal capitalism as the root cause of the crisis. This was also reflected in the rhetoric of the Merkel government, and most of all in that of her junior coalition partner, the Social Democrats (SPD). Merkel's Social Democratic Finance Minister Peer Steinbrück, who challenged her in the 2009 federal elections for the position of chancellor, put the distinction between what he branded as Anglo-American 'predator capitalism' and Germany's social market economy as a model of 'tamed capitalism' at the heart of his election campaign.[15] The Merkel government, and most of all the chancellor herself, promoted Germany's ordoliberal culture of state-regulated capitalism as a best practice model for the EU on the basis of the strong economic performance with which the German economy emerged from the 2009 recession.[16] Merkel herself spoke of the success of Germany's consensus-orientated culture in tackling the effects of the global financial crisis and prescribed the implementation of a German 'stability culture' as the remedy to overcome the eurozone sovereign debt crisis:

Germany emerged from the global financial crisis in a stronger position than it was in when it entered it ... This is why the paramount ambition of the federal government is to ensure that Europe also emerges from the crisis in a stronger position than the one it was in when it entered it. This means nothing more and nothing less than: Europe has to become a stability union.[17]

Merkel's Hesitant Ordoliberalism Meets Obama's Keynesianism

The promotion of Germany's ordoliberalism occurred in response to the deepening effects of the banking and sovereign debt crisis in a number of countries inside and outside the eurozone, especially in the liberal market economies of the United Kingdom and Ireland, as well as in the Southern European countries.[18] Initially Merkel considered these crises to be domestic issues which would have to be tackled by the respective national governments. Only when things turned from bad to worse in late 2009 did Merkel finally give in to the pressures from other member states to develop a collective approach to tackle the emerging eurozone crisis. This manifested itself in the six-pack eurozone governance mechanisms which at their core were focused on the strengthening of the existing budgetary rules of the stability and growth pact through enhanced policy coordination and supervision. Through the annual European Semester policy cycle which was introduced in 2011 under the Europe 2020 Strategy and the intergovernmental Fiscal Compact, which implemented a constitutional debt brake in the 25 participating countries, Merkel managed to stretch these measures beyond the euro core. This occurred in spite of the fundamental opposition of the British government under Prime Minister David Cameron, who vetoed the Fiscal Compact's inclusion in the EU treaty structure and demanded legal safeguards against further policy coordination.[19]

Merkel's initial inaction was seen as critical by the newly elected Obama administration. Obama's government wanted Germany to engage in a collective European crisis response. President Obama teamed up with British Prime Minister Gordon Brown and French President Nicolas Sarkozy in calling for joint action to tackle the crisis. At the G7 summit hosted by the UK government in London on 1 April 2009, Obama and Brown were at one in calling for global and European initiatives to stimulate growth, initiate better regulatory standards for the financial industry and to support the countries which were most affected by the crisis. In response to BBC journalist Nick Robinson's question how he would react to the German accusations that the US had caused the crisis, Obama emphasised that his administration was taking action to ensure that the crisis could be overcome:

> At this point, I'm less interested in identifying blame than fixing the problem. And I think we've taken some very aggressive steps in the United States to do so, not just responding to the immediate crisis, ensuring that banks are adequately capitalized, dealing with the enormous drop out from demand in the contraction that's been taking place.[20]

Angela Merkel initially rejected the joint calls of Brown, Sarkozy and Obama for collective action on stimulating the global economy. During the joint press conference with Sarkozy at the Franco-German Council of Ministers meeting in Paris on 24 November 2008 Merkel expressed lukewarm support for the calls for common

European action: 'For me the sequence is this: national measures as we have decided them, then coherent European action and then we will see'.[21] Sarkozy reacted by taking a dig at Merkel when he emphasised the need for more collective action: 'France is working on it. Germany is also thinking about it'.[22] As the impact of the financial crisis on European economies deepened, Sarkozy teamed up with Gordon Brown to nudge Germany towards agreeing to a European stimulus programme.[23] It took Merkel until after the federal elections in September 2009 to gradually adapt to the expectation in the EU that Germany would have to provide the lead to steer the eurozone collectively out of the crisis. Even in the run-up to the first piece in the puzzle of the six-pack governance reforms in response to the euro crisis, disagreements between Merkel and Sarkozy frequently resurfaced in the media. Sarkozy was rumoured to have been angered by Merkel's consistent refusal to agree to an EU-wide rescue package for affected banks, which was part of his general criticism that Merkel considered the crisis predominantly through the national lens.[24]

Merkel's preference for national measures and her insistence on prioritising austerity at the EU level was also criticised by US President Obama, who wrote a letter to his European partners on 16 June 2010 ahead of the G20 summit in Canada. In the letter Obama reminded EU leaders that his administration had made significant efforts to stimulate the US economy out of the 2008–09 recession that had followed the domestic financial crash. The American Recovery and Reinvestment Act (ARA) initiated by the Obama administration just after it had taken office in February 2009 injected a total of $787 billion into the US economy.[25] Obama was hence anxious that the US recovery could be undermined by a faltering eurozone which lacked a similar coordinated stimulus because of Germany's opposition: 'We worked exceptionally hard to restore growth; we cannot falter or lose strength now. This means that we should reaffirm our unity of purpose to provide the policy support necessary to keep economic growth strong'.[26]

Obama's approach to the crisis was first and foremost orientated towards stabilising financial markets. Merkel's failure to follow the calls from Paris and London for a coordinated European stimulus package in the initial phase of the eurozone sovereign debt crisis was widely criticised by American experts. Prominent US economist Adam Posen went as far as to question Merkel's grasp of 'the basic principles of economic policy'.[27] It was obvious that the Keynesian demand-management of the Obama administration was at loggerheads with Merkel's own approach, which was firmly grounded in the German ordoliberal tradition.[28] The culture of German ordoliberalism, which prioritises monetary stability and reduces the role of the state to that of a regulatory agent, clashes with the Keynesian view of an active state as an economic stimulator of demand through investment.[29] As Merkel gradually became increasingly active and moved into the role of reluctant hegemon[30] in the eurozone and the wider Single Market, she did so in the well-known German domestic tradition of the austerity-focused 'Swabian housewife'.[31] This approach is deeply embedded in the institutional culture of the German political economy through key actors such as the finance ministry, the Bundesbank and the Federal Constitutional Court (FCC). The FCC in its role as the guardian of the German constitution has been generally supportive in its rulings towards deeper policy coordination but also consistently protective of the principle of the budgetary sovereignty of the German Bundestag (*Haushaltsvorbehalt*).[32]

Germany's increasingly dominant role in the EU had become the obvious way before the onset of the financial crisis. The growing economic and political weight, which resulted from the reunification of the two German states in 1990, pushed the larger Germany into that of a 'benign'[33] or 'cooperative'[34] hegemon. The legitimacy of Germany's hegemony was predominantly built on the substantial financial contributions the country made to the EU budget. Under the conditions of the deepening eurozone sovereign debt crisis since 2009 the already previously existent and now substantially growing mismatch between Germany's economic strength and France's weakness turned Germany into the position of the hegemonic 'economic stabiliser', which initially reluctantly but ultimately determinately took the lead in shaping the policy response to the crisis.[35] The dominant role Germany has played in reshaping the eurozone governance framework under crisis conditions towards the ordoliberal parameters of Merkel's proclaimed 'stability union' has again transformed the perception of German hegemony. The formerly constructive view of German leadership, which was most openly expressed by partners in East-Central Europe, has most recently turned negative. As Merkel instilled the six-pack governance framework of multi-level policy coordination and unwaveringly insisted on the implementation of the accompanying austerity agenda for the Southern European crisis economies as being without alternative,[36] Germany's position has increasingly been considered as that of 'hegemonic self-righteousness'.[37]

Reinforcing the Importance of National Preferences

The emerging divide between Germany and the US over the management of the effects of the financial crisis reflects the importance of the domestic background to interstate bargaining. The ordoliberal tradition of Germany's post-World War II political economy has been profoundly shaping Berlin's response to the financial and the eurozone crisis. This is in accordance with Andrew Moravcsik's liberal intergovernmentalist approach, which considers states to play two-level games in their external relations, with national preferences emerging in the process of liberal preference formation on the primary domestic level. Moravcsik also stresses the importance of economic considerations in the formation of national preferences.[38] It has been obvious that under the adverse conditions of the financial crisis countries place greater emphasis on protecting what they perceive as their national comparative advantage. In the crisis context the rational assessment of the actual costs and benefits of existing bilateral economic relations, as well as the potential costs and benefits of enhanced multilateral cooperation has moved to the centre ground. Moravcsik points out in this respect that domestic constituencies carefully weigh up the potential advantages and disadvantages of deeper supranational policy coordination or integration before they are willing to give political elites the mandate to seal them in intergovernmental bargains.[39] Major disagreements and ultimately national vetoes in bilateral and multilateral external economic relations consequently are most likely to occur when the value base of the domestic constituencies of interacting countries substantially diverge.[40]

The fallout from the financial crisis has been an even greater divergence of domestic economic preferences between Germany and the United States than this had previously been the case. The mixed signals Washington perceived emerging from Berlin regarding Germany's commitment to the future of the eurozone, especially in the initial period of the crisis between late 2008 and 2010, caused at least some concern in the wider domestic debate on the crisis in America and in the incoming Obama administration.[41] The mood in the US regarding Merkel's austerity and ordoliberal stability mantra was reflected by the comments the prominent late former US presidential advisor Zbigniew Brzezinski made at the 2013 Annual Global Security Conference (GLOBSEC) in Bratislava, Slovakia. Brzezinski criticised that under the conditions of eurozone crisis the EU had turned into an organisation which lacked both solidarity and vision, in essence a 'largely financial union of nation states that lacks the popular commitment of genuinely European patriotism'.[42] Most of all Brzezinski warned about the negative consequences of the EU's inward-looking focus on austerity and the neglect of its external responsibilities: 'Europe's lack of global ambitions makes for excessive reliance on America and makes the American public more sceptical of Europe'.[43]

The German domestic constituency's preference for an ordoliberal regulatory framework, which is aimed at medium- to long-term economic stability is firmly grounded in the desire to maintain Germany's economic advantage as the leading export nation in the eurozone.[44] The German economy managed to emerge strongly from the financial crisis on the basis of its own domestic stimulus programme, which was predominantly initiated by SPD Finance Minister Peer Steinbrück during the 2005–09 grand coalition. The government not only initiated a guarantee for private savings deposited in banks up to the total value of €400 billion but also sponsored a trade-in scheme for older cars (*Abwrackprämie*). Germany managed to speedily recover from the brief dip into recession in 2009 through a combination of measures. These included the rescue package for the German plants of car manufacturer Opel,[45] targeted investment in infrastructure and most of all the temporary adaption of full-time employment contracts to allow employees to switch towards part-time work, which were agreed in cooperation with employers and trade unions as part of government-sponsored wage support for reduced working hours (*Kurzarbeitergeld*).[46] In the United States, the immediate priority under President Bush and subsequently under Obama from 2009 was to stabilise the financial industry, which is the crucial base for the domestic liberal market economy. Obama accompanied this by a massive economic stimulus programme which was considered critically by many Republicans but ultimately passed by Congress.[47] Similar policies never manifested in the eurozone or the wider EU due to the fundamental German opposition towards a system of permanent financial transfers. The German Federal Constitutional Court has unequivocally stated in its rulings that Germany could not participate in a European financial transfer union on constitutional grounds. At the same time the FCC supported Chancellor Merkel's concept of the eurozone as a stability union by permitting Germany to participate in the 2012 European Stability Mechanism (ESM), which effectively collectivises liability for debt in the eurozone but does not determine automatic financial transfers.[48]

New Challenges Over Military Burden-Sharing and Trade

Germany's ordoliberalism is also visible in the frugal approach towards defence spending, which is additionally grounded in Germany's traditional preference for non-military civilian instruments.[49] Germany has consistently spent less than the 2 per cent of its GDP that had been agreed as the minimum at the 2014 NATO summit in Wales. In the Wales summit declaration all NATO members committed themselves politically to spend at least 2 per cent of their annual GDP on defence. For countries like Germany that fail to meet this target the declaration confirmed the 'aim to move towards the two per cent guideline within a decade with a view to meeting their NATO Capability Targets and filling NATO's capability shortfalls'.[50]

Between 2009 and 2015 German government spending on defence actually fell from 1.39 to 1.18 per cent in 2015 and then only slightly increased to around 1.20 per cent in 2016.[51] The Obama administration was visibly critical of this approach and kept signalling to Berlin that it expected Germany to meet its commitment even under the burden of being preoccupied with the management of the eurozone crisis. In his departing speech at the NATO headquarters in Brussels in June 2011 at the peak of the eurozone crisis, Gates indirectly singled out Germany when he spoke of NATO having turned into a 'two-tier alliance' between members that prefer soft power and others that meet the demands of hard military burden-sharing: 'For all but a handful of allies, defense budgets – in absolute terms, as a share of economic output – have been chronically starved for adequate funding for a long time, with the shortfalls compounding on themselves each year'.[52]

Obama's call for a new era of enhanced free trade relations with the EU resulted in the initiation of official negotiations between his administration and the European Commission on the Transatlantic Trade and Investment Partnership Agreement (TTIP) on 8 July 2013. TTIP was aimed at creating a wide-ranging free trade area between the US and the EU which, according to economic experts, would benefit mostly the American economy but also the member states of the EU. According to a study conducted by the Bertelsmann Foundation, TTIP would add between 7 and 9 per cent in terms of GDP per capita to economies with a strong focus on the financial services industry, such as the UK, Ireland and Sweden. Germany's GDP per capita would only be boosted by around 5 per cent.[53] The US remains Germany's most important trading partner when it comes to the export of goods. Export trade with America amounted to €107 billion in 2016 (Figure 1). The German economics ministry points out in this respect that the American market is the most important export market for German products with 'around one-tenth of German export goods' heading towards the US.[54]

This explains the efforts the German government has made to realise the TTIP agreement. Merkel's Social Democratic Vice-Chancellor and former Economics Minister Sigmar Gabriel relentlessly promoted TTIP against growing opposition within his own party. His support only started to weaken in the summer of 2016 when it became clear that the agreement could not be completed before the end of President Obama's term in office because of persistent disagreements between Brussels and the EU. Gabriel finally announced that TTIP would be obsolete after both the Democratic presidential candidate Hillary Clinton and the Republican candidate Donald Trump had expressed fundamental doubts about the agreement.[55] In contrast to the EU-28 average, where a majority of the public (53 per cent) still support TTIP in the latest Eurobarometer poll conducted in the autumn of 2016, in Germany opposition to TTIP is now in the majority (52 per cent).[56] At the same time there is a profound sense of public concern in Germany that under Trump's leadership in Washington the crucial bilateral economic relations between the two countries could suffer and ultimately weaken the performance of the German economy. In the poll conducted by the German pollster Infratest Dimap in February 2017, 67 per cent of Germans expressed concern that Trump's policies could weaken the German economy.[57]

FIGURE 1
GERMANY'S MAJOR TRADING PARTNERS 2016

Germany's major trading partners, 2016
in EUR bn

Export			Import
United States	107	94	China
France	101	83	Netherlands
United Kingdom	86	66	France
Netherlands	78	58	United States
China	76	52	Italy
Italy	61	46	Poland
Austria	60	44	Switzerland
Poland	55	42	Czech Republic
Switzerland	50	39	Austria
Belgium	42	38	Belgium

© ⅃ Statistisches Bundesamt (Destatis), 2017

Source: German Statistical Office https://www.destatis.de/EN/FactsFigures/NationalEconomyEnvironment/ForeignTrade/ForeignTrade.html

GERMANY AND TRUMP'S NEW REALISM: TOWARDS DISENTANGLEMENT?

The presidency of Donald Trump, who defeated Hillary Clinton in the 2016 presidential election against all odds as a political outsider, poses fundamental new challenges for relations between Germany and the US. The election victory of Donald Trump on the basis of his populist and protectionist policy platform may seem like a distortion of the inherent free market culture of the US economy. However, considering the adverse effects of the financial crash on large sections of the working class, particularly in the economic periphery, the Trump agenda reflects the domestic preferences of a substantial and growing section of the US electorate. Trump's political style is not only unpredictable. The new president also seems to lack any deep-seated political convictions. He is therefore the first US president who may challenge the fundaments of transatlantic relations to which he lacks any deep-seated cultural affiliation. Trump has repeatedly questioned the future of NATO and attacked Germany for not meeting what he considers as the financial commitment to spend the required 2 per cent of GDP on defence.

The Trump presidency also poses fundamental questions about the future trade relations between the Germany and the US. Trump favours a protectionist economic nationalism which puts the future of the TTIP agreement in doubt. Moreover, Trump has openly attacked Germany for its economic surplus. During his first attendance at a G7 summit in Taormina, Italy, Trump plunged the summit into chaos by rejecting the Paris climate deal and refusing to rule out the imposition of protective measures in his economic policy. Trump showed great confidence in lecturing the European NATO members on the lack of burden-sharing during the summit. In this respect he emphasised that 23 of the 28 EU member states would fail to meet their financial obligations within NATO and that they 'owed massive amounts of money'.[58] It is obvious that this swipe was particularly aimed at Germany, which has never reached the minimum 2 per cent of GDP spending on defence since it was first agreed in 2009.

Trump was also reported to have branded Germany as 'very, very bad' over its persistent trade surplus.[59] His unmitigated concerns about Germany's export strength, especially in the automobile industry, pose a fundamental challenge for the future of German–US bilateral trade relations. If Trump resorts to protective measures this would have a noticeable impact on German exports. The German trade surplus has indeed grown to over €200 billion since 2012 (Figure 2). The German economics ministry rejects Trump's criticism and points out that the German trade surplus is accompanied by substantial German capital investment in America. According to the ministry's official figures, around $319 had been invested in the US by German companies in 2015, which amounts to around 10 per cent of the total foreign direct investment the US economy receives.[60]

Trump's strident conduct in dealing with America's European allies has initiated a new phase of realism in bilateral relations between Berlin and Washington which could fundamentally change the transatlantic relations for years to come. Public scepticism towards Trump's leadership and the future of bilateral relations with the US has reached record levels in Germany according to the latest opinion polls conducted by the pollster Forschungsgruppe Wahlen. According to the poll, 69 per cent of Germans consider America under Trump no longer to be a reliable ally; and 79 per cent even consider international multilateral cooperation to be threatened by the Trump presidency.[61]

Chancellor Merkel's public reaction to the difficult negotiations with Trump at the G7 summit in Taormina shows a distinctive change in the official German diplomatic approach towards Washington. During a general election rally in Munich the week after the summit Merkel warned her fellow leaders in the EU that they would have to regroup under the conditions of impending Brexit and Trump in the White House:

> The times in which we can fully count on others are somewhat over, as I have experienced in the past few days … Of course we need to have friendly relations with the US and with the UK, and with other neighbours, including Russia but we have to fight for our own future ourselves.[62]

Merkel's sentiments were also echoed by the new SPD leader Martin Schulz, who was the challenger of Merkel for the position of Chancellor at the September 2017 national elections. Schulz has adopted a firm line towards Trump and has called on the EU to rally together to 'challenge this man with everything we stand for, especially also his fatal logic of armament, which he wants to force upon us'.[63]

The fierce rhetoric that has recently emerged between leaders in Berlin and Washington, which has also been partly driven by the upcoming national election in

Germany, clashes with the reality of the continuing profound economic and political dependence between Germany and the US. In spite of Merkel hinting at a more independent European approach, it is unlikely that Berlin could risk jeopardising the trade relations with America which continue to be indispensable for Germany's export-driven economy. Even though the comprehensive trade agreement TTIP is most unlikely to materialise under the Trump presidency, imposing protective barriers towards trade with America's European partners would also fundamentally jeopardise the future of the US economy.

Since the onset of the global financial crisis a growing economic realism has taken hold in German–US relations. This has become ever more prominent in the context of the global financial crisis as domestic constituencies have become more narrowly focused on their economic self-interest and on maintaining what they perceive as their national comparative advantage. However, due to the strong linkages between the German and the US economy, the respective national constituencies cannot ignore bilateral trade relations and economic cooperation as an important factor in maintaining their domestic comparative advantage.[64] If one again adopts Moravcsik's liberal intergovernmentalist lens, it could on the one hand be argued that under Trump's leadership the traditional value base of transatlantic relations in general and of German–US

FIGURE 2
DEVELOPMENT OF GERMAN FOREIGN TRADE

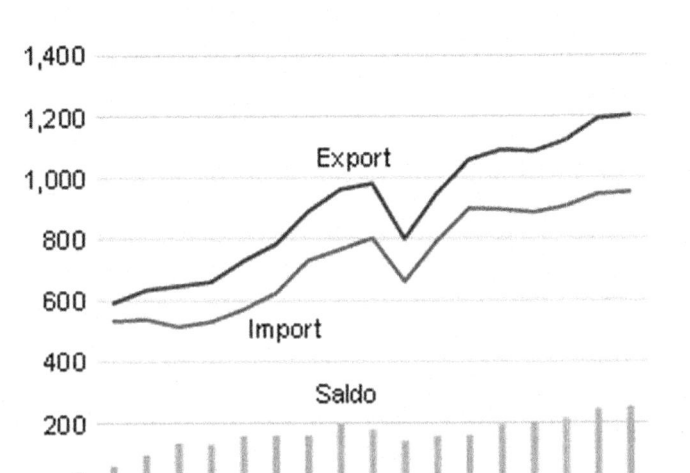

Development of German foreign trade
EUR bn

© lı Statistisches Bundesamt (Destatis), 2017

Source: German Statistical Office, https://www.destatis.de/EN/FactsFigures/NationalEconomyEnvironment/ForeignTrade/ForeignTrade.html (accessed 1 June 2017).

bilateral relations in particular has evaporated. Based on Moravcsik's expectation that corresponding values are an important prerequisite for interstate cooperation,[65] this should then lead to a pretty bleak assessment of the future of bilateral economic relations between Germany and the US. On the other hand, the persistently challenging external conditions of the global economy make it more likely that Berlin and Washington will continue to seek close economic and trade cooperation. The importance of the bilateral economic relations make it indispensable that both countries maintain their economic ties. This is in spite of their fundamental differences on how the global economy should be managed, including crucial issues such as free trade agreements and international climate deals. From Moravcsik's perspective, the realisation of the challenges resulting from external pressures can push countries towards deeper cooperation even when other factors, such as the lack of correspondence in values, are lacking.[66]

The biggest challenge for Germany and the US will be to overcome their persistent differences on military burden-sharing which have been accentuated more strongly as a direct consequence of the financial crisis. The new Trump administration is more vocal in emphasising that America is neither willing nor able to continue to shoulder the bulk of military spending within NATO. Trump famously singled out Germany as the weakest link in the group of European allies within NATO who do not pay their fair share in defence contributions.[67] Trump has even gone so far as to question continuing US military commitment towards defence in Europe if the European NATO partners fail to meet their financial commitments.[68] This should not come as a surprise to Berlin, as it was the unequivocal position of President Obama that the US has become financially overburdened within NATO. Since Merkel became German chancellor she has wavered between ignoring these demands and finding excuses for the persistently low German spending on defence. During the peak of the financial crisis Merkel's main excuse was the financial commitments made as part of the stabilisation of the euro-zone, particularly Greece.[69] More recently, Merkel and former SPD leader Sigmar Gabriel, who has now moved to the foreign office, are trying to counter Trump's aggressive demands by demanding that spending in the area of civilian aid is taken into account when assessing a country's overall defence spending within NATO.[70] Given Germany's strong economic and budgetary position in the wake of the eurozone crisis, this position will nevertheless be very difficult to maintain as calls for greater German burden-sharing in the area of hard military power will not vanish as long as NATO exists in its current form. Even if Trump remains a one-term president his successor is likely to continue to remind Berlin of its commitments on defence spending. This remains a fundamental challenge as political leaders in Berlin face a German public which is fundamentally sceptical towards prioritising increased military spending. An opinion poll conducted by the German weekly *STERN* in February 2017 shows that 55 per cent of the public oppose any increase in Germany's military budget.[71]

The complete disentanglement of Germany's and America's traditional close relations remains a possibility if leaders in Berlin and Washington decide to go down the path towards separation. Germans and Americans are however aware of the importance of their bilateral relations to maintain domestic economic success and political stability. Under the new realism that emerged from the crisis conditions of the past decade, domestic economic and political interests take priority on both sides of the Atlantic. Berlin and Washington therefore have become less emotionally attached to the path-dependent cultural foundation of the transatlantic relationship and are putting greater rational emphasis on the costs and benefits of their bilateral relations. In the future, German–American relations are therefore likely to become more contested, both in terms of hard bargains on economic and political interests and in terms of disagreements about fundamental values. The main challenge here lies in the expectation of Trump's electoral constituents to live up to his campaign promises and the growing pressure on Germany to offer a value-based agenda for the future of the EU which is distinctively different from Trump's nationalist realism.[72] Even under these constrained conditions Germans and Americans will realise that they have travelled far too long a path together to now be able to sever ties and go their separate ways. This is already noticeable in the fact that in spite of the overall deep-seated German scepticism towards the Trump presidency and the outright opposition towards the policies it promotes, in the latest opinion polls 79 per cent of Germans continue to consider bilateral economic relations with the US to be important.[73] In the words of Nobel Prize economist Joseph Stiglitz: 'In the end pragmatism is likely to win over ideology'.[74]

DISCLOSURE STATEMENT

No potential conflict of interest was reported by the author.

NOTES

1. Donald Rumsfeld, 'US Defense Secretary Speech at the 39th Munich Security Conference', 8 Feb. 2003, available from http://freerepublic.com/focus/news/838820/posts (accessed 25 May 2017).
2. Christian Schweiger, 'British–German Relations in the European Union after the War on Iraq', *German Politics* 13/1 (2004), p.46.
3. Rainer Apel, 'Clinton Affirms America's Partnership with Germany', *EIR International* 25/21 (May 1998), available from http://www.larouchepub.com/eiw/public/1998/eirv25n21-19980522/eirv25n21-19980522_042-clinton_affirms_americas_partner.pdf (accessed 25 May 2017); C.C. Schweitzer et al. (eds), *Politics and Government in Germany 1944–1994* (Oxford: Berghahn, 1995), p.116.
4. Vladimir Handl and William E. Paterson, 'The Continuing Relevance of Germany's Engine for CEE and the EU', *Communist and Post-Communist Studies* 46 (2013), pp.327–37.
5. Barack Obama Speech in Berlin, 24 Oct. 2008, available from http://edition.cnn.com/2008/POLITICS/07/24/obama.words/ (accessed 1 June 2017).
6. German Marshall Fund, *Transatlantic Trends 2009: Key Findings*, p.7, available from http://trends.gmfus.org/files/archived/doc/2009_English_Key.pdf (accessed 1 June 2017).
7. German Marshall Fund, *Transatlantic Trends 2014: Key Findings*, p.18, http://trends.gmfus.org/files/2012/09/Trends_2014_complete.pdf (accessed 1 June 2017).
8. Ibid, p. 20.
9. Nicholas Kitchen, 'The Obama Doctrine – Détente or Decline', *European Political Science* 10/1 (2011), p.32.
10. William Wallace and Christopher Phillips, 'Reassessing the Special Relationship', *International Affairs* 85/2 (2009), p.281.
11. Barack Obama Speech in Berlin.

12. Kori Schake, 'US Retrenchment is Right and Overdue', in F. Heisbourg et al. (eds), *All Alone? What US Retrenchment Means for Europe and NATO* (London: Centre for European Reform, 2012), available from https://www.cer.org.uk/sites/default/files/publications/attachments/pdf/2012/rp_089_km-6278.pdf (accessed 1 June 2017).

13. Robert M. Gates, 'Remarks by US Secretary of Defence at the NATO Strategic Concept Seminar', National Defense Unit, Washington, DC, 23 Oct. 2010, available from http://archive.defense.gov/Speeches/Speech.aspx?SpeechID=1423 (accessed 25 May 2017).

14. Alister Miskimmon, 'Foreign Security Policy', in S. Padgett, W.E. Paterson and R. Zohlnhöfer (eds), *Developments in German Politics 4* (Basingstoke: Palgrave MacMillan, 2014), p.217.

15. Peer Steinbrück, Speech at the SPD Party Conference in Hannover, 9 Dec. 2012, p.66, available from https://www.spd.de/fileadmin/Dokumente/Beschluesse/Bundesparteitag/2012_bpt_hannover_protokoll.pdf (accessed 27 June 2017).

16. Hubert Zimmermann, 'A Grand Coalition for the Euro: The Second Merkel Cabinet, the Euro Crisis and the Elections of 2013', *German Politics* 23/4 (2014), p.324.

17. Angela Merkel, *Official Declaration on the EU Council and the Euro Summit in the German Bundestag*, Berlin, 26 Oct. 2011, available from https://www.cdu.de/system/tdf/media/dokumente/26_10_2011_Regierungserklaerung.pdf?file=1 (accessed 27 May 2017).

18. Peter A. Hall, 'The Economics and Politics of the Euro Crisis', *German Politics* 21/4 (2012), p.362.

19. Christian Schweiger, *Exploring the EU's Legitimacy Crisis: The Dark Heart of Europe* (Cheltenham: Edward Elgar, 2016), pp.135–52.

20. Joint Press Conference by US President Barack Obama and UK Prime Minister Gordon Brown, 1 April 2009, available from http://edition.cnn.com/TRANSCRIPTS/0904/01/ltm.01.html (accessed 28 May 2017).

21. Joint Press Conference by Nicholas Sarkozy and Angela Merkel at the 10th Franco-German Council of Ministers, Paris, 24 Nov. 2008, available from http://www.deutschland-frankreich.diplo.de/Pressekonferenz-von,3764.html (accessed 29 May 2017).

22. Ibid.

23. Ben Hall, Jean Eaglesham and Bertrand Benoit, 'Sarkozy and Brown Turn up Heat on Merkel for More Action', *Financial Times*, 6 Dec. 2008, available from http://www.ft.com/cms/s/0/69691ca2-c33a-11dd-a5ae-000077b07658.html?ft_site=falcon&desktop=true (accessed 29 May 2017).

24. 'Sarkozy "stinksauer" auf Merkel', *Süddeutsche Zeitung*, 17 May 2010, available from http://www.sueddeutsche.de/wirtschaft/gefahr-fuer-deutsch-franzoesisches-verhaeltnis-sarkozy-stinksauer-auf-merkel-1.538014!amp (accessed 29 May 2017).

25. Geoffrey Garrett, 'G2 in G20: China, the United States and the World after the Global Financial Crisis', *Global Policy* 1/1 (2010), pp.31–2.

26. 'Merkel at Odds with Obama on Financial Policy', *Deutsche Welle*, 19 June 2010, available from http://www.dw.com/en/merkel-at-odds-with-obama-on-financial-policy/a-5710437 (accessed 29 May 2017).

27. Gregor Peter Schmitz and Gabor Steingart, 'Obama and Merkel: The Trans-Atlantic Frenemies', *SPIEGEL ONLINE*, 3 June 2009, available from http://www.spiegel.de/international/world/obama-and-merkel-the-trans-atlantic-frenemies-a-628301-2.html (accessed 29 May 2017).

28. Mark Landler and Nicholas Kulish, 'In Euro Crisis, Obama Looks to Merkel', *New York Times*, 15 June 2012, available from http://www.nytimes.com/2012/06/16/world/europe/in-euro-crisis-obama-tries-to-sway-merkel.html (accessed 29 May 2017).

29. V. Berghahn and Brigitte Young, 'Reflections on Werner Bonefeld's "Freedom and the Strong State: On German Ordoliberalism" and the Continuing Importance of the Ideas of Ordoliberalism to Understand Germany's (Contested) Role in Resolving the Eurozone Crisis', *New Political Economy* 18/5 (2013), p.775.

30. William E. Paterson, 'The Reluctant Hegemon? Germany Moves Centre Stage in the European Union', *Journal of Common Market Studies* 49/S1 (2011), pp.57–75.

31. Franz-Josef Meiers, *Germany's Role in the Euro Crisis: Berlin's Quest for a More Perfect Monetary Union* (Berlin: Springer, 2015), p.19.

32. Simon Bulmer and William E. Paterson, 'Germany and the Crisis: Asset or Liability?', in D. Dinan, N. Nugent and William E. Paterson (eds), *The European Union in Crisis* (London: Palgrave, 2017), pp.218–19.

33. Melanie Morisse Schilbach, '"Ach Deutschland!" Greece, the Euro Crisis and the Costs and Benefits of Being a Benign Hegemon', *Internationale Politik und Gesellschaft 1* (2011), pp.26–41.

34. Simon Bulmer and William E. Paterson, 'Germany as the EU's Reluctant Hegemon? Of Economic Strength and Political Constraints', *Journal of European Public Policy* 20/10 (2013), p.1392.

35. Ibid., p.1397.

36. Angela Merkel, Official Declaration on the EU Council and the Euro Summit, 26 Oct. 2011.

37. Wolfgang Streeck, 'Scenario for a Wonderful Tomorrow', *London Review of Books* 38/7 (2016), p.8.

38. Andrew Moravcsik, 'Preferences and Power in the European Community: A Liberal Theory of International Politics', *International Organization* 51/4 (1993), p.480.
39. Ibid., p.495.
40. Andrew Moravcsik, 'Taking Preferences Seriously: A Liberal Theory of International Politics', *International Organization* 51/4 (1997), p.528.
41. Amelia Hadfield, 'The EU's Global Image', in D. Dinan, N. Nugent and W.E. Paterson (eds), *The European Union in Crisis* (London: Palgrave, 2017), p.304.
42. Zbigniew Brzezinski, *Keynote at GLOBSEC 2013*, 24 April 2013, available from http://www.globsec. org/globsec2013/highlights-news/globsec-2012-summary3/ (accessed 1 June 2017).
43. Ibid.
44. Andreas Busch, 'Germany and the Euro', in S. Padgett, William E. Paterson and R. Zohlnhöfer (eds), *Developments in German Politics* (Basingstoke: Palgrave MacMillan, 2014), p.204.
45. Kenneth Dyson, 'In the Shifting Shadows of Crisis: Pivot Points, Crisis Attribution, and Macro-Economic Policies under Grand Coalition', *German Politics* 19/3–4 (2010), p.401.
46. Lothar Funk, 'Germany: Sweeping Structural Reforms Can Work', in V. Novotny (ed.), *From Reform to Growth: Managing the Economic Crisis in Europe* (Amsterdam: Eburon, 2013), pp.201–24.
47. Norman Birnbaum, 'American Progressivism and the Obama Presidency', *The Political Quarterly* 81/4 (Oct.–Dec. 2010), p.473.
48. Friedrich Heinemann, 'Germany: Constraints in the Crisis', in K. Dervis and J. Mistral (eds), *Europe's Crisis, Europe's Future* (Washington, DC: Brookings Institute, 2014), p.112.
49. Sebastian Harnisch and Hanns W. Maull, *Still a Civilian Power? The Foreign Policy of the Berlin Republic* (Manchester: Manchester University Press, 2001).
50. NATO, 'Wales Summit Declaration', 5 Sept. 2014, para. 14, available from http://www.nato.int/cps/ic/ natohq/official_texts_112964.htm (accessed 19 June 2017).
51. NATO, 'Defence Spending of NATO countries', 13 March 2017, p.9, available from http://www.nato. int/nato_static_fl2014/assets/pdf/pdf_2017_03/20170313_170313-pr2017-045.pdf (accessed 26 May 2017).
52. 'Remarks by Secretary Gates at the Security and Defense Agenda', Brussels, Belgium, 10 June 2011, available from http://archive.defense.gov/Transcripts/Transcript.aspx?TranscriptID=4839 (accessed 26 May 2017).
53. Fritz Breuss, 'European Union in a Globalised World', in Kyriakos N. Demetriou (ed.), *The European Union in Crisis: Explorations in Representation and Democratic Legitimacy* (London: Springer, 2015), p.246.
54. *Bundeswirtschaftsministerium*, 'Der deutsche Leistungsbilanzüberschuss im Lichte der deutsch-amerikanischen Beziehungen', *Monatsbericht* 05/2017 (2017), p.2, available from http://www.bmwi.de/ Redaktion/DE/Downloads/Monatsbericht/2017-05-leistungsbilanzueberschuss.pdf?__blob= publicationFile&v=8 (accessed 1 June 2017).
55. 'Gabriel Gegen TTIP – Alle Gegen Gabriel', *Frankfurter Allgemeine Zeitung*, 29 Aug. 2016, available from http://www.faz.net/aktuell/wirtschaft/ttip-und-freihandel/gabriel-gegen-ttip-alle-gegen-gabriel-14411031.html (accessed 1 June 2017).
56. European Commission, *Standard Eurobarometer 86: National Report Germany* (2016), p.8, available from http://ec.europa.eu/commfrontoffice/publicopinion/index.cfm/ResultDoc/download/DocumentKy/ 77126 (accessed 1 June 2017).
57. 'ARD DeutschlandTREND Februar 2017', *Infratest Dimap*, https://www.infratest-dimap.de/umfragen-analysen/bundesweit/ard-deutschlandtrend/2017/februar/ (accessed 1 June 2017).
58. Peter Baker, 'Trump Says NATO Allies Don't Pay Their Share. Is That True?', *New York Times*, 26 May 2017, available from https://www.nytimes.com/2017/05/26/world/europe/nato-trump-spending.html? _r=0 (accessed 30 May 2017).
59. Anthony Faiola, '"The Germans are Bad, Very Bad": Trump's Alleged Slight Generates Confusion, Backlash', *Washington Post*, 26 May 2017, available from https://www.washingtonpost.com/world/ trumps-alleged-slight-against-germans-generates-confusion-backlash/2017/05/26/0325255a-4219-11e7-b29f-f40ffced2ddb_story.html?utm_term=.a2cdf924bcb4 (accessed 30 May 2017).
60. *Bundeswirtschaftsministerium*, 'Der Deutsche Leistungsbilanzüberschuss', p.2.
61. *Forschungsgruppe Wahlen Politbarometer*, 2 June 2017, available from https://www.zdf.de/politik/ politbarometer/170602-bilder-100.html#gallerySlide=0 (accessed 2 June 2017).
62. Patrick McGee and George Parker, 'Europe Cannot Rely on US and Faces Life Without UK, Says Merkel', *Financial Times*, 28 May 2017, available from https://www.ft.com/content/51ed8b90-43b9-11e7-8519-9f94ee97d996 (accessed 30 May 2017).
63. 'Kritik an Trump: Schulz Ruft zu Widerstand auf, Lindner Warnt vor Entfremdung', *SPIEGEL ONLINE*, 30 May 2017, available from http://www.spiegel.de/politik/ausland/martin-schulz-ruft-zu-widerstand-gegen-donald-trump-auf-a-1149795.html (accessed 30 May 2017).

64. Sanford Henry, 'The Transatlantic Trade and Investment Partnership: TTIP', in *Transatlantic Relations: A European Perspective, The Regent's Report 2014* (London: Regent's University, 2014), available from http://www.regents.ac.uk/pdf/TransatlanticRelations-%20AEuropeanPerspective.pdf (accessed 1 June 2017), p.44.
65. Moravcsik, 'Taking Preferences Seriously'.
66. Moravcsik, 'Preferences and Power in the European Community'; Andrew Moravcsik, 'The European Constitutional Compromise and the Neofunctionalist Legacy', *Journal of European Public Policy* 12/2 (2005), p.358.
67. Philip Rucker and Robert Costa , 'Trump Questions Need for NATO, Outlines Noninterventionist Foreign Policy', *Washington Post*, 21 March 2016, available from https://www.washingtonpost.com/news/post-politics/wp/2016/03/21/donald-trump-reveals-foreign-policy-team-in-meeting-with-the-washington-post/?utm_term=.36d8888f9617 (accessed 1 June 2017).
68. Carol Morello and Adam Taylor, 'Trump Says U.S. Won't Rush to Defend NATO Countries If They Don't Spend More on Military', *Washington Post*, 21 July 2016, available from https://www.washingtonpost.com/world/national-security/trump-says-us-wont-rush-to-defend-nato-countries-if-they-dont-spend-more-on-military/2016/07/21/76c48430-4f51-11e6-a7d8-13d06b37f256_story.html?utm_term=.c1814ac266a4 (accessed 1 June 2017).
69. Tom Dyson, 'German Defence Policy Under the Second Merkel Chancellorship', *German Politics* 23/4 (2014), p.461.
70. 'Rede von Außenminister Sigmar Gabriel bei Eröffnung der Deutsch-Amerikanischen Konferenz "The Marshal Plan and Its Legacies – Towards a Strong Transatlantic Partnership"', 16 May 2017, available from http://www.auswaertiges-amt.de/DE/Infoservice/Presse/Reden/2017/170516_BM_Marshall.html (accessed 1 June 2017).
71. 'Mehr Geld für Verteidigung? Mehrheit der Deutschen Sagt Nein', *STERN*, 15 Feb. 2017, available from http://www.stern.de/politik/ausland/stern-umfrage-mehrheit-der-deutschen-gegen-aufruestung-und-kampfeinsaetze-gegen-is-7326810.html (accessed 1 June 2017).
72. Klaus Brinkbäumer, 'Trump as Nero: Europe Must Defend Itself Against a Dangerous President', *DER SPIEGEL*, 5 Feb. 2017, available from http://www.spiegel.de/international/world/a-1133177.html (accessed 1 June 2017).
73. *Forschungsgruppe Wahlen Politbarometer*, 2 June 2017.
74. Sven Prange, 'Germany Must Lead International Opposition to Trump', Interview with Joseph Stiglitz, 20 Jan. 2017, available from https://global.handelsblatt.com/politics/germany-must-lead-international-opposition-to-trump-686878 (accessed 1 June 2017).

Different Approaches to Russia: The German–American–Russian Strategic Triangle

STEPHEN F. SZABO

Russia has been both a divisive and a unifying force in the German–American relationship. It has been the focal point in this relationship since the end of World War II. During the cold war, the Soviet threat held Washington and Bonn together despite some important divergences in interests and policies. During the 1950s Adenauer's 'policy of strength' emphasised western solidarity and a strong military approach based on NATO and the European Community (EC), reinforced by the stationing of over 200,000 American military personnel in West Germany and West Berlin. Adenauer believed this policy of western solidarity would allow West Germany to draw East Germany (DDR) toward unification through the magnetism of western economic success combined with its military resolve. A corollary to this was the Hallstein Doctrine which barred the Federal Republic from having diplomatic relations with any country which recognised the DDR.

THE LEGACY OF THE COLD WAR

This policy of strength was compatible with the approach of the Eisenhower administration and its policy of 'roll back'. This unity was tested by the Kennedy administration's lack of a strong response to the building of the Berlin Wall and its beginnings of a détente policy, which came to fruition during the Nixon administration. The shift toward détente opened the door for the Brandt policy of *Ostpolitik* which modified the policy of strength. Although the *Ostpolitik* raised some concerns with Washington, the two capitals were in broad agreement on the need to ease tensions with the USSR.[1]

Tensions developed later when the Reagan administration took a much harder line in its policy toward the USSR and returned to a policy of strength. Here again German policy followed that of the United States as Helmut Schmidt and the SPD were replaced by the CDU chancellorship of Helmut Kohl and the deployment of the Euromissiles. The culmination of the Kohl–George H.W. Bush administration's cooperation on German unification and the end of the cold war was a high-water mark in the German–American relationship and was further evidence of a joint approach toward Russia which carried over to the Clinton administration and the enlargement of the North Atlantic Treaty Organization (NATO).[2]

The most glaring example of divergence came with the George W. Bush administration and the split over the Iraq war. This was the first case since the beginning of the cold war in which Germany sided with Russia and against the United States on an issue of vital national interest to an American administration.[3] The Russia factor was not crucial for the decision of the Schröder government to break with Washington as the alliance with France was more decisive, but it opened up a split which Moscow was able to utilise in playing on divisions within Europe. The coming to power of Angela Merkel in 2005 saw a rapprochement with Washington, although tensions over Germany's Russia policies continued, with American concerns that Germany was 'soft' on Russia.[4]

The legacy of these years regarding Russia policy was one which saw the security imperative trumping the built-in structural divergences between Washington and Bonn/ Berlin. Differences in geographic proximity, history and culture and economic interests were substantial. Russia was and remains Germany's big neighbour and is not separated by mountains or oceans. Germans must live with Russia while the US has the luxury of geographic distance and limited interdependence. Splits which did occur were often due to these geographic interests. In the Adenauer–Kennedy split over the response to the Berlin Wall as well as that regarding Intermediate Range Nuclear Force (INF) deployments, the US tended to take a global view while Germany had a regional focus. German governments viewed détente as divisible, meaning that if Europe was stable that was enough, while US administrations linked Soviet actions outside of Europe to their broad approaches to the USSR.

Geography was also behind the deep economic and energy relationship Germany developed with the USSR and then Russia, a relationship which goes back centuries. While German stakeholders in Russia policy are largely economic and commercial, American stakeholders were in the national security state, and they tended to view the USSR as a threat rather than an economic opportunity. The unavoidable fact of the Russian nuclear arsenal set this relationship apart from all others. The continuing splits during the cold war period were over the West German–Soviet energy relationship and over nuclear deterrence.

Finally, there was always a divergence in strategic cultures following *Ostpolitik*. German leaders and the German public came to believe that it was engagement with the USSR which opened the door for the peaceful unification in 1990, leaving a legacy of engagement rather than confrontation as a hallmark of the German approach to difficult countries. The US under Reagan and then again under George W. Bush was willing to take a more confrontational approach and to alternate between détente and deterrence.

These strategic cultures were also shaped by very different historical legacies. Germany, both as a unified state and as a collection of principalities and city states before 1871, has been dealing with Russia for seven centuries. Recent memories have included the devastation of World War II, the Soviet occupation of East Berlin and East Germany and then the more positive one of the Soviet role in German unification. Many Germans still hold a favourable view of Russia and the role of Gorbachev in allowing Germany to unite peacefully. Many of the 12 million East Germans who lived under Soviet occupation still have more positive views of Russia than their western compatriots. The American experience with Russia, in contrast, has been brief and limited. While America had not fought a war with Russia, it viewed the USSR as an ideological rival and threat. It has a relatively small Russian community, many of whom are Jews who wanted out of the USSR. Partisan affiliations mattered as well.

As a general rule, Republican administrations worked better with Christian Democrats while Democrats and Social Democrats had world views which were more closely aligned.

Given all these divergences, it is remarkable how well the US and German governments have been able to cooperate on Russia policy. During the cold war this was a result of the division of Germany and Bonn's dependence on the US for its security. This strategic glue held the two sides together when divergences threatened unity. Many realists questioned whether this alliance would survive the end of the division of Germany and Europe.[5] The expectation was that Germany would become a more independent realist power and freed from strategic dependence it would assert itself more as a traditional power. These expectations were not realised.[6]

THE OBAMA LEGACY

The German–American relationship had begun to recover from the split over the Iraq war during the final years of the George W. Bush term. Bush and Angela Merkel had a surprisingly warm personal relationship and felt comfortable working with each other. They diverged over the question of NATO enlargement to Georgia and Ukraine at the NATO Bucharest summit in 2008, with both the German chancellor and French President Sarkozy opposing Bush's proposal to offer Membership Action Plan (MAP) status to the two nations. While Merkel pushed back, she did accept the principle that both Ukraine and Russia would one day become members of NATO. The Russian–Georgian war which followed changed German thinking in many ways and marked the beginning of a much more critical view of Putin and his policies among the German elite.[7]

Although the working relationship had improved, the Obama administration came into power at a low point in the German public's assessment of the relationship.[8] Obama aimed at restoring the image of American power to one which was multilateral rather than unilateral and which took the views of its allies seriously. However, Obama was not an Atlanticist or even a liberal internationalist but rather a liberal realist.[9] His view of Europe was not one based on close personal associations but rather one of a purely pragmatic worldview. He believed that the central problem of American foreign policy was the over-stretch of American commitments and resources and a proclivity to use military force to deal with the threats which did not involve vital American interests. This was compounded by a tendency for allies to free ride on American power.[10]

The Russian use of force to change borders in Ukraine and the growing crisis of the liberal order in Europe, aggravated by the influx of refugees, forced the administration to reassess its European strategy. The Europe that existed when Obama entered office was very different than the one he faced at the end of his term. Obama had started with the famous 'reset' of relations with Russia based on the Medvedev presidency and the hope that Russia would become, if not a partner, at least a constructive player in the international system. While rejecting the acceptance of a Russian sphere of influence, the Obama administration recognised Russian sensitivities about the regions it bordered and cancelled an anti-missile deployment that Bush had planned for Poland and the Czech Republic. Obama gave priority to working on issues outside of Europe where US and Russian interests coincided, most notably on Iran and Afghanistan as well as in the arms control area.[11] Following the return of Putin to the presidency in 2012 and the disappointments which followed, Obama came to consider Russia as a declining 'regional power' before its actions in Ukraine; and even after Russia's violation of Ukraine's territorial sovereignty, American policy was based on a realist assessment that Russia had reacted defensively and had escalation dominance and a greater strategic interest in Ukraine than did the West.[12] This implied that Europe was now just one of many regions and no longer the preeminent one in American strategic thinking.

Obama thought Europe should take the lead on dealing with the Ukraine crisis as Europeans had a more direct stake in this challenge than did the United States. As it turned out this leadership role was taken by Angela Merkel, with Germany shaping both the European and transatlantic responses to the Russian violation of Ukrainian territorial integrity. This in turn solidified the Obama–Merkel relationship as not only the central one in the transatlantic world but as one of the key relationships for the Obama administration more broadly. It also boosted Merkel's image in the US, culminating in her being named *Time* magazine's person of the year in 2015 for 'asking more of her country than most politicians would dare, for standing firm against tyranny as well as expedience and for providing steadfast moral leadership in a world where it is in short supply'.[13]

This solidarity clearly surprised Putin, who regarded the West as weak, decadent, divided and uninterested. One of Putin's major goals has been and continues to be to divide Europeans from each other and Europe from the United States. His most important target was and will continue to be the German–American relationship. Putin tried to capitalise on the Snowden effect during the Obama years in German public opinion, hoping to feed a sense among Germans that both the US and Russia are equivalent in their behaviour and that Washington was trying to drag Germany and Europe into a confrontation. He has used his extensive business and criminal network, including former members of the East German secret police who worked for him when he was a KGB agent in East Germany, to foster corruption and to buy favour among German decision makers.[14] The rise of the Alternative für Deutschland (AfD) is another case of a right-wing populist party which is pro-Putin to go along with a number of *Putinverstehers* in both Die Linke and the SPD.

The two western leaders had to manage this partnership carefully and bridge the divergences between a military and classic great power in the United States and a rising geo-economic power in Germany. This was most clear in the development of the main tool used to respond to Russia's aggression, economic sanctions. Geo-economic Germany was more vulnerable to the impact of sanctions on Russia given its ten-fold greater economic relationship with Russia than that of the United States. Yet this close economic relationship and Berlin's lack of real military options due to its strategic culture and low level of military capabilities, made an economic response, diplomacy and Germany's leadership role in the EU the major ones available in its toolbox.

While Merkel worked closely with the Obama administration, a number of key Republicans like Senators John McCain and Lindsey Graham were openly critical of her handling of the crisis. Upon her return from negotiating the Minsk agreement in February 2015 she was heavily criticised by both McCain and Graham at the Munich

Security conference.[15] There were many in both parties at the time who were calling for military aid to Ukraine, most notably in a joint report issued by the Brookings Institution, the Chicago Council on Global Affairs and the Atlantic Council of the US and signed by prominent Democrats like Ivo Daalder, Michele Flournoy and Strobe Talbott.[16] That all three were close to Hillary Clinton reflected a difference in emphasis between Clinton and Obama on the role of military instruments in US foreign policy more generally and in Ukraine more specifically.[17] Following the release of this report and a joint Merkel–Obama press conference on 9 February 2015 on Ukraine, McCain issued the following statement: 'Russia's invasion of Ukraine has not only continued, but intensified in the face of political and economic sanctions. Yet President Obama and Chancellor Merkel are offering a "more of the same" diplomatic strategy that is doomed to fail'.[18]

The US and German governments came out of the Ukraine crisis united in their assessment that Russia now posed a significant and long-term threat to the European order. The 2016 German Defence White Book, the first issued in a decade, offers a reassessment of the threat posed by Russia.

> Russia is openly calling the European peace order into question with its willingness to use force to advance its own interests and to unilaterally redraw borders guaranteed under international law, as it has done in Crimea and eastern Ukraine. This has far-reaching implications for security in Europe and thus for the security of Germany.[19]

It goes on to point out that Russia is rejecting a close partnership in favour of strategic rivalry and is extensively modernising its armed forces, and re-emphasises the centrality of the EU, NATO and the relationship with the United States. However, while stressing defence, the emphasis of the Foreign Ministry was also on a cooperative relationship with Russia.

> Without a fundamental change in policy, Russia will constitute a challenge to the security of our continent in the foreseeable future. At the same time, however, Europe and Russia remain linked by a broad range of common interests and relations. … Sustainable security and prosperity in and for Europe cannot therefore be ensured without strong cooperation with Russia. It is therefore all the more important that, in our relations with Russia, we find the right balance between collective defence and increased resilience on the one hand, and approaches to cooperative security and sectoral cooperation on the other.[20]

This is a reformulation of the Harmel doctrine of NATO from the late 1960s of defence and détente now rephrased as deterrence and dialogue. The decision to build a second Nord Stream gas pipeline from Russia to Germany and the statements of a number of leading German politicians calling for an end to sanctions make clear the potential for divergence on Russia over the long run.[21] Nord Stream 2 was the main area of divergence between Washington and Berlin during this period. It was seen within the Obama administration as weakening the sanctions regime and European solidarity, as well as undermining the financial base of Ukraine. However, German and American defence policies came together in the wake of the Ukraine crisis, with both countries committing to troop deployments in the Baltics at the

NATO summit in Warsaw in 2016 combined with an increase of 8 per cent in German defence spending. The German decision to deploy into the Baltics was a major strategic signal to Russia.

While the legacy of the Obama–Merkel years saw a number of divergences on economic policy and tensions remained on burden sharing and the role of American intelligence agencies in Germany, the close cooperation on Russia policy was a major achievement and was crucial in Germany's shaping of a unified EU sanctions regime.[22]

THE TRUMP FACTOR

The election of Donald Trump as president in 2016 and his openly sympathetic attitude regarding Putin and Russia is an entirely new factor in the German–American approach toward Russia. In the past, strains over Russia arose from a confrontational Washington facing a reluctant and cautious Berlin. Had Hillary Clinton been elected rather than Trump, this dynamic might have reasserted itself given Clinton's generally tougher approach to a Russia which had actively tried to undermine her candidacy. As it turned out, the Trump–Merkel relationship might more resemble that between Adenauer and Kennedy, Schmidt and Carter or Schröder and Bush, all cases where German chancellors clashed with American presidents and turned to France.[23]

Trump's views on Russia remain in the minority in the US. Most polls of American opinion found little sympathy for Russia prior to the Trump campaign for president, while Germans tended to think western policies were too tough. A 2015 Pew survey found:

> More than half of Americans (54 per cent) believe that U.S. policy toward Russia is not tough enough. And 59 per cent say the EU is not being strong enough. At the same time, roughly six-in-ten Germans (62 per cent) think the U.S. position with regard to Russia is too tough (27 per cent) or about right (35 per cent). Similarly, 62 per cent of Germans believe that EU actions against Russia are too strong (18 per cent) or about right (44 per cent). Only 23 percent of Germans think Washington is not tough enough. And 26 per cent believe the European Union is not aggressive enough.[24]

However, a 2016 Gallup poll found that American attitudes toward Russia had moderated somewhat.

> After reaching a new low in 2015, Americans' impressions of Russia have recovered somewhat this year, with 30 per cent viewing the country favorably versus 24 per cent in 2015. A majority of Americans continue to view the nation unfavorably, and their favorability rating is still half as high as it was a decade ago.[25]

In general, the public in both Germany and the United States remain negative on Putin and Russian policies and are in broad convergence on Russia. However, the 2016 US presidential campaign and Donald Trump's praise for Putin introduced a new element. The Trump and Republican emphasis upon the 'strong man' style of leadership and their virulent opposition to Obama have led to significant numbers of Republicans regarding Putin as a stronger leader than Obama and reduced the numbers of Republicans regarding Putin unfavourably. In addition, many on the

American right saw Putin as a defender of Christian and conservative values such as traditional marriage and, to some, as a defender of whites in an increasingly diverse world.[26] These new attitudes in the United States are linked not only to a tendency toward authoritarianism and to Putin's appeal to traditional values, but also to the belief that cutting a deal with Russia will lower the costs of international burdens and free up the country to focus on its domestic problems. Many do not regard the Baltic states or Ukraine as worth fighting a war over.[27] A number of these American *Putinverstehers* see Russia as an ally in the fight against Islamic extremism which emerged as the top priority in the early days of the new administration. This is a remarkable shift for a party which has been the most critical of Russia and whose 2012 presidential candidate, Mitt Romney, called Russia America's greatest geopolitical threat.[28]

Reports of Russian interference in the 2016 campaign left a broadly negative view of Russia among the American public.[29] Gallup surveys taken since 1990 on the favourability of American opinion on Russia found that it peaked in 2002, that is just at the beginning of the Putin era, at 66 per cent favourable against 28 per cent unfavourable. The unfavourable number spiked beginning around February 2014, jumping from 44 per cent unfavourable in 2012 up to 70 per cent in February 2017.[30] While most of the public and the Congress remain sceptical about Russia, the president will continue to be the most important player in Russia policy. The public is more concerned about immigration, jobs and health care than it is about Russia. In addition, Russia has become a partisan issue to a degree that it never was during the cold war. The role of Russia in the American elections and the inability of the Obama administration to get bipartisan support for a response to Russian interference marks a major break in what was a strategic consensus on Russia.[31] A 2017 Pew survey found that 39 per cent of Democrats compared to only 21 per cent of Republicans listed Russia as the greatest threat to the United States.[32]

The German public shares this highly negative view of Putin. Polls commissioned by the Bertelsmann Foundation in 2016 found that that 64 per cent did not consider Putin's Russia a credible partner for Germany, with a similar number finding German–Russian relations bad (up from 40 per cent in 2013). In regard to Germany's policy toward Russia, 44 per cent supported it compared to 25 per cent who found it too anti-Russian and 19 per cent too friendly to Russia. Support for continuation of economic sanctions against Russia remained high, with 62 per cent in favour of the current or even strengthened levels.[33] Eastern Germans and supporters of both die Linke and the Alternative für Deutschland stood out as more pro-Putin.[34] However, even prior to the election of Donald Trump, these negative attitudes on Russia did not translate into a desire for closer relations with the US, with a clear preference rather to work with Germany's European partners. The early days of the Trump administration resulted in Trump's negatives being greater than Putin's. An April 2017 survey found that only 29 per cent of Germans considered the US a trustworthy partner compared to 20 per cent viewing Russia in this light. A June 2017 Pew survey was even more devastating.[35]

TOWARD A ZERO-SUM WORLD

The new president and some of his team hold a highly transactional and über-realist view of the world. Trump's national security advisor and top economic advisor explained the Trump administration's view of foreign policy as one in which 'the world is not a "global community" but an arena where nations, nongovernmental actors and businesses engage and compete for advantage'.[36] This is a clearly zero-sum view of the world and is much closer to the Putin world view than that of Angela Merkel. The new president's relations with Russia and Russians prior to his assuming office was based on financial and business links and not on strategic concerns. In this he is close to the views of the German Russia business lobby and former Chancellor Gerhard Schröder. Given Trump's emphasis on combatting the Islamic State in Iraq and Syria and what he called 'Islamic extremism', it is not surprising that he was open to Russian arguments that the two countries shared a common threat which over-rode differences in other policy areas. Added to this was the upheaval concerning allegations of collusion between the Trump campaign and Russia which made Trump defensive over this relationship, in large part as it threatened the legitimacy of his election.

The contrast between those in the White House associated with Stephen Bannon and the more traditional national security team was striking and has led to confusion regarding policy. In addition, the Congress is more sceptical and has tried to place some limits on the president's ability to relax sanctions on Russia, a clear sign of distrust in his Russia policies. While the instability in American policy and especially in the White House is likely to continue, the Trump administration marks a turning point in post-war American foreign policy, taking with it the hopes in Berlin that the president would be moved by his more centrist foreign policy team. As Edward Luce and others have pointed out, Trump ignores their advice on key policies like climate change and NATO and has deeply held views of a world which he sees as continually taking advantage of America.[37]

This stands in contrast to the situation in Germany where the main political parties remain much closer on Russia policy. The Social Democrats, with their tradition of *Ostpolitik* and its follow-on, *Modernisierungspartnerschaft*, have always favoured engagement over confrontation and have been the most pro-Russia of the major German parties. The continuing influence of former Chancellor Gerhard Schröder, with his close ties to Gazprom and to Putin, has been evident in the support of both the SPD-led Economics and Foreign ministries for the building of the Nord Stream 2 gas pipeline with Russia.[38] The chancellery did not block this project although the chancellor clearly did not support it as she feared it would undermine her broader policy on sanctions within the EU. Both the business wing of the CDU and the CSU have also favoured loosening sanctions under certain conditions but the overall Merkel policy is generally supported. While leading members of the SPD have expressed an openness to easing sanctions on Russia, there is no significant split between the two major parties on this topic.

The Nord Stream 2 case highlights another important potential source of German–American divergence over Russia, and that is the differential dependence on Russian energy and the broader economic relationship. As Angela Stent has pointed out, the US has few economic stakeholders in the Russia relationship while the German economic relationship with Russia is far more extensive. US trade with Russia totalled about $20 billion in 2016, down from pre-Ukraine highs of $40 billion in 2012.[39] German trade during the same period fell from $80 billion to $40 billion, with exports in

2016 totalling $22 billion. Over 5200 German companies were operating in Russia in 2016.[40] The US has no real dependence on Russian energy and the only major joint venture which involved Exxon Mobil and Rosneft has been suspended due to the Ukraine-related sanctions.[41] Germany in contrast gets about 36 per cent of its gas and 39 per cent of its oil from Russia and this relationship has created a formidable lobby in Berlin for good economic relations with Russia.[42]

Although the White House and Secretary of State Rex Tillerson would like to weaken sanctions, the new Russia sanctions passed by the US Senate in June 2017 threatened penalties on European companies financing Nord Stream 2. This caused an angry reaction from Germany's Foreign Minister Gabriel, who issued a joint statement with the Austrian chancellor which stated: 'To threaten companies from Germany, Austria and other European states with penalties in natural gas projects such as Nord Stream 2 with Russia or finance them introduces a completely new and very negative quality into European–American relations'.[43] A new factor is the energy boom in the United States due to the development of shale oil which has now made the US an energy exporter that would like to sell Liquified Natural Gas (LNG) to Europe. While the American president and his secretary of state would clearly prefer to conduct a more commercially oriented policy toward Russia, the suspicion in the Congress over his campaign's Russia dealings have clearly limited this option, at least for the short term. This will avoid a split with Chancellor Merkel on sanctions policy, a key element of the Minsk Agreement on Ukraine. What seems clear is that the Trump administration has placed the US on the same level as Russia in its proclamation of a zero-sum world and its open pursuit of national interest which seems value free. This has reinforced the tendency in Germany toward equidistancing between Washington and Moscow.

END OF AN ALLIANCE?

The strategic glue which held the transatlantic relationship together has been weakening since German unification, most notably during the Iraq war and the rise of the neo-conservatives in the second Bush administration. Despite the closeness of German–US cooperation over Ukraine, this glue further weakened during the Obama years. The Trump era and the president's ambivalence over the Article 5 security guarantee of the NATO treaty has been decisive in announcing the end of an era, as noted by Chancellor Merkel in her speech in Bavaria in May 2017.[44] Her main opponent in the 2016 Bundestag election campaign, Martin Schulz, made her lack of stronger resistance to Trump an issue and revived the America factor, as did Schröder in the 2002 campaign.[45] The June 2017 global survey conducted by the Pew Center found that the image of both President Trump and the US has dropped in all countries except Russia and Israel, with Germany having one of the most negative views of the new administration.[46] The same survey found confidence in both Trump and Putin at very low levels, although Trump came in lower than Putin.

The Trump ambivalence over NATO and the American security guarantee poses a major challenge for German foreign and security policy, with implications for its posture toward Russia. The nuclear guarantee which lay behind the strategy of deterrence has now come into question at a time when the Putin regime has increased its emphasis on the role of nuclear weapons in its defence doctrine. The old cold war issue of the decoupling of the American deterrent from European security which was at the heart of the Euromissile INF deployment in the 1980s has returned and with it the beginning of a debate in Germany over the future of nuclear deterrence.[47]

Chancellor Merkel's declaration that the days that Europe could rely on the United States were most likely over was a declaration that the German–US partnership as it had developed since the beginning of the cold war and then renewed after German unification is over. This has major implications for all aspects of German foreign and security policy, especially regarding its relations to Russia. Germany has tried to combine both deterrence and détente, a combination of elements of *Ostpolitik* and the policy of strength.[48] Berlin has responded to Russian aggression in Ukraine with both diplomacy and hard power, through sanctions and the deployment of a German military contingent to Lithuania. At the same time, German leaders continue to talk to their Russia counterparts even though Russian credibility in Berlin is near zero. These policies have depended on both a united European and a transatlantic base. The transatlantic pillar of German policy toward Russia is now in serious question and is resulting in what John Foster Dulles once referred to as an 'agonizing reappraisal' of policy.[49] This policy has relied on the threat of American military force backing up diplomacy, a threat which is now in substantial doubt. As Edward Luce observed,

> Since the end of the Cold War, it has become ever harder for U.S. leaders to convince voters of the old Kennedy exhortation to 'pay any price, bear any burden'. The very notion that an aspiring U.S. president could urge Americans to sacrifice on behalf of other countries seems fanciful.[50]

German policy now faces a choice of either strengthening the European pillar, based on a revitalised Franco-German core, supported by Poland, the Baltics and the Scandinavian states, or turning toward an accommodation with Moscow.[51] It has already taken steps to enhance its defence through increased spending, an enlarged frigate and submarine presence in the North Sea, the creation of a cyber command and its role in the NATO Baltic Joint Task Force. It has enhanced measures to counter Russian hybrid warfare and disinformation efforts in Germany. At the same time in keeps its channels to Russia open, including the Petersburg Dialogue, support for more military transparency and a revitalised NATO–Russia Council. However, the decision to go ahead with Nord Stream 2 makes energy diversification and a Europeanisation of energy policy less likely. This policy of hugging and hedging, of sanctions and dialogue will continue to be at the centre of Germany's approach, but will it be sustainable without American support? Germany risks once again becoming the land between, but this time a multilateralist and open country without partners due not to its own policies but to those of its closest allies.[52]

DISCLOSURE STATEMENT

No potential conflict of interest was reported by the author.

NOTES

1. For good overviews of West German foreign policy during this period, see Wolfram Hanrieder, *Germany, America, Europe* (New Haven, CT: Yale University Press, 1989); Helga Haftendorn, *Deutsche Aussenpolitik zwischen Selbstbeschränkung und Selbstbehauptung* (Munich: Deutsche Verlags Anstalt, 2001) or the English version, *Coming of Age: German Foreign Policy Since 1945* (Oxford: Rowman and Littlefield, 2008); also Christian Hacke, *Die Aussenpolitik der Bundesrepublik Deutschland: von Konrad Adenauer bis Gerhard Schröder* (Frankfurt: Ullstein, 2003)
2. See Stephen F. Szabo, *The Diplomacy of German Unification* (New York: St. Martin's Press, 1992); Philip Zelikow and Condoleezza Rice, *Germany Unified and Europe Transformed: A Study in Statecraft* (Cambridge, MA: Harvard University Press, 1995); Horst Teltschik, *329 Tage: Innenansichten der Einigung* (Munich: Siedler, 1991); Derek Chollet and James Goldgeier, *America Between the Wars: From 11/9 to 9/11, The Misunderstood Years Between the Fall of the Berlin Wall and the Start of the War on Terror* (New York: Public Affairs, 2008). On NATO enlargement see Angela E. Stent, *Russia and Germany Reborn: Unification, The Soviet Collapse and the New Europe* (Princeton, NJ: Princeton University Press, 1999), pp.212–35.
3. See Stephen F. Szabo, *Parting Ways: The Crisis in German–American Relations* (Washington, DC: Brookings Press, 2004); and Philip Gordon and Jeremy Shapiro, *Allies at War: America, Europe and the Crisis over Iraq* (Washington, DC: Brookings Institution Press, 2004); for an account from the German side see Günther Joetze, *Der Irak als deutsches Problem* (Baden Baden: Nomos 2010). For the French role see Frederik Bozo, *A History of the Iraq Crisis: France, the United States and Iraq, 1991–2003* (Washington, DC: Woodrow Wilson Center Press, 2016).
4. See Angela E. Stent, *The Limits of Partnership: U.S.–Russian Relations in the Twenty First* Century (Princeton, NJ: Princeton University Press, 2014), pp.165–8; Erik Kirschbaum and Hans Edzard Busse-mann, 'Germany Dismisses Suggestions It's Soft on Russia', *Reuters*, 28 March 2014, available from http://www.reuters.com/article/us-ukraine-nato-germany-idUSBREA2R17520140328 (accessed 12 June 2017); Alexander Motyl, 'Why are so Many German Leaders Soft on Putin's Aggression?', *Newsweek*, 23 June 2016, available from http://www.newsweek.com/why-are-so-many-german-leaders-soft-putin-aggression-472882 (accessed 12 June 2017).
5. John J. Mearsheimer, 'Back to the Future: Instability in Europe After the Cold War', *International Security* 15/1 (1990), pp.5–56; Hans Peter Schwarz, *Die Zentralmacht Europas: Deutschlands Rückkehr auf die Weltbühne* (Munich: Siedler, 1998); for an excellent short treatment of this discussion see Hans Kundnani, *The Paradox of German Power* (Oxford: Oxford University Press, 2015); for a collection of contemporary reactions to German unification see Harold James and Marla Stone (eds), *When The Wall Came Down: Reactions to German Unification* (New York: Routledge, 1992).
6. See Kundnani, *The Paradox of German Power.*
7. See Condoleezza Rice's account in her memoir, *No Higher Honor: A Memoir of My Years in Washington* (New York: Crown, 2011), pp.671–5. See also Stent, *The Limits of Partnership*, p.261.
8. In 2008 only about 20 per cent of Germans polled had confidence that the US president would do the right thing; That number skyrocketed to 93 per cent in Obama's first year in office and never fell lower than 71 per cent following the revelations of NSA intelligence gathering from German citizens.

See Frédéric Bozo et al., *Suspicious Minds: U.S.–German Relations in the Trump Era* (Washington, DC: Transatlantic Academy, 2017), p.20, available from http://www.transatlanticacademy.org/sites/default/files/publications/Suspicious_Minds_Final_0.pdf (accessed 12 July 2017).

9. Jeffrey Goldberg, 'The Obama Doctrine', *The Atlantic* (April 2016), available from http://www.theatlantic.com/magazine/archive/2016/04/the-obama-doctrine/471525/ (accessed 12 July 2017). For a broad overview of the Obama legacy see Derek Chollet, *The Long Game: How Obama Defied Washington and Redefined America's Role in the World* (New York: Public Affairs, 2016).

10. As he stated in his interview with Jeffrey Goldberg in *The Atlantic* near the end of his time in office, '"Free riders aggravate me," he told me. Recently, Obama warned that Great Britain would no longer be able to claim a "special relationship" with the United States if it did not commit to spending at least 2 percent of its GDP on defense. "You have to pay your fair share," Obama told David Cameron, who subsequently met the 2 per cent threshold. "We don't have to always be the ones who are up front," he told me. "Sometimes we're going to get what we want precisely because we are sharing in the agenda. The irony is that it was precisely in order to prevent the Europeans and the Arab states from holding our coats while we did all the fighting that we, by design, insisted that they lead during the mission to remove Muammar Qaddafi from power in Libya. It was part of the anti-free rider campaign"'. Goldberg, 'The Obama Doctrine'.

11. See Peter Rudolf, 'Amerikanische Russland Politik und europäische Sicherheitsordnung', in *SWP Studie, S17* (Berlin: Stiftung Wissenschaft und Politik, Sept. 2016), pp.18, 19.

12. 'Obama's theory here is simple: Ukraine is a core Russian interest but not an American one, so Russia will always be able to maintain escalatory dominance there. "The fact is that Ukraine, which is a non-NATO country, is going to be vulnerable to military domination by Russia no matter what we do," he said. I asked Obama whether his position on Ukraine was realistic or fatalistic. "It's realistic," he said. "But this is an example of where we have to be very clear about what our core interests are and what we are willing to go to war for. And at the end of the day, there's always going to be some ambiguity".' Goldberg, 'The Obama Doctrine'.

13. During the height of the Ukraine crisis, between February 2014 and November 2015, Merkel talked with French President François Hollande 38 times (13 one-on-one), and with Obama 15 times (11 one-on-one), and British Prime Minister David Cameron 14 times (8 one-on-one), more than those the American president had with any other leader. She in turn talked with Putin 65 times (35 of those conversations one-on-one) in addition to numerous meetings with Putin. Ulrich Speck, *The West's Response to the Ukraine Crisis: A Transatlantic Success Story*, 2015–2016 Policy Paper, No.4 (Washington, DC: The Transatlantic Academy, 2016), p.4, available from http://www.transatlanticacademy.org/sites/default/files/publications/Speck_WestResponseUkraine_Apr16_web.pdf (accessed 12 July 2017). These figures came from the German chancellery and the White House, available from http://time.com/time-person-of-the-year-2015-angela-merkel-choice/ (accessed 12 July 2017)

14. Stephen F. Szabo, *Germany, Russia and the Rise of Geo-economics* (London: Bloomsbury, 2015), pp.61–82.

15. Graham stated, 'At the end of the day, to our European friends, this is not working', Graham said of Merkel''s diplomatic efforts. 'You can go to Moscow until you turn blue in the face. Stand up to what is clearly a lie and a danger.' McCain added: 'The Ukrainians are being slaughtered and we're sending them blankets and meals. Blankets don''t do well against Russian tanks'. Stephen Brown and Noah Barkin, 'Merkel Defends Ukraine Arms Stance in Face of U.S. Criticism', *Reuters*, 7 Feb. 2015, available from http://uk.reuters.com/article/uk-ukraine-crisis-idUKKBN0LA13N20150207 (accessed 12 July 2017).

16. Ivo Daalder et al., *Preserving Ukraine's Independence, Resisting Russian Aggression: What the United States and NATO Must Do* (Washington, DC: The Atlantic Council of the United States, 2015, available from https://www.brookings.edu/wp-content/uploads/2016/06/UkraineReport_February2015_FINAL.pdf (accessed 26 June 2017).

17. For more on the Clinton–Obama relationship on foreign policy see Mark Landler, *Alter Egos: Hillary Clinton, Barack Obama, and the Twilight Struggle Over American Power* (New York: Random House, 2016).

18. Statement by Senator John McCain on the Obama–Merkel Press Conference on Ukraine', 9 Feb. 2015 available from http://www.mccain.senate.gov/public/index.cfm/press-releases?ID=92836DC1-6730-4FBB-A218-B0E3CB2F1494 (accessed 26 June 2017).

19. *White Paper2016: On German Security Policy and the Future of the Bundeswehr* (Berlin: Federal Ministry of Defence, 2016), p.31, available from https://www.bmvg.de/resource/resource/MzEzNTM4MmUzMzMyMmUzMTM1MzMyZTM2MzIzMDMwMzAzMDMwMzAzMDY5NzE3MzM1MzEzOTMyNmUyMDIwMjAyMDIw/2016%20White%20Paper.pdf (accessed 26 June 2017) (hereafter referred to as the 2016 White Book).

20. *2016 Defence White Book*, p.32. A June 2016 Pew poll found that 58 per cent of Germans believe having a strong economic relationship with Russia is more important than being tough with Russia on foreign policy disputes (35 per cent); Pew Research Center, *Europeans Face the World Divided* (Washington, DC, June 2016), p.19.

21. Hannes Adomeit, *Germany's Russia Policy: From Sanctions to Nord Stream 2?*, Policy Paper No. 3 (Washington, DC: Transatlantic Academy, March 2016), available from http://www.transatlanticacademy. org/sites/default/files/publications/Adomeit%20-%20web.pdf (accessed 12 July 2017).

22. For more on the ambivalence of the Obama legacy on German–US relations see Bozo et al., *Suspicious Minds*, pp.6–13.

23. For an examination of the German–French–US triangle see Helga Haftendorn et al. (eds), *The Strategic Triangle: France, Germany and the United States in the Shaping of the New Europe* (Washington, DC: Woodrow Wilson Center Press, 2007).

24. Pew Research Center, Global Attitudes and Trends, *Germany and the United States: Reliable Allies* (Washington, DC: Pew Research Center: 7 May 2015), available from http://www.pewglobal.org/ 2015/05/07/germany-and-the-united-states-reliable-allies/ (accessed 26 June 2017).

25. Art Swift, 'Americans See Russia Less Negatively, as Less of a Threat', Gallup Poll Social Series, 18 Feb. 2016, available from http://www.gallup.com/poll/189284/americans-russia-less-negatively-less-threat.aspx (accessed 26 June 2017).

26. David Weigel, 'Trump Not Alone in GOP with his Praise for Putin', *The Washington Post*, 10 Sept. 2017, p.A1. For Putin's use of religion see Alicja Curanovic, 'The Guardians of Traditional Values: Russia and the Russian Orthodox Church in the Quest for Status', in Michael Barnett et al. (eds), *Faith, Freedom and Foreign Policy: Challenges for the Transatlantic Community* (Washington, DC: Transatlantic Academy, 2015), pp.191–212.

27. Secretary of State Tillerson asked his European counterparts why American taxpayers should care about Ukraine and Trump confidant Newt Gingrich referred to Tallinn as a suburb of St Petersburg. 'Tillerson Asks why U.S. Taxpayers Should Care About Ukraine', *Bloomberg News*, 11 April 2017, available from https://www.bloomberg.com/news/articles/2017-04-11/tillerson-asks-why-u-s-taxpayers-should-care-about-ukraine (accessed 12 July 2017); Andrew Stuttaford, 'Estonia, Newt Gingrich and Strategery', *The National Review*, 23 July 2016, available from http://www.nationalreview.com/corner/438260/estonia-newt-gingrich-and-strategery (accessed 12 July 2017).

28. Alicia M. Cohn, 'Romney Calls Russia "Our No. 1 Geopolitical Foe"', *The Hill*, 26 March 2012, available from http://thehill.com/video/campaign/218201-romney-calls-russia-our-no-1-geopolitical-foe (accessed 17 July 2017).

29. Scott Clement, 'Russia's Popularity among Americans Sinks to Thirty Year Low, New Poll Finds', *The Washington Post*, 21 Dec. 2016, available from https://www.washingtonpost.com/news/worldviews/wp/ 2016/12/21/russias-popularity-hits-30-year-low-in-u-s-new-poll-finds/?utm_term=.d1b11282cdbc (accessed 12 July 2017).

30. Gallup, 'Russia'.

31. See Greg Miller, Ellen Nakashima and Adam Entous, 'Hacking Democracy: Obama's Secret Struggle to Retaliate Against Putin's Election Assault', *The Washington Post*, 25 June 2017, p.A1.

32. Rob Suls, *Share of Democrats Calling Russia 'Greatest Danger' to U.S is at its Highest since the End of the Cold War* (Washington, DC: Pew Research Center, 20 April 2017), available from http://www. pewresearch.org/fact-tank/2017/04/20/share-of-democrats-calling-russia-greatest-danger-to-u-s-at-its-highest-since-end-of-cold-war/ (accessed 12 July 2017). 'The new survey is the latest indication of growing concern among Democrats, in particular, about Russia in the wake of reports that the Russian government interfered in the 2016 U.S. election. A January survey found that Democrats were far more likely than Republicans to say that Russia was behind the hacks of the Hillary Clinton campaign and the Democratic National Committee. That survey also found that 38 per cent of Democrats viewed Russia as an "adversary," compared with 20 per cent of Republicans.'

33. Bertelsmann Stiftung, *Frayed Partnership: German Public Opinion on Russia* (Gutersloh: April 2016), available from https://www.bertelsmann-stiftung.de/fileadmin/files/user_upload/EZ_Frayed_Partnersh ip_2016_ENG.pdf (accessed 26 June 2017). 'Our survey shows that the phenomenon of consistent "Russland-Versteher" has a relatively small representation within the society at large. This can be demonstrated by looking at the percentage of Germans who consistently responded to the questions in a pro-Russian way. Thus, the percentage of those who at the same time believe that Putin's Russia is a credible international partner for Germany, do not see Russia as a military threat, and would like the sanctions to be eased is only 13 per cent. If we take into account those who positively view Putin's intervention in Syria, the number of thus defined "Russland-Versteher" shrinks to 8 per cent of Germans' (p.15).

34. See Josef Joffe, 'Die bizarre Russland-Apologetik der Linken', *Die Zeit*, 19 March 2014, available from http://www.zeit.de/politik/deutschland/2014-03/sahra-wagenknecht-krim-russland (accessed 26 June

2017); Sahra Wagenknecht, 'Rot–Rot–Grün: Politik- statt Personalwechsel', *Blätter für deutsche und internationale Politik* 2 (2015), pp.73–81; cited in Andreas Heinemann-Grüder, 'Kalter Krieg Oder Neue Ostpolitik? Ansätze deutscher Russlandpolitik', *Aus Politik und Zeitgeschichte* 21–22 (2017), p.5.

35. ARD Deutschland Trends polls conducted by Infratest Dimap and cited in Bozo et al., *Suspicious Minds*, p.20; Richard Wike et al., *U.S. Image Suffers as Publics Around World Question Trump's Leadership* (Washington, DC: Pew Global Research, 26 June 2017), available from http://www.pewglobal.org/2017/06/26/u-s-image-suffers-as-publics-around-world-question-trumps-leadership/ (accessed 3 July 2017).

36. H.R. McMaster and Gary D. Cohn, 'America First Does Not Mean America Alone', *The Wall Street Journal*, 30 May 2017; available from https://www.wsj.com/articles/america-first-doesnt-mean-america-alone-1496187426 (accessed 26 June 2017).

37. Edward Luce, 'The New World Disorder', *The Financial Times*, 24/25 June 2017, FT Weekend, p.18. See also Yascha Mounk, *Wake Up Berlin: To Save the Transatlantic Alliance German Foreign Policy Needs to Change Radically*, Policy Paper No.4 (Washington, DC: Transatlantic Academy 2017), available from http://www.transatlanticacademy.org/sites/default/files/publications/Mounk%20-%20Wake%20Up%20Berlin.pdf (accessed 3 July 2017).

38. See the comprehensive study of Nordstream 2, Kai-Olaf Lang and Kirsten Westphal, 'Nord Stream 2-Versuch einer politischen und wirtschaftlichen Einordung', in *SWP Studien*, S21 (Berlin: Stiftung Wissenschaft und Politik, December 2016), available from http://www.auswaertiges-amt.de/EN/Aussenpolitik/Laender/Laenderinfos/01-Nodes/RussischeFoederation_node.html (accessed 3 July 2017).

39. US Census Bureau, available from https://www.census.gov/foreign-trade/balance/c4621.html#2016 (accessed 3 July 2017).

40. Source: German Foreign Office, available from http://www.auswaertiges-amt.de/EN/Aussenpolitik/Laender/Laenderinfos/01-Nodes/RussischeFoederation_node.html (accessed 3 July 2017).

41. Andrew E. Kramer and Clifford Kraus, 'Rex Tillerson's Company, Exxon, Has Billions at Stake Over Sanctions on Russia', *The New York Times*, 12 Dec. 2016, available from https://www.nytimes.com/2016/12/12/world/europe/rex-tillersons-company-exxon-has-billions-at-stake-over-russia-sanctions.html?action=click&contentCollection=Energy%20%26%20Environment%20&module=RelatedCoverage&region=Marginalia&pgtype=article; https://www.nytimes.com/2017/04/21/business/energy-environment/treasury-exxon-mobil-sanctions-waiver.html?_r=0 (accessed 3 July 2017).

42. See Szabo, *Germany, Russia and the Rise of Geo-Economics*, chapter 4; and Tom Dyson, 'Energy Security and Germany's Response to Russian Revisionism: The Dangers of Civilian Power', *German Politics* 25/4 (2016), pp.500–581.

43. Christian Krug and Kalina Oroschakoff, 'Germany and Russia Warn U.S. Over Expanded Russia Sanctions', *Politico Europe*, 15 June 2017, available from http://www.politico.eu/article/germany-and-austria-warn-u-s-over-expanded-russia-sanctions/ (accessed 3 July 2017); Karoun Dimirjian, 'Senate Overwhelmingly Passes New Russia and Iran Sanctions', *The Washington Post*, 15 June 2017, available from https://www.washingtonpost.com/powerpost/senate-overwhelmingly-passes-new-russia-and-iran-sanctions/2017/06/15/df9afc2a-51d8-11e7-91eb-9611861a988f_story.html?utm_term=.040879077d80 (accessed 3 July 2017). The Austrian–German statement is misleading as Europe is deeply divided over the NS 2 project with many eastern European states and Italy bitterly opposed to the project.

44. Michael Birnbaum and Rick Noack, 'Following Trump's Trip Merkel Says Europe Can't Rely on "Others". She Means the U.S.', *The Washington Post*, 28 May 2017, available from https://www.washingtonpost.com/world/following-trumps-trip-merkel-says-europe-cant-rely-on-us-anymore/2017/05/28/4c6b92cc-43c1-11e7-8de1-cec59a9bf4b1_story.html?utm_term=.0f66c0b2ad22 (accessed 3 July 2017).

45. For the impact of the Iraq war on German politics see Stephen F. Szabo, *Parting Ways: The Crisis in German–American Relations* (Washington, DC: Brookings Institution Press, 2004).

46. Wike et al., *U.S. Image Suffers*.

47. Rudolf, 'Amerikanische Russland Politik und europäische Sicherheitsordnung', p.23; and Ulrich Kühn and Tristan Volpe, 'Keine Atombombe, Bitte', *Foreign Affairs* 96/4 (July/Aug. 2017), pp.103–12.

48. Heinemann-Grüder, 'Kalter Krieg Oder Neue Ostpolitik?'

49. 'John Foster Dulles – An Agonizing Reappraisal', *The Harvard Crimson*, 22 May 1956, available from http://www.thecrimson.com/article/1956/5/22/john-foster-dulles-an-agonizing-reappraisal-pfor/ (accessed 3 July 2017).

50. Luce, 'The New World Disorder', p.19.

51. For the range of options facing German foreign policy see the papers listed on http://www.transatlanticacademy.org/ (accessed 3 July 2017).

52. See Gideon Rachman, *Multilateralism in One Country: The Isolation of Merkel's Germany*, Policy Paper No.6 (Washington, DC: Transatlantic Academy, 2017), available from http://www.transatlanticacademy.org/sites/default/files/publications/Rachman%20-%20Multilateralism%20in%20One%20Country.pdf (accessed 3 July 2017).

Trading Places: Securitising Refugee and Asylum Policics in Germany and the United States

JOYCE MARIE MUSHABEN

Given their radically different historical approaches to immigration and refugees, one would expect Germany and the United States to have adopted diverging policies in these domains following the '9/11' attacks. More surprising is the extent to which they have 'traded places' regarding their respective 'leadiator' and 'laggard' roles concerning asylum rights. Although both countries embraced restrictive practices during the 1980s, US law now concentrates on 'security first', relying heavily on exclusionary border control and national security framing. Whereas the old FRG used complex, exclusionary laws to limit all forms of migration prior to 1998, united Germany has redefined itself as a 'welcoming culture', upholding human rights, open borders and pro-active resettlement policies. Focusing on the 'migration—security' nexus, this study compares fundamental changes in the admission and resettlement policies each now applies to persons seeking international protection. It reviews securitisation dynamics in the USA, followed by a treatment of developments at the European level that have conditioned reforms in German since 2005. The refusal of some EU member states to accept their fair share of the humanitarian burden invoked by the 2015–2016 refugee crisis has ironically contributed to Chancellor Angela Merkel's new image as Lady Liberty, 'lifting her lamp besides the golden door'.

Keep, ancient lands, your storied pomp!' cries she
With silent lips. 'Give me your tired, your poor,
Your huddled masses yearning to breathe free,
The wretched refuse of your teeming shore.
Send these, the homeless, tempest-tost to me,
I lift my lamp beside the golden door!
(Emma Lazarus, 'The New Colossus' (1883), inscribed on the US Statue of Liberty)

Thwarted Arab Springs, the rise of ISIS (Islamic State) and sectarian conflicts stretching from Libya to Afghanistan have led mass waves of migrants to seek refuge in the West. Surviving perilous land and sea journeys, roughly 860,000 people filed European asylum applications in 2014, rising to 1.26 million in 2015; another 1.2 million applied in 2016, a year marked by 5000 drowning deaths (Eurostat 2016). While some states have opened their hearts, borders and public coffers to these 'huddled masses', others are jettisoning generous acceptance polices in favour of lengthy terrorist-vetting processes, leaving thousands in legal limbo.

US-American openness to people fleeing oppression has deep historical roots, although some groups hoping to enter were always 'more equal' than others prior to the elimination of national quotas in 1954. Responsibility for Nazi atrocities that displaced over 12 million Europeans after World War II led Germany to embrace a simple but elegant promise to future victims of violent conflict. Article 16 of the 1949 Basic Law declared: *Persons persecuted on political grounds shall have the right of asylum.* Over the last 10 years Germany and the United States have ironically traded places regarding their willingness to admit refugees victimised by disastrous foreign policies towards Iraq, Afghanistan, Libya and the Middle East. Particularly at risk are persons who aided the US military as translators and contractors in Iraq and Afghanistan. Despite promises made to countless at-risk candidates, few have been granted refuge in a timely fashion. Obama's promise to accept 10,000 Syrians *nationally* by 2016 compared poorly to the 35,000 Bosnians welcomed by St. Louis, a single mid-western *city*, between 1993 and 1995 (International Institute 2016).

Donald Trump's recent executive orders, bent on 'rounding up' undocumented migrants and banning 'Muslim' admissions, have darkened the picture further (White House 2017). Once known for opening its 'golden door' to millions, the United States now seems willing to ignore its obligations under international human rights conventions. Although Trump cut the federal cap on refugee admissions by almost half, to 45,000, in 2017, experts now estimate that only 21,300 are likely to be admitted in 2018 (Yuhas 2018). Chancellor Angela Merkel, by contrast, is perceived as a new Lady Liberty, having welcomed 1.1 million refugees to Germany since 2015.

This article compares refugee and asylum policies in the United States and Germany, highlighting fundamental changes in the laws, procedures and resettlement benefits each now applies to persons seeking international protection. I contend that while both adopted ever more restrictive practices during the 1980s, US law, in theory, continued to uphold inclusive, humanitarian principles. Since the terrorist attacks of 11 September 2001, however, American policy has been driven by the precept *security first*, relying ever more heavily on exclusionary 'border control' and 'national security' framing. The Federal Republic has also witnessed a change in course, albeit in the opposite direction. Whereas the old FRG stubbornly adhered to complex, exclusionary laws intended to limit all forms of migration, united Germany has become a 'welcoming culture' building on human rights, open borders and pro-active resettlement policies.

Commencing with a discussion of the 'migration—security' nexus, I address the extent to which securitisation dynamics in the USA have chipped away at the human rights foundation. I then turn to the other side of the Atlantic, outlining developments at the European level, as well as major reforms in FRG migration/asylum policy since 2005. I contend that Germany, formerly a 'laggard' in this domain, has now become a 'leadiator' working to secure supranational solutions, despite the refusal of some EU member states to accept their fair share of the humanitarian burden. I conclude with reflections on factors contributing to Merkel's new image as the 'Mother of Exiles ... lifting her lamp besides the golden door'.

SECURITY VERSUS SAFETY: THE LIBERAL DEMOCRATIC PARADOX

The end of the cold war marked both 'the disappearance of a powerful external threat' to the West and 'the loss of an important source of cohesion' among states formerly aligned with two opposing blocs (Faist 2004, 5). No longer captive to a US—Soviet 'balance-of-terror', national leaders had to find new rationales for their military-industrial complexes as new security dilemmas became opaque, diffuse and divorced from real state actors. 'Religious' radicalisation, ethnic violence, environmental disasters, energy scarcities, human trafficking, drug smuggling and organised crime pose 'ontological threats to the borders of sovereign states, bodily security, moral values, collective identities and cultural homogeneity' (Faist 2004, 1). Easily exploited by politicians and fake-news pundits, migration is framed as a metaphorical challenge 'to the ability of a nationally bound society to maintain and reproduce itself'; it is widely blamed for falling wages, rising crime and structural unemployment, all evidence to the contrary (Faist 2004, 2–3).

The 9/11 attack on the World Trade Towers triggered a backlash against foreigners *not* seen after the 1993 bombing of that capitalist landmark, master-minded by a 'blind cleric' admitted during the Reagan years. Nor was there much Islamophobia when thousands of nominal Muslims from Bosnia and Kosovo arrived in Germany and the USA through 1999. Concerns over mass waves of refugees back then were sooner quantitative and financial in nature. Adding 12 new central-east European (CEE) states rendered EU borders more porous after 2004, intensifying post-9/11 'security' worries, although subsequent terrorist bombings in Madrid and London sooner reflected 'failed integration' problems in the old member states. *Securitisation*, according to Georgis Karyotis, 'occurs when a political actor pushes an area of "normal politics" into the security realm by using the rhetoric of existential threat ... to justify the adoption of "emergency" measures outside the formal and established procedures of politics'. A societal problem can be rendered a security issue 'not necessarily because of the nature or the objective importance of a threat, but because the issue is presented as such' (Karyotis 2007, 3).

Rather than focus on the discursive elements shaping national migration debates since 2001, this article examines the policy changes born of such shifts. I define *securitisation* as a process that increasingly seeks to 'manage migration' by utilising mechanisms, procedures and technologies generally associated with crime fighting (like fingerprinting, profiling) or military defence (e.g. sharing intelligence, technical surveillance, fortifying borders). In doing so, it relegates human rights norms to the backburner, obscuring obligations under international law. I concur with Niemann and Schmidthäussler (2012, 8) that 'security logic ... has a tendency to be self-sustaining in that it produces insecurity that requires counter-measures to handle it, while creating further insecurity'. I nonetheless find their alternative, 'the logic of risk', less compelling than the framing offered by Peter Marcuse, distinguishing between 'safety' and 'security'.

Marcuse (2006, 919) contends that politicians manipulate the terrorist threat to produce 'a sense of existential insecurity which displaces the insecurities stemming from the social relations of a neo-liberal capitalist system'. Defining *security* as 'the perceived protection from danger', he construes *safety* as the protection from real risks of bodily harm, property losses and socio-economic rights essential to personal well-being. It is easier to alleviate real causes of danger than to eliminate diffuse sources of angst. I argue that leaders intent on securing populist majorities intentionally conflate security and migration problems at the expense of safety. Rather than reduce the dire poverty, sectarian strife or failed foreign policies that drive millions to seek refuge in the West, politicians present *their arrival* as an existential threat to national identities that are, at best, 'imagined'.

Despite its clear geographical advantages, the United States routinely adopts military metaphors in response to any threat to national well-being. The 'war on drugs', for example, has been used to turn urban police forces into paramilitary special weapons and tactics (SWAT) teams, who purchase military surplus at discounted prices. Since 9/11, the Defense Department has distributed over \$4.2 billion worth of equipment, including 500 military aircraft, 93,763 assault weapons and Mine-Resistant Ambush Protected vehicles (MRAP tanks); use of the latter by local law enforcement officers significantly escalated the 2014 protests against the Michael Brown shooting in Ferguson, Missouri.[1] US citizens nonetheless remain curiously oblivious to the heightened surveillance powers rooted in the USA PATRIOT Act (*Uniting and Strengthening America by Providing Appropriate Tools Required to Intercept and Obstruct Terrorism Act*, 2001). Nor do they question 'the flimsy connection' between government spending and real terrorist targets. After 9/11, the new Homeland Security Department (DHS) cut funding for New York City and Washington, DC, for example, while granting 'priority protection' to sites frequented by Republican voters, including 3773 malls, 1305 casinos, 163 water parks, 244 jails, 571 nursing homes and 718 mortuaries (Marcuse 2006, 920–921).

Hot and cold war experiences led Germans, especially, to protest against heightened state surveillance and to reject police outfitted as walking arsenals. Most FRG citizens are nowadays irritated by UK, Polish and Hungarian denunciations of EU responses to the refugee crisis as assaults on their national sovereignty. The physical 'safety' of the latter is sooner threatened by welfare cuts mandated by neo-liberal 'Troika' austerity policies than by putative 'Sharia' takeovers in Dresden, Warsaw or Budapest. CEE member states were happy to accept generous EU funding to expedite their accession but conveniently ignore the fact that rights come with responsibilities.

The securitisation of migration has given rise to two liberal democratic paradoxes. First, the tougher the stance pursued by national governments, e.g. tighter border controls, domestic surveillance, onerous airport check-in procedures or 'extreme vetting', the more citizens are duped into believing that the state *can eliminate insecurity*, although the latter reflects abstract fears, not real physical dangers. Correspondingly, the more money and resources leaders commit to such measures, the more proof they need to deliver that *these policies really work*, i.e. by reporting terrorist plots they have nipped in the bud, which usually evokes new fears. The second paradox is that the more leaders pursue 'collective security', the more they lose sight of, and even violate the very values that these actions are supposed to protect: privacy, religious freedom and human rights.

FROM BEACON TO BUSHEL BASKET: REFUGEE POLICIES IN THE UNITED STATES

Introducing national origin quotas to restrict entry to the United States, the 1924 Immigration Act did not differentiate between refugees and other migrants. World War II shaped the international refugee regime, setting the parameters for national protection policies. President Roosevelt's War Relief Control Board prioritised settlement for displaced persons and orphaned children; merely 38,000 were admitted during the first three years, each of whom had to be sponsored by a 'financially competent' individual. Unwilling to impose new burdens on US taxpayers in 1945, President Truman granted sponsorship rights to organisations capable of covering travel and resettlement costs. The Displaced Persons Act of 1948 opened the gate to 202,000 arrivals by 1950; the federal government covered travel from Europe to US ports of entry, while private associations and charities assumed the costs to a final destination (Brown and Scribner 2014, 104). The 1952 Immigration and Nationality Act (INA) defined a refugee commensurate with the 1951 UN Convention and 1967 Protocol, as any person 'unable or unwilling to avail himself or herself of the protection of [the home] country because of persecution or a well founded fear of persecution on account of race, religion, nationality, membership in a particular social group, or political opinion'.

The 1956 invasion of Hungary offered the first major test of evolving US refugee policy. President Eisenhower accepted 35,000 Hungarians, paying $1.5 million to warrant their safe arrival. From January 1959 through December 1960, he admitted 100,000 Cubans, most of whom were expected to return home following a 'quick collapse' of Fidel Castro's socialist regime. Instead, *El Comandante* confiscated the property of those who fled, forcing President Kennedy to allocate $5 million for their resettlement. In 1962, the Migration and Refugee Assistance Act appropriated $260 million for reception, health, education, employment and support benefits through 1967. A 1966 Cuban Adjustment Act granted that group special status and legal permanent residence (LPR) after one year. Following the fall of Saigon (Vietnam), the Indochina Refugee Assistance Act of 1975 allocated $500 per refugee, soon reduced to $350 for relocation. President Ford added state grants to cover mounting employment and job-training costs. Refugees fleeing the Soviet Union cost the government $1100 each, with private organisations supplying $1100 in matching funds (Brown and Scribner 2014, 105). Under the 1980 Refugee Act, the USA took in roughly 3 million refugees, a new high, then granted permanent asylum to over 400,000 'tempest-tost' individuals (Kerwin 2015, 205).

Amended in 1990, the INA extended recognition to 'a person who has been forced to abort a pregnancy or to undergo involuntary sterilization, or who has been persecuted … for other resistance to a coercive population control program'; rape, sex trafficking and female genital mutilation (FGM) were not included, however. Openness to refugee populations changed over time, owing to shifts in the countries of origin. Cold war interests favoured persons 'fleeing communism' from the mid-1970s to the early 1990s. Another 380,000 Russians were the biggest winners from 1992 to 2012, followed by 182,000 from Vietnam, 169,000 from Yugoslavia, 106,000 from Iraq and 104,000 from Myanmar. Officials only accepted 1500 of the 2.3 million victims force to flee the Rwandan genocide of 1994, inferring that political 'security' trumps physical 'safety' even in extreme cases (Gordon 2013).

Supporting authoritarian regimes in Central and South America, the United States was loathe to accept 'well founded fears' of persecution among applicants from that region; a 1987 Supreme Court ruling (*INS v. Cardoza-Fonseca*) forced the Reagan administration to adopt a Nicaraguan Review Program.[2] President Bush, Sr. granted Chinese applicants special status after the 1989 Tiananmen Square massacre, but US attorneys-general (with the exception of Janet Reno) have stone-walled against Haitians facing military coups; denied even temporary protection, most were subject to *refoulement*, despite the 1998 Haitian Refugee and Immigration Fairness Act. Their pro-spects did not change until a cataclysmic earthquake killed 316,000, injured 301,000 and displaced another 1.3 million people in January 2010 (Kerwin 2014, 53). In 2018 Donald Trump issued an executive order ending 'temporary protection' for up to 280,000 beneficiaries from El Salvador and Haiti, many of whom have been in the United States for over 20 years (Miroff and Nakamura 2018).

The 1980s imposed egregious conditions on people seeking international protection not only regionally but also in financial terms. Reagan's aversion to welfare policies triggered serious cuts across the board under the 1985 Balanced Budget Emergency and Deficit Control Act. 'Supply-side economics' invoked a discursive shift intended to reduce the flow of 'regular' migrants; the 1986 Immigration Reform and Control Act (IRCA) was nonetheless packed with so many loopholes that the 33 million who arrived between 1990 and 2001 literally outnumbered the great migration wave of 1880 to 1920.

The 1980 Refugee Act initially required federal authorities to reimburse the states for all benefits accorded during the first 36 months, including cash and medical aid; the provision exempting new arrivals from work registration during the first 60 days was reversed in 1982. Opportunities for language and vocational training, along with healthcare access, were curtailed in an obsessive push for 'self-sufficiency' (Brown and Scribner 2014, 85). From 1985 to 1989, aid provided by the Health and Human Services Department declined from $6921 to $3600 (48 per cent) per refugee (Brown and Scribner 2014, 109). Reagan transferred many responsibilities to the states but failed to 'pass the buck' needed to support them.[3] Reduced to 18 months in 1982, reimburse-ments were limited to eight months in 1991 (Brown and Scribner 2014; Nezer 2014). Federal officials stopped compensating the states for refugees drawing on Aid to Families with Dependent Children, Medicaid, and Supplemental Security Income (SSI).

Reform plans under President Clinton were undercut by House leader Newt Gin-grich and the 1992 revolt of the 'angry white males', eliminating bi-partisan consensus and fostering 'fortress America' thinking. Under the 1996 Illegal Immigrant Reform and Immigrant Responsibility Act (IRIRA), individuals can be stopped *within 100 miles* of US coastal areas or lands, *before* they even cross the border. Central Americans face expedited removal or mandatory detention. Under Operation Streamline, many are charged with illegal entry before they can request a 'credible fear interview', violating both US law and the UN Refugee Convention which bars criminal penalties for persons seeking protection. Few are apprised of their rights, and local officials often insist that 'the US is full', or threaten would-be applicants with family separation or incarceration (Kerwin 2014, 12–13).

Recent humanitarian crises have created new problems for communities willing to take in refugees. State and local authorities must submit funding applications well before federal figures are set, rendering them unequipped for a sudden influx. Already steeped in fiscal crisis, Michigan saw a 400 per cent increase in new arrivals, 2006–2008, but the Office of Refugee Resettlement had only 'scheduled' a 72 per cent funding increase for 2007–2009 (Brown and Scribner 2014, 115). Resettlement funding doubled under the Obama administration, however (Bruno 2015).

The 1990 Immigration Act undermined the legal permanent residence (LPR) norm in favour of temporary protection (TP), according legal status and work authorisation for 6—18 months, depending on homeland conditions (Bergeron 2014). Some are admitted as 'designated groups', subject to presidential discretion, but TP beneficiaries are rarely entitled to family unification or means-tested welfare aid. American variations include 'parole', extended voluntary departure (EVD), deferred enforced departure (DED), as well as 'T' or 'U' visas (for trafficking or crime victims cooperating with law enforcement).

Assuming office in 2000, George W. Bush was soon consumed with 9/11 and its aftermath, i.e. NATO attacks on Afghanistan and the invasion of Iraq. The 'war on terrorism' has marginalised human rights framing for migration in general by vetting for 'terrorism-related inadmissibility grounds' (TRIG). Two legislative measures bookmark this paradigm shift: the USA PATRIOT Act (2001) and the Emergency Supplemental Appropriations Act for Defense, the Global War on Terror and Tsunami Relief, known as the REAL ID Act (2005). Deemed the biggest reorganisation of the federal bureaucracy since World War II, the Department of Homeland Security (DHS) commenced operations in 2003, pulling together 22 national agencies, including the Immigration Naturalization Service (INS), Immigration and Customs Enforcement (ICE) and Customs and Border Protection (CBP). Securitisation is best measured in terms of the changing allocations for 'resettlement' versus 'border control' and processing requirements. The CPB and ICE budgets alone totalled $18 billion, excluding costs at other levels (Kerwin 2015, 206).

While 68,921 refugees were resettled in 2000, the figure plunged to 27,131 in 2002 and 28,403 in 2003 (Bruno 2015, 3). 'Sequestration' imposed after the 2008 Wall Street meltdown has compounded the problem: because federal allocations depend on actual arrivals, 58 per cent of non-state resettlement agencies stretching from New Jersey to Guam were forced to cut staff or shut down. Anti-migration vitriol in recent years has led Arizona and Texas to take unauthorised ICE powers into their own hands. State legislatures in Tennessee, New Hampshire and Georgia voted to block any new resettlement.

The top four sending countries in 2010 were Iraq, Burma, Bhutan and Somalia (Brown and Scribner 2014, 107). Despite growing restrictions, the United States resettled 70 per cent of all UNHCR-certified refugees between 2009 and 2013, less than one-fourth of all persons displaced by sectarian violence, natural disasters and development-induced hazards. America now lags behind its European allies in per capita entries, however: the ratio of asylum-seekers per 100,000 residents stands at 1.3 for the US, compared to 24.4 in Sweden, 17.5 in Malta, 12.3 for Switzerland and 5.3 in Germany.[4] The immigration-enforcement system has given birth to a massive, opaque 'homeland security' Hydra. As Kerwin reports (2015, 224):

> UNHCR assesses refugee claims and refers persons for resettlement. The Population, Refugees and Migration (PRM) division of DOS [State Department] proposes admissions ceilings and priorities, and contracts with nongovernmental Resettlement Support Centers to screen persons for admission and prepare cases for review. USCIS reviews refugee applications for eligibility and admissibility, interviews applicants, and coordinates background checks, which are conducted by DOS, the Federal Bureau of Investigation, and the Central Intelligence Agency. CBP agents screen refugees for admission at ports of entry. The

International Organization for Migration organizes refugee travel, which is funded through loans from PRM. The US Department of Health and Human Services (HHS) Office of Refugee Resettlement (ORR) coordinates domestic resettlement services.

In 2008 Congress approved special permanent visas and resettlement benefits for Iraqi and Afghan nationals (along with spouses and minor children) who had assisted US military forces or private contractors for at least one year after March 2003 (Kerwin 2015, 135). The total admitted to date (11,599 Iraqis and Afghans) falls very short of the qualified applicants imperilled by ISIS takeovers (Falluja, Mosul); another 12,000 applications submitted by Afghan linguists were still pending in 2015. Over 230,300 Iraqis were referred for settlement over a seven-year period; 119,202 were accepted, yet only 84,902 entered US territory.[5]

Even before Trump's policy reversals, all migrants had to be vetted for 'TRIG factors', a 13-step process, before they could be 'woven into the rich fabric of American society' (White House 2015). Under those regulations, pro-democracy groups opposing repressive regimes could be classified as 'undesignated Tier II terrorist organisations' (Attix 2015). Even if threatened with death, applicants could be accused of providing 'material support' for complying with terrorists' demands.[6] Because screening takes up to two years, the validity period of one evaluation can expire by the time another is completed, forcing refugee families to repeat the process, while subsisting in camps that impede their prospects for quick integration, especially for school-aged children (Nezer 2014, 284).

High evidentiary standards are coupled with scarce court resources, a dearth of legal representation and questionable judicial competency: judges know little about conditions in the countries of origin, much less about especially vulnerable 'social groups'. Women reluctant to reveal instances of rape, FGM or domestic violence to male border guards and translators, often in front of family members, are deemed 'not credible' (Fletcher 2006; Bonewit and Shreeves 2016). Some 45 per cent of all individuals subjected to judicial review had no legal representation in 2014. The Executive Office for Immigration Review (EOIR) received only $312 million to carry out its duties, rising to $347 million in 2015, compared to $18 billion for the CBP/ICE generating its caseload. The 260 EOIR judges 'cannot keep pace with incoming cases, much less make headway against a backlog of 449,001 cases' (as of June 2015), left 'pending' for 612 days, on average (Kerwin 2005, 2015, 38–39).

Having sparked 'Islamic' radicalisation, US military engagements have actually provoked the *need for securitising* asylum and refugee policies. As 2016 Republican presidential contender Mike Huckabee said of Syrians: 'Are they really escaping tyranny, are they escaping poverty, or are they really just coming because we have cable TV?' (Brantly 2015). Obviously the cable channels ex-Governor Huckabee watches in Arkansas are not devoted to world news; otherwise he would know that Bashar al-Assad has killed up to 470,000 and displaced 11 million Syrians since 2011 (BBC 2016).

Purportedly intent on fighting organised trafficking rings, 'states regularly combine rationales by raising the spectre that hardened terrorists will use smugglers – and endure life-threatening journeys by land or by sea – to facilitate their travel' (Kerwin 2015, 211;

and see Hathaway and Gammeltoft-Hansen 2014). The children of refugee spouses are no longer treated as 'derivative beneficiaries'; children separated from parents or relatives during flight who do not otherwise qualify cannot be resettled (Nezer 2014, 127). Although UN provisions permit detentions only as a last resort, US figures rose from 198,307 in 2002 to 477,523 in 2012, falling to 441,000 in 2013 (Kerwin 2015, 221). Under fire for stopping 'Dreamer' deportations (children brought in illegally, but educated in the US), Obama approved construction of massive family detention centres along the border with Mexico. In 2009–2010, almost half of the 29,000 asylum applicants meeting the 'credible fear' threshold were physically detained for extended periods (Kerwin 2015, 220). Negotiated by a bipartisan 'Gang of Eight' in 2013, two Senate bills (Refugee Protection Act: Border Security, Economic Opportunity and Immigrant Modernization Act) would have meliorated some of these hardships. Republican John Boehner refused to let them onto the floor of the House of Representatives.

My aim is not to judge whether this long list of securitisation measures is/is not justifiable in view of 9/11 but rather to show the extent to which a self-reinforcing 'culture of insecurity' has replaced a historically rooted American commitment to safeguarding freedom-seekers. The United States no longer affords the greatest protection to victims of sectarian violence, religious persecution and political oppression. We now turn to another value community, the EU, and its efforts to harmonise migration and asylum policies.

SECURITISATION AND 'FREEDOM OF MOVEMENT' IN THE EUROPEAN UNION

Germany's asylum policy turnaround is rooted in supranational developments. Unification accelerated the *Europeanisation* of migration, visa and asylum policies, once western governments realised that Germany would no longer serve as the big, bad gatekeeper along the eastern front, following two EU enlargements.[7] Wars intensified by high-tech weapons sales to underdeveloped countries, coupled with cheaper air travel to Europe, contributed to new waves of asylum-seekers, rising from 13,000 in 1972 to 158,500 by 1980. Its generous constitutional guarantee and geographical proximity to the east led Germany to see more applications than other Community states; it accounted for 60 per cent of all first-submissions between 1988 and 1990 (Mainwaring 2012, 46).

A surge in state-centred, ultra-leftist terrorism (e.g. Baader Meinhof Gang, Brigade Rosso, ETA) moved European interior ministers to push for intergovernmental cooperation among law enforcement structures in 1975.[8] Known as the Trevi Group, they invited their justice minister counterparts to join their twice-yearly meetings in 1976. They came together in 1986 as the Ad Hoc Group on Immigration and Asylum, blurring the boundaries between these two domains. Adopted by five EC countries *before* the Berlin Wall fell, the 1985 Schengen agreement was intended to facilitate the 'passport-free' movement of citizens, goods, services and capital across the Single European Market; this treaty-external 'ad hockery' drove the institutionalisation of many Community policies through the 1980s. Dublin I brought a major reorientation *after* the Iron Curtain collapsed; the Council sought the common regulation of external borders, under a Justice and Home Affairs 'pillar' embedded in the Maastricht

Treaty. By 1991, they had drafted an External Frontiers Convention, paving the way for border control as a standalone EU policy.

The JHA Council linked migration and asylum to cooperation among police, judicial and border control agencies, as well as to the fight against drugs, terrorism, human trafficking and organised crime. Securitisation intensified via changes introduced by Dublin II and the 2004 Hague Programme, intended to strengthen 'freedom, security and justice'. Formulated after the 11 September 2001 attacks, both are heavy with security language, offering only token references to the *free movement of people*. Despite the EU's gender mainstreaming mandate, women are only mentioned as potential victims of trafficking.

By the time it was incorporated into the Amsterdam Treaty (1997), the Schengen-turned-Dublin system encompassed 13 EU states (Marschang 1998; Angenendt 1999). The EU established a Common European Asylum System (CEAS), the parameters of which were specified in several directives adopted between 1999 and 2005. Claiming to offer 'enhanced effectiveness and higher standards for protection', Dublin III (2013) revised provisions regarding family members and unaccompanied minors (European Commission 2008).

The 9/11 attacks politicised migration and external controls, pitting 'internal security' and 'asylum rights' against each other. The post-9/11 years brought a proliferation of EU agencies, information systems and funding mechanisms linking asylum, migration and border control, most subject to 'ordinary legislative procedure'. The JHA's Extraordinary Meeting of 20 September 'invited' the Commission to balance internal security with international protection obligations, which Karyotis (2007, 7) construed as an effort 'to find legal ways to deprive asylum seekers' of Geneva Convention protections by 'scrupulously and rigorously applying exclusion clauses pertaining to domestic security'. Linked to Dublin, the European Dactyloscopy System (EURODAC) stores and shares various types of biometric data; its holdings are increasingly used to hinder 'asylum shopping', blocking anyone over 14 from filing multiple applications. Although Helmut Kohl pressured Council members to allow its use in tracking 'illegal migrants', member states were barred from using EURODAC data to initiate criminal investigations against asylum-seekers until 1998.

Using funding as a concrete indicator of EU priorities, one finds a heavy emphasis on information gathering and data exchanges. According to its 2016 work programme, the EU contributed €9,610,500 to the Schengen Information System II, €9,610,500 to the Visa Information System and €100,000 for EURODAC finger-printing. Total European Border and Coast Guard Agency (FRONTEX) revenues rose from €93.95 million in 2013 to €114.1 million in 2015, while the European Police Office received €95.5 million. By contrast, the budget for the European Asylum Support Office only grew from €10.5 million (2013) to €15.7 million (2014), declining to €14.99 million in 2015.[9] Combining the European Refugee Fund, Solidarity and Management of Migration Flows, the Eurofund for Integration of Third Country Nationals and the European Return Fund, the 2014–2020 allocation for the Asylum, Migration and Integration Fund (AMIF) totals €3.1 billion, 88 per cent of which goes to individual member states adopting multi-annual programmes. Only €360 million of AMIF goes directly to relocation and transfers, not surprising given the failure of member states to live up to even voluntary resettlement pledges Commission Work Programme 2016 (2015).

The number of first-time asylum applications across the EU hit 435,450 in 2013, then 625,000 in 2014, filed by citizens from 144 countries. Kosovars, Syrians and Afghanis initially comprised the largest groups, but proportions shifted after the Balkans were declared 'safe states of origin'. In spring 2015 the EU revised its Asylum Procedures, Reception Conditions and Qualification Directives, along with Dublin and EURODAC regulations to ensure that new arrivals would be 'treated equally in an open and fair system – wherever they apply'. In 2016, only five EU countries offered resettlement programmes; others abide by the Temporary Protection Directive. Only 5115 of the 68,000 who made it to Greece, and 28,500 of the 67,500 who landed in Italy by mid-2015 filed for asylum in those countries; 43 per cent moved on to apply in Germany or Sweden, despite Dublin 'first arrival' rules.[10]

None of the CEAS directives have been applied adequately much less equally across the EU. The 'militarisation of the Mediterranean' is reflected in the shift from search-and-rescue operations to FRONTEX policing and tougher return policies. One-size-fits-all efforts presented as harmonisation have shifted the burden away from wealthier, northern members to poorer, southern and eastern states with small populations, highly exposed boundaries and limited institutional capacity; new processing 'hotspots' like Kos (Greece) lack the internet access needed for EURODAC reporting. We now turn to Germany's effort to replace a traditionally very exclusionary asylum regime with a new 'welcoming culture'.

FROM FESTUNG DEUTSCHLAND TO THE WILLKOMMENSKULTUR

Given the highly restrictive policies pre-dating unification, it hard to imagine how FRG refugee regulations could have been made tougher after 2001 (Mushaben 2008). Despite the 'unqualified' nature of *political* asylum rights, some persecution victims were treated more equally than others. Most beneficiaries were males fleeing communist regimes devoid of western freedoms. Averaging 4000 per year, the application numbers rose and fell in accordance with Soviet crackdowns, ranging from 16,284 in 1956 (Hungary), to 11,664 in 1969 (Prague Spring), peaking at 107,818 in 1980 under martial law in Poland. Between 1980 and 1992, the average *recognition* rate under Art. 16 criteria stood at 8.37 per cent, ranging from 29 per cent in 1985 to 4.9 per cent the year the Wall fell (BAMF 2016, 3ff.). The rights of women and children depended entirely on the legal status of (presumptive) male breadwinners (Mushaben 2017). In 2000 the Constitutional Court finally accorded independent asylum rights to women facing gender-specific persecution, holding that 'war parties' exercising stable domination and a monopoly of force over core territories (e.g. in Afghanistan) do exercise 'state power'.[11]

Although real asylum rights were extended to very few, FRG lawmakers were bound by international no-return *norms*. So-called *Convention refugees* ('little asylum') received 'passports' and residency permits good for two years, renewable at six-month intervals if homeland conditions had not improved. Rejected but non-deportable applicants were accorded renewable, six-month residency permits but denied social assistance. 'Tolerated' for years on end under various Alien Acts, desperate individuals often resorted to undocumented labour, giving rise to public resentment.

Germany recognised a special historical responsibility towards groups like Soviet Jews ('quota refugees'), whose ranks swelled dramatically after the Iron Curtain collapsed.

West Germany's insistence that it remained an organic community based on *jus sanguinis* was rooted, in part, in hopes that eventual unification would not only restore ties between easterners and westerners but also with 'co-ethnics' in territories held prior to 1945. Unable to enter under a real *immigration* law, foreigners arrived by way of guestworker contracts, family unification policies or international crises. Many other laws (*Ausländergesetze, Aufenthaltsgesetze*) strictly regulated foreigners' behaviour once they were *in* the country but provided no option beyond asylum and family claims for others to *enter*.

Helmut Kohl introduced an unsuccessful guestworker repatriation programme in 1984, but asylum-seekers and refugees were shielded, in theory, under international law (Mushaben 2008). Conservatives tried to deter new applicants through leaner, meaner benefits under a revised Asylum Law (*AsylG*, 1982) and the Asylum-Seekers Benefits Act (*AsylbG*, 1993), long before the EU mandated better reception conditions and common asylum procedures. Although breadwinners with pending cases could access temporary work permits prior to 1980, the Bundestag imposed a five-year work ban on all would-be applicants (except east Europeans) in 1987, despite the fact that two-thirds were males of prime working age (Mushaben 2008, 2017). Applicants were relegated to designated dwelling sites, even if family or friends offered to sponsor them elsewhere. Denounced as 'pseudo-applicants', 'asylum parasites' and 'economic refugees', their dependence on state aid fuelled public perceptions that most were only coming 'to exploit the welfare system' – because they had no other choice.

The hard-line approach failed to halt new surges fleeing martial law in Poland, another coup in Turkey, the Soviet invasion of Afghanistan and the Khomeini revolution in Iran. Residing in hostels, school gymnasiums and even shipping containers, their living conditions worsened over time: though families were initially entitled to grocery vouchers, authorities removed kitchens from hostel facilities to prevent them from cooking.[12] Small cash allocations were replaced with in-kind benefits and limited healthcare. Working applicants could not earn more than the equivalent of €1.05 per hour (Thränhardt 2015, 13). The labour ban effectively increased illegal employment, welfare costs and crime rates during long processing periods, averaging three to five years (Der Spiegel 1985). In 1989, the Bundestag adopted restrictive quotas for Southeast Asians, Chileans, Cubans, Argentineans and Kurds.

Negative state policies evoked rising hostility towards foreigners, climaxing in unprecedented xenophobic violence, just as the collapse of the Iron Curtain rendered Germany vulnerable to new refugee flows (Mushaben 1998, 329ff.). The implosion of Yugoslavia triggered three new waves of asylum-seekers; the number of first-time applications rose from 193,063 in 1990, to 256,112 in 1991, to 438,191 in 1992.[13] Bosnian arrivals peaked at 345,000 in 1996, falling to 28,000 by late 2000; by April 1999 nearly 100,000 Kosovars also landed in Germany. Classified as *collective victims of war*, many were only granted temporary protection status, especially after 1993 (Kühne 2001). Nearly 85,500 were repatriated by March 2001, including 7400 against their will. Invoking Dublin logic, Bavaria was quick to declare that order and safety had been restored back in the Balkans. Only 20,000 remained as of 2002 (Ausländerbeauftragte 2001, 50).

Sooner motivated by voter antipathy than by EU trends, lawmakers revised Art. 16 of the Basic Law in 1993, undermining 'unqualified' political asylum. They moreover restricted the right of return extended to 'late resettlers' under Art. 116 BL, setting a maximum annual quota of 225,000 (later 100,000). Families separated by someone's need to flee ahead of the rest lost their automatic right to reunification. Municipal authorities restricted applicants' physical mobility, granting only temporary residency. Financial aid dropped to less than 30 per cent of Social Assistance payments as authorities shifted to in-kind benefits for war refugees. Tighter employment rules exacerbated the numbers dependent on welfare, rising from 81,000 in 1980 to 524,000 in 1995. As the number of Bosnians and Kosovars peaked, asylum approval rates under Art. 16 criteria dropped from 9 per cent to 1.63 per cent (2004). Only 124,000 of the 370,000 *de facto refugees* secured residency rights needed for regular work permits. The government's need to cover DM 5 billion in welfare costs for applicants-in-waiting and rejected-but-not-deportable groups coincided with extraordinary transfers to eastern Germans rendered jobless by failed *Treuhand* policies. Families were offered up to DM 9000 to return home; local authorities in their countries of origin received DM 8000 if they stayed away at least four months, purportedly saving Germany DM 5000 per month in benefit costs (Mushaben 1998, 321–322; Angenendt 1999).

But they kept on coming: Between 1996 and 2002, the number of *convention refugees* rose from 16,000 to 75,000 (Mushaben 2008, 132). Hoping to populate its own territory, Israel ironically urged Germany to 'redirect' post-Soviet Jewish migrants: their numbers fell from 12,000 in 1996 to 6800 in 2002. Stemming the flow did little to remedy growing bureaucratic backlogs, economic dependency and missing integration policies. The Independent Commission on Migration reported in 2000 that only 17 per cent of asylum cases were 'decided' in six months or less; 40 per cent took six months to two years; 32 per cent remained in limbo for two to five years; while 11 per cent waited more than five years for a verdict (Independent Commission 2000, 125). By the time a new SPD—Green coalition began rethinking citizenship and migration policies in 1998, asylum provisions were increasingly subject to EU purview.

The Red—Green response to the 9/11 attacks was an impressive exercise in self-restraint; Schengen and Dublin requirements precluded a national, gate-shutting reaction. Parliamentarians bundled heightened intelligence and surveillance measures into a 2001 'Security Package', valid through 2012. A further 'Anti-Terrorism Package' allocated €3 billion to enhance the capacities of the Bundeswehr, the Federal Intelligence Service (BND), the Federal Border Control and Criminal Agencies (BGS, BKA). It created a Federal Office for Civil Protection and Catastrophe Assistance in 2004. Thomas Faist claims that 9/11 delayed adoption of the 2004 *Zuwanderungsgesetz* (ZWG) but the migration—security nexus was limited to requiring the Federal Agency for Migration and Refugees (BAMF) and *Ausländerbehörde* to share personal data with relevant agencies with respect to suspicious cases.[14] Securitisation efforts became increasingly 'European' in nature.

With Dublin (I, II) regulations firmly in place, Germany assumed the EU Council presidency in January 2007 under a CDU chancellor heading a grand coalition. Its six-month Conclusions called for Schengen enlargement, a European Border

Surveillance System under CEAS, combating organised crime, enhancing biometric-document security and a slew of Balkan 'readmission' agreements. The real paradigm shift in German refugee protection policies occurred between 2007 and 2014, *before* thousands began crossing the Mediterranean. Using EU directives to justify a few ZWG rollbacks in 2007, the Bundestag approved a right to remain for 50–60,000 'tolerated' persons but imposed welfare sanctions against those failing to enrol in mandatory integration courses; only spouses over 18 with knowledge of German could enter (overturned by the European Court of Justice in 2014). Since 2011, youth completing German schooling receive their own work permits; those in residence for 15 months can secure educational stipends and work permits after training. In 2012, the Constitutional Court impelled lawmakers to raise cash benefits, to warrant refugees' human dignity and the chance 'to participate actively in normal social and cultural life'.[15] In 2014, lawmakers granted applicants freedom of movement after four months, enabling their children to participate in school trips. Benefits remained tied to designated dwelling sites, but applicants and 'tolerated' individuals could seek jobs after three months. In December 2014, the grand coalition approved permanent residency for persons denied asylum who have lived in Germany at least eight years (six for children, four years for youth).

Shifting to 'welcoming practices and intercultural opening', Germany initiated a humanitarian resettlement programme, to admit 300 'especially needy' persons per year, trapped in first-arrival countries, rising to 500 in 2015. Beginning with Tunisians, Iraqis, Iranians and Syrians, the 2014 list added refugees from Somalia, Sri Lanka, China, Afghanistan and Indonesia; officials warranted another 100 places for African trafficking victims, pledging to accept 800 in 2016 and 2017. The refugee flow into Europe swelled from 369,300 (2012) to 714,300 (2014), compared to US and Canadian increases from 98,900 to 134,600 (combined) (Sachverständigenrat deutscher Stiftungen für Integration und Migration 2015; United Nations Human Rights Commission 2015, 3, 11). Initial claims submitted in Germany rose from 41,330 in 2010 to 173,070 in 2014, outpacing US applications for the first time.

From January to June 2015, the FRG registered 171,797 new applications, compared to total of 202,834 in 2014 (UNHRC 2015, 3, 11). On 1 August, it adopted the Law to Redefine the Right to Stay and the Termination of Residence. Declaring that 'asylum knows no upper limits', Merkel boldly suspended the Dublin rules on 31 August, allowing thousands who had not filed asylum applications in their first EU state to do so in Germany. In November, the Bundestag approved a first Asylum Package, including a law on the Acceleration of Asylum Procedures and the Act to Improve the Housing, Care, and Treatment of Foreign Minors and Adolescents (Der Spiegel 2015).

The federal government contributed €2 billion to help state and local authorities cover accommodation, meals and medical costs. In 2016, it began paying €670 per person (monthly) from the time of registration until a decision is rendered. Anticipating 800,000 per year with a five-month processing period, the states received a €2.68 billion advance. Allocating €500 million to build additional social housing and 150,000 more reception places, Merkel's government temporarily suspended strict construction and renewable energy requirements. Refugees were distributed among the Länder, using the Königsteiner Key developed in the 1990s.[16] Cash payments were replaced with in-kind benefits at the receiving centres; to expedite the integration of those likely to be approved, skilled labourers could seek temporary jobs after three months. State insurance funds issued health cards to new arrivals for immediate treatment, to be reimbursed later.

By December 2015, the administrative backlog numbered 350,000 applications (Gathmann and Hagen 2015). The mood shifted dramatically in the wake of over 500 reported sexual assaults by 'North African-looking' men in multiple cities on New Year's Eve (Mushaben 2016). The Bundestag approved a second Asylum Package in February, rolling back some 'welcoming measures'. Applicants must stay in 'first admission' centres for six (previously three) months, where they will receive more benefits in kind. Free movement rules have been tightened as well: refugees cannot leave the districts in which their respective Foreigners' Registration Offices are situated, even to visit relatives in neighbouring counties. If caught outside their districts, they will lose benefits and their proceedings will be terminated. Asylum Package II reduces 'pocket money' benefits (€143) by charging applicants €10 per month to cover the cost of language instruction (most Afghanis are not eligible) (Schüler 2016). It is unclear whether these changes conform to EU 'reception' requirements, much less to the Constitutional Court verdict obliging lawmakers to provide refugees with sufficient cash 'to participate in social, cultural and political life' (Der Spiegel 2012). Persons granted 'subsidiary protection' (distinct from Art. 16 or UN status) only become eligible for family unification after two years. Exceptions involve family members held in refugee camps in Turkey, Jordan and Lebanon to be admitted under quotas subject to EU regulation.

By January 2016, only 272 Syrians and Eritreans had been transferred from Greece and Italy – 0.17 per cent of the 160,000 the member states had promised to accept in 2015 (Kingsley 2016). An Accelerated Asylum Procedure law, adopted in 2016, has significantly reduced processing times. German 'securitisation' measures are still a far cry from those of the United States, despite a new statute Simplifying Expulsion of Foreign Criminals and the Broadened Suspension of Refugee Recognition for Criminal Asylum Applicants. Hoping to expedite deportations, the Law Improving Registration and Exchange of Data for Residence and Asylum Law Purposes created a new federal police unit to procure replacement documents. Persons from 'safe' countries (e.g. Balkan states) are placed in special reception centres for fast-track processing (three weeks). Persons violating 'voluntary' deportation deadlines receive significantly reduced maintenance benefits; only very serious illnesses warrant a right to stay (Frankfurter Allgemeine Zeitung 2016).

CONCLUSION: 'TRADING PLACES' IN CHANGING CONTEXTS

While securitisation has dominated most US migration debates since 2001, the migration—security nexus has followed a very different trajectory in Germany, despite a consistent legislative stream focusing on many facets of terrorism since 2001.[17] The real threats to citizen *safety* in the USA – the national obsession with guns, unaffordable healthcare and unsustainably low wages – are domestic in nature. Annual homicides in the US far exceed the death toll inflicted by foreign terrorists since 2001; indeed, the first major terrorist attack, against the Alfred P. Murrah Federal Building (Oklahoma City), was executed by a white US military veteran, Timothy McVey.

Inextricably linked to World War II atrocities, Germans perceived migration and asylum policies as a threat to ethno-national identity until 1990, when unification proved that *jus sanguinis* was conflicting with other national needs. CDU policies of the 1980s perpetuated collective insecurity about *what it means to be German*, although the real threat to citizen safety rested with the chance of 'being destroyed in order to be defended' under NATO's Flexible Response strategy (Mushaben 1998, 203–208). Propelled by generational change, the end of the cold war created new space for human rights concerns largely shared by easterners and westerners, despite their diverging experiences. Most no longer accept the USA as an indisputable role model regarding democracy and human rights, given its support for rendition/torture, Guantánamo Bay detentions devoid of due process and NSA spying, snaring even the chancellor's cell-phone. Angela Merkel would rather solve real problems than foster paranoia for political gain.

One consequence of securitisation on both sides of the Atlantic is that tougher border controls have increased 'illegality', leading to sophisticated smuggling techniques and 'dangerously diversified' migration routes which provoke calls for further restrictions (Mainwaring 2012, 54). This confirms the *security-versus-safety paradox* highlighted at the outset: exaggerated threats to western identity and affluence exacerbate abstract citizen fears in the receiving countries, impelling politicians to pursue counter-measures that merely increase the real perils for persons in need of physical safety. A second, Dublin-driven development is the emphasis on data-sharing among law enforcement, intelligence gatherers, migration aid agencies and foreigner registration offices, within Germany and across member state boundaries. The prospects for abuse are greater in a poorly monitored, gun-toting, states' rights context like the US than in a supranational EU network, famous for issuing 'shame and blame' reports and National Action Plans to bring laggard countries up to Community standards.

Recent terrorist incidents (lone wolves claimed by ISIS) in Paris, Nice, Brussels and Berlin enhanced securitisation trends as reflected in Germany's third Anti-Terror Law, enacted in 2016. Border control is a key theme, but where the US has militarised border controls in ways that potentially criminalise the efforts of *all* groups desiring admission, Germany has taken a kinder, gentler approach, relatively speaking, towards peoples seeking refuge against violence, oppression and abject poverty. Although Dublin provisions will allow Germany to reject and return more refugees based on an expanding list of 'safe countries', the fact remains that 98 per cent of Syrians and 85 per cent of Iraqis have been granted formal asylum since 2014, an extraordinary development, compared to the abysmally low rates registered prior to unification. Even if their claims are denied, 'non-deportable' Afghanis, Sudanese and Pakistanis stand a far better chance of building new lives in Germany today than they did from 1980 to 2000.

The hard-line US approach has intensified *perceived insecurities* among millions of Americans, who ignore their own Bill of Rights while embracing Trump's repeated campaign pledge to ban 'all Muslims ... until the government can figure out what is going on'. Merkel, by contrast, has openly denounced the fear-mongers driving Pegida and AfD protests, attacks on refugee reception centres and arson assaults on asylum hostels. Germany and the United States have indeed traded places regarding their respective willingness to accept 'huddled masses yearning to be free' since 2001. The 14,000 volunteer centres established across the FRG since 2015 moreover suggest that citizens' embrace of a 'welcoming culture' is not just a passing phase. A 2015 study involving 460 participants and 79 organisations found that 72 per cent of these volunteers are female, 61 per cent held a tertiary degree, 69 per cent are economically secure and 34 per cent were aged between 20 and 30 (Karakayali and Kleist 2015). One could argue that their well-educated female chancellor has served as an excellent role model for younger citizens open to pro-active socio-political engagement in an economically secure Germany. The new Lady Liberty has probably done more to inspire them with a few well-placed 'refugee selfie' photos than her statuesque counterpart does these days, standing alone on an island across from a taller but colder memorial skyscraper in Lower Manhattan.

DISCLOSURE STATEMENT

No potential conflict of interest was reported by the author.

NOTES

1. The 'DOD 1033' programme was initiated under the 1997 National Defense Authorization Act. See the photos, 'Ferguson protests: National Guard sent to Missouri unrest', BBC report, 18 August 2014, http://www.bbc.com/news/world-us-canada-28832462.
2. The CIA supplied military training and equipment to right-wing governments, snaring Reagan himself in the criminal Iran-Contra web. Unaccompanied minors from Central America face incredible violence tied to drug-cartels and gang wars. See Campos and Friedland (2014), Cantor (2014), as well as Carlson and Gallagher (2015).
3. Annual presidential 'ceilings' do not match federal allocations made two to three years in advance. See Kerwin (2014, 18).
4. UNHCR (2015) figures, cited in Kerwin (2015).
5. Posted in 'The Cable', *Foreign Policy*, September 17, 2015.
6. Attix (2015, 683) cites the example of a villager who could be barred as a 'terrorist' from seeking refuge in the US even if he had been forced to ferry local rebels across the river.
7. Only first-pillar policies (e.g. single market) require automatic implementation by all members; under the CFSP and JHA pillars, actions are only required for EU states that embrace them. The Lisbon Treaty ended the pillar structure, but supranational versus intergovernmental rules still apply.
8. The name is variously attributed to a nearby Roman landmark, to the first Dutch chair or to its charge, combatting *terrorisme, radicalisme, et violence internationale.*
9. See the Commission decision concerning the adoption of the 2016 work programme for procurements within the framework of the second generation Schengen Information System (SIS II), the VISA Information System (VIS), the DubliNET and the Eurodac system serving as a financing decision (Brussels: 26 Jan. 2016).
10. Eurostat data, 'Asylum in the EU Member States' (44/2016 – 4 March 2016).

11. BVerfG Beschluss der 1. Kammer des Zweiten Senats vom 10. August 2000, 2 BvR 1353/98 – RN. (1–23), http://beverfg.de/e/rk20000810_2bvr026098.html. Earlier verdicts had declared female Afghanis ineligible for individual protection insofar as the Taleban regime, recognised by only two rogue polities, did not comprise a real state Beck (2002, 2003).
12. Radio report, 'Flüchtlinge in Deutschland: Leben in Containern', Deutschlandfunk, 11 October 2014.
13. Data from the Bundesamt für die Anerkennung ausländischer Flüchtlinge.
14. Faist (2004, 4). The main controversy centred on dual nationality. Abou-Taam (2011).
15. BverfG, Urteil des Ersten Senats vom 18. Juli 2012, I Bvl 10/10-Rn.(1-40).
16. The Key uses population size, per capita income and employment rates to distribute refugees across the Länder.
17. For a summary, see https://www.tagesschau.de/inland/sicherheitsgesetze108.html.

REFERENCES

Abou-Taam, Marwan. 2011. "Folgen des 11. September 2001 für die deutschen Sicherheitsgesetze." *Aus Politik und Zeitgeschichte* 27 (30 June): 9–14.

Angenendt, Steffen, ed. 1999. *Asylum and Migration Policies in the European Union.* Bonn: Europa Union Verlag.

Attix, Cheri. 2015. *Making Sense of the New TRIG Exemptions.* San Diego: American Immigration Lawyers' Association.

BAMF (Bundesamt fur Migration und Flüchtlinge). 2016. *Aktuelle Zahlen zu Asyl,* January 2016.

BBC. 2016. Syria: The Story of the Conflict. March 11. Accessed July 10, 2017. http://www.bbc.com/news/world-middle-east-26116868.

Beck, Marie Louise, ed. 2002. *Bericht zur Lage der Ausländer,* 23 August. Berlin.

Beck, Marie Louise, ed. 2003. *Migrationsbericht der Ausländerbeauftragten im Auftrag der Bundesregierung 2003,* Berlin.

Bergeron, Claire. 2014. "Temporary Protected Status after 25 Years: Addressing the Challenge of Long-Term 'Temporary' Residents and Strengthening a Centerpiece of US Humanitarian Protection." *Journal on Migration and Human Security* 2 (1): 22–43.

Bonewit, Anne, and Rosamund Shreeves. 2016. *Reception of Female Refugees and Asylum in the EU. Case Study of Germany,* sponsored by the Directorate-General for Internal Policies, PE 536.497.

Brantly, Max. 2015. "Huckabee's Religion Doesn't Cover Refugees." *Arkansas Times,* September 15. http://www.arktimes.com/ArkansasBlog/archives/2015/09/15/huckabees-religion-doesnt-cover-refugees.

Brown, Anastasia, and Todd Scribner. 2014. "Unfulfilled Promises, Future Possibilities: The Refugee Resettlement System in the United States." *Journal on Migration and Human Security* 2 (2): 101–120.

Bruno, Andorra. 2015. *Refugee Admissions and Resettlement Policy.* Washington, DC: Congressional Research Service. http://fas.org/sgp/crs/misc/RL31269.pdf.

Bundesbeauftragte für Ausländer. 2001. *Migrationsbericht der Ausländerbeauftragten 2001.* Berlin: Bundesbeauftragte für Ausländer.

Bundesverfassungsgericht. 2012. BverfG, Urteil des Ersten Senats vom 18. Juli 2012, I Bvl 10/10-Rn.(1-40).

Campos, Sara, and Joan Friedland. 2014. *Mexican and Central American Asylum and Credible Fear Claims: Background and Context.* Washington, DC: American Immigration Council.

Cantor, James David. 2014. "The New Wave: Forced Displacement Caused by Organized Crime in Central America and Mexico." *Refugee Survey Quarterly* 33 (3): 34–68.

Carlson, Elizabeth, and Anna Marie Gallagher. 2015. "Humanitarian Protection for Children Fleeing Gang-Based Violence in the Americas." *Journal on Migration and Human Security* 3 (2): 129–158.

Commission Work Programme 2016. 2015. COM (2015) 610 final, Strasbourg, 27 October, https://ec.europa.eu/info/sites/files/cwp_2016_en_0.pdf.

Der Spiegel. 1985. "ASYL: Grüne Algenpolster." April 1.

Der Spiegel. 2012. "Entscheidung des Bundesverfassungsgerichts: Asylbewerber müssen ab sofort mehr Geld bekommen," July 18.

Der Spiegel. 2015. *Flüchtlingskrise: Kabinett beschließt neues Asylgesetz.* September 29.

European Commission. 2008. "Policy Plan on Asylum: An Integrated Approach to Protection Across the EU." [COM (2008) 360 final]. Brussels: June 17, 2008.

Eurostat, Asylum statistics. 2016. http://ec.europa.eu/eurostat/statistics-explained/index.php/Asylum_statistics.

Faist, Thomas. 2004. "The Migration-Security Nexus. International Migration and Security before and after 9/11." Willy Brandt Series of Working Papers 4/03. Malmö University.

Fletcher, Aubra. 2006. "The Real ID Act: Furthering Gender Bias in US Asylum Law." *Berkeley Journal of Gender, Law & Justice* 21 (1): 111–131.

Frankfurter Allgemeine Zeitung. 2016. "Flüchtlingskrise: Was steht im Asylpaket II?" January 29.

Gathmann, Florian, and Kevin Hagen. 2015. "Was jetzt gilt – und was noch kommt." *Der Spiegel*, January 12.

Gordon, Claire. 2013. "Coming to America: The 5 Biggest Refugee Groups of the Last 20 Years." *Al Jazeera America, Flagship Blog*, 14 October 2013. Accessed July 10, 2017. http://america.aljazeera.com/watch/shows/america-tonight/america-tonight-blog/2013/10/13/the-5-biggest-refugeegroupsofthelast20years.html.

Hathaway, James C., and Thomas Gammeltoft-Hansen. 2014. "Non-Refoulement in a World of Cooperative Deterrence." *Law & Economics Working Papers*, No. 1062014, http://repository.law.umich.edu/law_econ_current/106.

Independent Commission. 2000. *Structuring Immigration, Fostering Integration.* Berlin: Bundesregierung.

International Institute of St. Louis, Annual Report. 2016. https://www.iistl.org/.

Karakayali, Serhat, and Olaf Kleist. 2015. *Strukturen und Motive der ehrenamtlichen Flüchtlingsarbeit (EFA) in Deutschland.* Berlin: BIM/Humboldt Universität.

Karyotis, Georgios. 2007. "European Migration Policy in the Aftermath of September 11th: The Security Migration Nexus." *Innovation: The European Journal of Social Science Research* 20 (1): 1–17.

Kerwin, Donald. 2005. "The Use and Misuse of 'National Security' Rationale in Crafting U.S. Refugee and Immigration Policies." *International Journal of Refugee Law* 17 (4): 749–763.

Kerwin, Donald. 2014. "Creating a More Responsive and Seamless Refugee Protection System: The Scope, Promise, and Limitations of US Temporary Protection Programs." *Journal on Migration and Human Security* 2 (1): 44–72.

Kerwin, Donald. 2015. "The US Refugee Protection System on the 35th Anniversary of the Refugee Act of 1980." *Journal on Migration and Human Security* 3 (2): 205–254.

Kingsley, Patrick. 2016. "Refugees: EU Relocates Just 0.17% of Pledged Target." *The Guardian*, January 5.

Kühne, Peter. 2001. *Zur Lage der Flüchtlinge in Deutschland*. Bonn: Friedrich Ebert Stiftung. September.

Mainwaring, Cetta. 2012. "Resisting Distalization? Malt and Cyprus' Influence on EU Migration and Asylum Policies." *Refugee Survey Quarterly* 31 (4): 38–66.

Marcuse, Peter. 2006. "Security or Safety in Cities? The Threat of Terrorism After 9/11." *International Journal of Urban and Regional Research* 30 (4): 919–929.

Marschang, Bernd. 1998. "Miβtrauen, Abschottung, Eigensinn—Entwicklung der europäischen Asylrechts - Harmonisierung bis zum Amsterdamer Vertrag." *Kritische Justiz* 31 (1): 69–83.

Miroff, Nick, and David Nakamura. 2018. "200,000 Salvadorans May Be Forced to Leave the U.S. as Trump Ends Immigration Protection." *Washington Post*, January 8.

Mushaben, Joyce Marie. 1998. *From Post-War to Post-Wall Generations: Changing Attitudes toward the National Question and NATO in the Federal Republic of Germany*. Boulder, CO: Westview.

Mushaben, Joyce Marie. 2008. *The Changing Faces of Citizenship: Integration and Mobilization among Ethnic Minorities in Germany*. New York: Berghahn Books.

Mushaben, Joyce Marie. 2016. "The Sad Truth Highlighted by Germany Assaults," *CNN*, 12. January 2016, http://www.cnn.com/2016/01/11/opinions/mushaben-cologne-attacks/.

Mushaben, Joyce Marie. 2017. "*Wir schaffen das!* Angela Merkel and the European Refugee Crisis." *German Politics* 26 (4): 516–533.

Nezer, Melanie. 2014. "An Overview of Pending Asylum and Refugee Legislation in the US Congress." *Journal on Migration and Human Security* 2 (2): 121–143.

Niemann, Arne, and Natalie Schmidthäussler. 2012. "The Logic of EU Policy-Making on (Irregular) Migration: Securitisation or Risk?" Paper presented at the UACES conference, Passau, Germany, September 3-5.

Sachverständigenrat deutscher Stiftungen für Integration und Migration. 2015. "Krise der europäischen Asylpolitik: Kollektive Aufnahmeverfahren mit fairen Quoten einrichten" (Kurz-info SVR- Forschungsbereichs 2015-1).

Schüler, Katharina. 2016. "Asylpaket II: Viel Härte, wenig Wirkung." *Die Zeit*, February 25.

Thränhardt, Dietrich. 2015. *Die Arbeitsmigration von Flüchtlingen in Deutschland: Humanität, Effektivität, Selbstbestimmung*. Bertelsmann Stiftung. May. https://www.bertelsmann-stiftung.de/fileadmin/files/Projekte/28_Einwanderung_und_Vielfalt/Studie_IB_DieArbeitsintegration_von_Fluechtlingen_inDeutschland2015.pdf.

United Nations Human Rights Commission (UNHRC). 2015. "The Sea Route to Europe: Mediterranean Passage in the Age of Refugees." http://www.unhcr.org/protection/operations/5592bd059/sea-route-europe-mediterranean-passage-age-refugees.html.

White House. 2015. Infographic Screening Process 2015. https://www.whitehouse.gov/blog/2015/11/20/infographic-screening-process-refugee-entry-united-states.

White House. 2017. "Executive Order: Protecting the Nation from Foreign Terrorist Entry into the United States." posted on January 27, 2017. https://www.whitehouse.gov/the-press-office/2017/01/27/executive-order-protecting-nation-foreign-terrorist-entry-united-states.

Yuhas, Alan. 2018. "Trump Administration Set to Admit Far Fewer Refugees Than Plan Allows For." *The Guardian*, January 26.

More Similar Than Different: Of Checks, Balances, and German and American Government Responses to International Terrorism

D. HELLMUTH

This paper examines German and American responses to international terrorism from the end of the cold war to today. While terrorism was not a priority for much the 1990s, the 9/11 attacks generated a long list of domestic counterterrorism measures in both countries. In the international realm, the German government ended up participating in many US initiatives designed to hunt down al-Qaeda operatives and prevent them from launching another attack inside the United States. However, German support was often secret and cooperation in the context of the 'war on terrorism' was considered controversial at home. When comparing German and US counterterrorism approaches, the paper takes a unique approach by analysing how parliamentary and presidential government structures affected responses in terms of content and scope. The comparative analysis illustrates various similarities between German and US decision-making processes and argues that checks and balances continue to balance executive power gains in both countries.

This paper analyses German and American responses to international terrorism from the end of the cold war to today. With few exceptions, international terrorism seemed on the backburner for much the 1990s. By contrast, the 9/11 attacks triggered a long stream of domestic counterterrorism laws and executive programmes in *both* countries. In terms of international responses, the German and US states did not see eye to eye. The United States sought to externalise the terrorism threat by means of a wide variety of different approaches, all designed to deter or prevent terrorists from coming to US shores, which included military invasions in Afghanistan and Iraq, offshore detention in Guantanamo, extraordinary renditions (used to kidnap terror suspects and render them to other countries for interrogations involving torture), and surveillance programmes. The German government ended up participating in many of these initiatives (the Iraq invasion being the most prominent exception), but German support was often not known to the German public and cooperation in the context of the 'war on terrorism' was considered controversial at home.

When comparing German and US counterterrorism responses, this contribution takes a unique look at how parliamentary and presidential government structures affected domestic and international counterterrorism approaches in terms of content and scope. It thus illustrates the various similarities between German and US government systems, especially when it comes to domestic measures. Germany's structural veto points (inter alia, a powerful Bundesrat made up of the Länder which retain veto powers with regard to many domestic security issues) and intra-executive restraints (for example, coalition partners) brought about counterterrorism decision-making features similar to those associated with the US separation of powers system.[1]

This structural focus places the article at the centre of a debate about the domestic sources of national security/foreign policy decision-making, with one school focusing on how different domestic governmental structures produce variations in decision-making processes and policy output[2] and another stressing the motivations and workings of bureaucracies and organisations.[3] However, the paper does not assume that structural variables are the only factors at play. In Germany, bureaucratic influences in the form of executive interagency battles between the Federal Ministries of the Interior and Justice (Bundesministerium des Inneren, BMI, and Bundesministerium der Justiz, BMJ) and coalition partners also shaped counterterrorism responses, among others. Their input is made possible in the first place, though, by the particular type of parliamentary system Germany represents, one that relies more on power-sharing arrangements than on fusion of power features typically associated with parliamentary systems.[4] All of this is reminiscent of the US system as the separation of power system is, by its very design, based on power sharing.

The article further argues that the balance between executive and legislative/judicial branches in the US did not change as much or as permanently as is often claimed by those who emphasise the increase in presidential/executive branch power and/or the extra-legal nature of US counterterrorism programmes post-9/11. When dissecting German responses, the paper draws attention to executive power gains and unilateral decision-making, especially when it comes to international counterterrorism responses, even if legislative and/or judicial controls continue to exist in many areas.

The article is organised in three parts. A first part on counterterrorism responses after the cold war is quickly followed by a detailed examination of US and German domestic[5] counterterrorism reforms after 9/11. The third part focuses on international issues of contention and cooperation, followed by the conclusion.

COUNTERTERRORISM AFTER THE COLD WAR

With few exceptions, counterterrorism was not a priority for much of the 1990s. US counterterrorism authorities focused on international terrorism and the emerging al-Qaeda network. In this context the military strikes in response to the 1998 US embassy bombings in Africa represented the most high-profile counterterrorism operation during the first post-cold war decade, including air strikes against a terrorist training camp in Afghanistan as well as a pharmaceutical plant in Sudan. By contrast, the Khobar Towers attacks against American servicemen in Saudi Arabia in 1996 and the attack against the USS Cole warship in Yemen in 2000 triggered criminal investigations and indictments but no military responses. Operation Infinite Reach thus was the notable exception to the US law-and-order counterterrorism approach in the 1990s.[6]

In the meantime, German counterterrorism services concentrated on domestic terrorism, notably a few remnants of the left-wing Red Army Faction (RAF) as well as the re-emerging right-wing neo-Nazi scene. RAF activities, which peaked in the 1970s and

1980s with a series of assassinations and bombings, largely ceased after the declaration of a ceasefire in 1992; the group disbanded for good in 1998. However, German reunification triggered a wave of right-wing violence and arson attacks against immigrants and refugees, killing a total of 17 people.[7]

Counterterrorism after 9/11: Responses at Home

New domestic security measures. What legislative and executive programmes did the United States and Germany adopt?

United States: Having suffered a substantial terrorist attack on home soil, the United States responded swiftly and forcefully. Domestic reforms, which can be separated into new counterterrorism authorities and institutions, were a vital part of an overarching strategy designed to externalise the terrorist threat. As part of a first effort to prevent future attacks and apprehend terrorists, the US government passed the 2001 Patriot Act. Mainly designed to improve the collection of counterterrorism data as well as information sharing among law enforcement and intelligence services, various other reforms also broadened domestic counterterrorism authorities: Patriot reauthorisations in 2005, 2006, 2011, and 2015; parts of the 2004 Intelligence Reform Act; the 2008 Foreign Intelligence Surveillance Act (FISA) Amendments Act; as well as its 2012 renewal.[8]

In terms of new institutions designed to facilitate counterterrorism coordination, the Department of Homeland Security and Director of National Intelligence must be mentioned. In 2002, the Homeland Security Act was passed, consolidating 22 agencies, among them the US Coast Guard, Transportation Security Administration, Secret Service, Customs Service, and Federal Emergency Management Agency, under one organisational roof. Only two years later, the Intelligence Reform Act created the position of Director of National Intelligence in an effort to help coordinate the 16 members of the intelligence community.

Consistent with the aforementioned externalisation approach, the US further focused on detecting and defusing threats *before* they reached US borders; the 9/11, Madrid, and London attacks served as justifications for stricter border security initiatives. At the centre of various executive and legislative programmes, border security was closely monitored by Congress. In the aftermath of the November 2015 Paris attacks, the US Congress thus pushed to further tighten the visa waiver programme and considered ways to keep Syrian refugees, considered potential Islamic State of Iraq and the Levant (ISIL) sleeper cells, out of the country.[9] Key border security measures included a revised US-Visit (Visitor and Immigrant Status Indicator Technology) programme that stored the biometric data of people entering the country and in 2009 was supplemented by the pre-flight ESTA (Electronic System for Travel Authorization) requirement for citizens of all visa waiver countries; and the SEVIS (Student and Exchange Visitor Information) system, which kept tabs on foreign nationals who entered the US on student or work visas.[10] In addition, US authorities began compiling passenger name records from all international flights arriving in the United States and checking them against government watch lists, such as the no-fly list. Borders were further reinforced by the building of actual border fences, symbolising the ultimate protection of the homeland. As is well known, President Donald Trump has been looking to continue this tradition. While going beyond previous approaches, the January 2017 Trump travel ban on individuals from six mostly Muslim countries – which continues to be subject to Supreme Court review and limitations[11] – also falls within the well-known confines of 'pushing US borders out' by insisting on intensified security vetting *before* granting entry to the United States. The strategy does not just focus on people but also cargo: as part of the Container Security Initiative (CSI) initiative, US authorities in 2002 began working with more than 50 foreign ports to identify any high-risk containers before they were shipped to the United States.[12]

In line with the focus on external threats, there has been a tendency to attribute Jihadi radicalisation to non-American factors – dangerous influences and people coming from *outside* the United States. Against this backdrop, it is perhaps not surprising that the United States got a late start to preventive counter-radicalisation initiatives at home. Only after experiencing a spike in home-grown Jihadi attacks and plots did the US government switch gears in 2009. However, 'softer' de-radicalisation measures, intended to assist and rehabilitate those who have already become infected with the Jihadi virus, were kept on the backburner, with the 2015 San Bernadino and 2016 Orlando attacks adding new urgency to the matter.[13]

Germany: The overall scope of German counterterrorism responses after 9/11 is noteworthy; especially since German security services were not new to domestic terrorism and already had significant counterterrorism tools available. Nonetheless, existing policies were adjusted and/or supplemented to counter the new networked Jihadi threat. Counterterrorism measures – adopted as part of the 2001 Counterterrorism Act, the 2006 Counterterrorism Supplemental Act (Terrorismusbekämpfungsergänzungsgesetz, TBEG), the 2008 Federal Criminal Police (Bundeskriminalamt, BKA) Act, the 2011 and 2015 TBEG reauthorisations, as well as the 2015 Data Retention Act – thus expanded data collection powers of law enforcement and intelligence services; facilitated the sharing of data with and among security services; and increased preventive policing powers. The 2001 reforms centralised certain law enforcement powers at the federal level, tasking the BKA with data collection and cyber-terrorism authorities. The 2008 BKA reform further equipped the federal BKA with a list of new investigative powers in the counterterrorism realm.[14] Since 2009, various other laws have focused on German foreign fighters: in addition to terrorist training camp visits, travel attempts to Syria and Iraq became punishable by law;[15] counterterrorism services could revoke ID cards and passports to prevent foreign fighter travel;[16] domestic intelligence and law enforcement authorities were expanded, as was their ability to share data with foreign intelligence services.[17] The more recent laws sought to prevent Germans joining ISIL on Iraqi and Syrian battlegrounds; returning foreign fighters with newly acquired terrorist skills presented a major concern as well.

Another focus has been on counter- and de-radicalisation methods. Since 2009, Germany has made an effort to prevent violent Jihadi radicalisation and also to de-radicalise individuals who have started embracing violent ideas and/or actions. German authorities have thus been looking to help and reintegrate individuals via family-assisted counselling, phone hotlines, targeted interventions, and exit programmes.[18] In this context, it is important to note that the string of Jihadi-motivated attacks that have occurred in Germany since summer 2016 involved individuals who had recently arrived in Germany amid the refugee wave; they did not constitute home-grown attacks.

Two new institutional arrangements, the joint counterterrorism centre (Gemeinsames Terrorismusabwehr Zentrum, GTAZ) and the joint anti-terror database

(Antiterrordatei), centralised German counterterrorism analysis and data capacities in 2004 and 2006, respectively. This was considered necessary due to the particularly fragmented nature of the German security architecture where, in addition to the BKA and the Federal Office for the Protection of the Constitution (Bundesamt für Verfassungsschutz, BfV), the 16 Länder have unique competences. In fact, the 16 State Criminal Police Offices and State Offices for the Protection of the Constitution bear resemblance to miniature FBIs and MI5s with complete authority in their states. The relationship between law enforcement and intelligence is further guided by the *Trennungsgebot* principle, which prescribes the strict separation of intelligence and police powers.

The GTAZ represented a network-centric body that relied on co-location and voluntary information exchange between the BKA and BfV, which were moved to the same location in Berlin but maintained their institutional independence. Members of the federal intelligence service (Bundesnachrichtendienst, BND), other federal services, as well as the law enforcement and intelligence bureaus of the 16 Länder soon attended all meetings. Similarly, the database represented a network-centric, technological compromise that preserved the federal security architecture but allowed intelligence and law enforcement services of the states and the federal government to more or less jointly store and access counterterrorism data.[19]

Executive power gains. What do the post-9/11 counterterrorism reforms reveal about the balance between executive power vis-à-vis legislative and judicial oversight?

United States: Without question, executive branch agencies in the United States gained significant powers; reforms thus appear to have been at the expense of judicial and legislative oversight. On second view, however, Congress forced important legal restrictions on all new institutions and counterterrorism policies. Lawmakers also periodically reauthorised the most controversial parts of the Patriot, Intelligence Reform, and FISA Reform Acts, which otherwise would have lapsed.[20] A National Security Agency (NSA) surveillance programme that was adopted by means of secret executive order in 2001, subject to only limited congressional oversight through the Gang of Eight – the House and Senate leaders from both parties, plus the Chairmen and Ranking Members of the House and Senate Intelligence Committees[21] – was first contained by means of the temporary 2007 Protect America Act (PAA),[22] which was soon replaced by the 2008 FISA Amendments Act. The latter retained many PAA provisions that were considered a legislative victory for the Bush administration. The FISA reform, however, also increased safeguards for US citizens and came with new oversight powers, ensuring that Congress would become a key player in FISA-related decision-making and implementation.[23] More recently, the USA Freedom Act, passed in June 2015, enacted new restrictions on federal intelligence powers, ending NSA bulk collection of US phone records and internet metadata and introducing new oversight measures.[24] All in all, even though executive branch powers after 9/11 expanded, lawmakers continue to play a more or less active role in any of the new counterterrorism programmes and institutions examined in this article – the level of congressional involvement and influence hinges on whether lawmakers find their voice and vote to hold the executive branch accountable.[25]

Similar to Germany, executive versus legislative power plays were particularly noticeable with regard to institutional reforms. The initial executive branch response after 9/11 merely consisted of creating new coordination mechanisms, in the form of a new White House Office of Homeland Security, or new data-sharing entities, like the Terrorist Threat Integration Center or the Terrorist Screening Center. Representing network-centric arrangements, like the German GTAZ and anti-terror database, these centres came with flat institutional designs and served as new nodal points of contact between agencies. Gradually, however, more 'heavyweight' congressional solutions replaced these 'lightweight' executive models, like the new Department of Homeland Security and the Office of the Director of National Intelligence.[26] In other words, law-makers pushed for more far-reaching reforms that would pull them into the decision-making arena, to ensure tangible electoral results as well as permanent congressional involvement through budgetary decisions and oversight hearings.

Slowly but surely, all those institutions and programmes the White House implemented by executive order thus became checked by congressional legislation. At times, the White House was forced to act because Congress threatened to use the power of the purse; in other instances, Supreme Court rulings and the 9/11 Commission report provided an opening for legislative action as well as important political cover.[27] However, even though Congress had to wrestle the White House into the legislative arena on many occasions, the latter had tremendous influence over the details of the bills – the White House either assumed command of the legislative process (in the case of the Homeland Security and FISA Reform Acts)[28] or kept a conspicuously low profile that translated into watered-down reforms (as illustrated by the Intelligence Reform Act).[29]

Germany: All in all, considerable executive power gains must be noted, but these frequently remained subject to parliamentary and/or judicial oversight. For example, the 2001 counterterrorism package contained sunset provisions that had to be renego-tiated in 2006, 2011, and 2015.[30] Reauthorisations offered opportunities for renewed debate and reform. The parliamentary G10 Commission (G10-Kommission, where G10 stands for Article 10 of the Basic Law), which approves all foreign, domestic, and military surveillance measures affecting the privacy of correspondence, continued to take a central role.[31] BKA counterterrorism continued to be strictly delineated and exclusively reserved for *international* terrorism, with states retaining responsibility for domestic terrorism cases, despite the fact that the federal BKA was granted new pre-ventive powers as part of the 2008 BKA reform. Finally, several counterterrorism laws became subject to constitutional court review, forcing the revamping of the Data Reten-tion, Anti-terror Database, and BKA Acts, in 2010, 2014, and 2016 respectively, with additional safeguards.

Decision-making actors and obstacles. These checks can help illuminate the key actors and obstacles in the decision-making process, as well as the importance attributed to them within the two presidential and parliamentary systems.[32]

United States: Both branches faced substantial obstacles inherent to the decision-making process when initiating reforms. Resistance took the form of interbranch oppo-sition, for example when the White House and Senate faced off over the 2002 Homeland

Security and 2005 Patriot Reauthorization Acts, or when the House opposed the 2008 FISA Amendments Act and the 2010/11 Patriot Act Reauthorization.

Obstacles to decision-making also included interagency/bureaucratic battles which were not only waged inside the executive branch (for example, when cabinet members rejected the White House border agency proposal in 2001)[33] but also as proxy wars in Congress, whenever the agendas of executive departments aligned with the interests of oversight committees. The chairmen of the House Armed Services and Judiciary Committees thus served as the Pentagon's most potent allies in the battle against the intelligence reform bill in the House.[34]

In an effort to prevent this kind of bureaucratic meddling, the White House opted to block all bureaucratic stakeholders from the decision-making process over the 2002 Homeland Security legislation. As noted above, the White House pursued additional strategies to ensure implementation of executive branch agendas, including concerted lobbying efforts or disengagement. Legislative decision-making processes surrounding the 2001 Patriot and 2002 Homeland Security Acts illustrate that White House officials were able to tailor the rules of the game so they would serve executive interests best, particularly in the House of Representatives. The typically fragmented decision-making procedures were thus avoided; they were also circumvented in the markup of the Patriot Act and the 2007 PAA.[35] Disjointed decision-making procedures were left in place, however, when it was time to pass the intelligence reform bill in 2005, with the White House taking a decidedly hands-off approach to the sweeping proposal deemed an encroachment on executive national security prerogatives.[36]

Germany: The Ministry of the Interior typically encountered opposition when starting pre-legislative coalition and/or interagency negotiations within the executive branch, which left room for turf battles. The Justice Department represented one such key stakeholder, determined, inter alia, to defend the *Trennungsgebot* principle against BMI infringements.

Moreover, the Länder imprint on counterterrorism reforms was considerable. While interagency players had a chance to stake their claims as part of executive proposals, these could still be rejected or held up by the Bundesrat Länder, which had veto powers with regard to most counterterrorism legislation. Länder preferences thus superseded coalition/bureaucratic interests whenever the two did not see eye to eye – in other words, whenever any of the proposed measures threatened to encroach on Länder jurisdiction. When reviewing decision-making processes leading to, for example, the 2001 anti-terror and 2008 BKA acts, it becomes especially obvious that 'the Länder have been dealt a strong hand in the legislative bargaining process'.[37] In 2001, the Länder thus gained the same new security powers for their 16 domestic intelligence agencies as the federal agencies did, against the opposition of the Green coalition party.[38] In 2008, the Bundesrat, fearing federal BKA encroachment on Länder turf, went as far as to veto a counterterrorism bill submitted by the lower house – despite the fact that the CDU–SPD coalition government still had a majority in the Bundesrat at the time.[39] Others have referred to the 2008 veto as a bureaucratic[40] or partisan decision, arguing that the SPD coalition partner, in particular Justice Minister Brigitte Zypries, incited the rebellion by encouraging the SPD-governed Länder to reject the bill. Even though SPD opposition to the bill may have carried over to the Bundesrat, explanations focusing on party loyalties show a largely incomplete picture of the standoff; several

CDU-ruled Länder also abstained from the vote as concerns about infringement on Länder sovereignty dominated Bundesrat debates and official statements.

In many ways, the Bundesrat 'provided Länder representatives with the structural cover'[41] to defend their own interests. The Länder thus not only significantly influenced the blueprint of the anti-terror database but also ensured their unfettered right to use the database.[42] In light of Länder opposition, federal centralisation plans gave way to the loose organisational makeup of the GTAZ.[43] At the end of the day, the GTAZ and database designs validated the federal security architecture and Länder sovereignty in the counterterrorism realm, keeping the established balance of power between the federal government and Länder.[44]

Summary. After granting the president significant leeway in the immediate months after 9/11, the US Congress did swing into action in 2002: first, lawmakers insisted on a full-fledged reorganisation of homeland security-related agencies and tasks; second, they also pushed for an intelligence coordinator to better orchestrate intelligence community resources and missions. In addition, lawmakers reviewed, reauthorised, and reformed Patriot Act provisions on no fewer than four occasions,[45] most recently to end the mass collection of American telecommunication data, install new internal audits and enhance legislative oversight; Congress also oversaw a FISA overhaul in 2008.[46] Decision-making obstacles came in form of interbranch battles but also bureaucratic/interagency meddling; both were kept at bay only when the White House engaged in concerted lobbying.

In Germany, new-won executive counterterrorism powers remained under legislative and judicial watch, while federal centralisation attempts were prevented. With the exception of the new GTAZ, all counterterrorism measures were put on a statutory basis. Legislative processes opened the gate for numerous intra-executive (interagency and coalition partner) and structural (Bundesrat Länder) hurdles among which the Länder played the most pronounced role.

COUNTERTERRORISM AFTER 9/11: INTERNATIONAL RESPONSES

As will become obvious, parliamentary/congressional involvement and/or oversight were often lacking or only minimal when it came to international counterterrorism responses. With the exception of military operations, German assistance in US intelligence collection or extraordinary renditions was an executive branch prerogative, allowing for the kind of flexibility that did not exist in the domestic realm due to civil liberty concerns. Likewise, many US counterterrorism measures targeting non-Americans outside the US homeland were not held to domestic standards. A fundamental part of the separation of powers system, congressional and/or judicial oversight of international responses was arguably more pronounced, however, even if, at times, legislative control only involved the Gang of Eight.

Military Operations

United States: While the prevention of terrorist attacks at home became the predominant counterterrorism objective, this was to be achieved by battling the terrorists *abroad*. On the evening of 11 September 2001, President George W. Bush declared a war on terrorism, explaining that the attacks 'were on a scale that has created a state of armed conflict that requires the use of the United States Armed Forces'.[47] The war proclamation was more than just a powerful rhetorical instrument as it also involved a legal component that triggered presidential war powers.

As commander in chief, the president was responsible for the safety of the nation in times of crisis. In times of war Congress also tended to withdraw from the spotlight to facilitate quick decision-making. By implication, lawmakers became more accepting of presidential unilateral tools, such as executive orders and presidential directives. Similarly, the Authorization for the Use of Military Force (AUMF), a joint congressional resolution passed in October 2001,[48] represented a 'blank cheque': it delegated far-reaching war powers to the president, and thus was condemned as an abdication of congressional checks on presidential war powers by the critics.[49] Interestingly, in addition to the US invasion in Afghanistan, the AUMF subsequently was cited to legally justify a series of other counterterrorism programmes, including drone strikes, Guantanamo detention, and NSA surveillance.[50]

By December 2001 the Taliban was driven from power, but Operation Enduring Freedom (OEF) remained in place to chase down all those al-Qaeda and Taliban leaders who escaped. Moreover, the mission of the UN-mandated International Security Assistance Force (ISAF) was established in December 2001 and, while initially limited to Kabul, expanded across the country between 2003 and 2006, now under NATO leadership. Only 18 months after launching OEF, the Bush administration started a second military invasion in Iraq, justified as a last-minute effort to prevent Saddam Hussein's regime from building nuclear weapons and selling them to al-Qaeda. Use of military force in Iraq was authorised by a second joint congressional resolution passed in autumn 2002, once again illustrating strong bipartisan support.[51] As is widely known, a number of key European allies were strongly opposed to the war – with Germany being among the most vocal critics – giving rise to one of the most severe transatlantic crises since the end of the cold war. Operation Iraqi Freedom continued until the end of 2011. As part of Operation Inherent Resolve, incidentally also justified by the 2001 AUMF, US forces have since returned to Iraq in an effort to counter the Islamic State; the United States has led the anti-ISIL coalition of 60-plus states since 2013.[52] US military operations have also involved drone strikes against high-value terrorist targets in, for example, Afghanistan, Pakistan, Somalia, and Yemen.[53]

Germany: Even though the US pledged to use every instrument of national power in the pursuit of the 9/11 terrorists, military means arguably played a prominent role in the ensuing war on terror. Germany, by contrast, is often referred to as a civilian power that views the use of force as an absolutely last resort.[54] The 2016 Bundeswehr White Paper thus cited military responses as the last of five instruments of statecraft needed to effectively combat terrorism, in addition to political, legal, intelligence, and police resources.[55] Regardless, both 2006 and 2016 White Papers identified transnational terrorism as 'the most immediate danger to (German) security',[56] with the 2016 strategy specifically referencing al-Qaeda, its regional affiliates, and ISIL as the most prominent threats.[57] The 2006 White Paper previously stated that military counterterrorism functions fall under the umbrella of international conflict prevention and crisis management, considered the Bundeswehr's topmost function.[58]

While Germany refused to participate in the 2003 US-led invasion of Iraq, long-time German involvement in Afghanistan and, more recently, Iraq/Syria must be mentioned. German military deployments in Afghanistan started as early as November 2001 when German special forces and naval assets began contributing to the US-led OEF. Germany also served as the third largest troop contributor of NATO's ISAF campaign from 2005 to 2014 (after the US and United Kingdom).[59] The entire time, however, German ISAF troops were stationed in the Northern provinces, the ones least affected by insurgency violence; the German constitution only allows for limited German military engagements outside the NATO area, all of which require annual Bundestag approval.

Germany has since served as a key contributor of NATO's Resolute Support mission, designed to offer additional training, advice, and assistance to Afghan security forces and institutions.[60] Furthermore, in December 2014 the German parliament approved military contributions to the US-led anti-ISIL coalition in Iraq, albeit only in the form of weapons and training to Kurdish Peshmerga forces.[61] Germany stepped up its assistance after the Paris terrorist attacks in November 2015, offering additional logistical and reconnaissance support.[62]

Guantanamo Detention and Torture

United States: Following the externalisation strategy, senior al-Qaeda and Taliban leaders were transferred to and held at a US military base in Guantanamo Bay, Cuba, a location that was precisely chosen because it was surrounded by ocean, far away from US communities and court jurisdiction.[63] Categorised as so-called unlawful enemy combatants, suspected al-Qaeda operatives were detained in accordance with a newly formulated detention regime. The Military Order signed by President Bush in November 2001 authorised indefinite detention without charge and established military commissions that would eventually be used to prosecute the detainees. The military commissions were designed to facilitate convictions, meaning they favoured the prosecution and significantly lowered the standards of evidence required for conviction. In creating these new detention procedures, the Bush administration not only suspended habeas corpus rights but also the Geneva Conventions.[64]

Unlawful enemy combatants were also detained in Afghanistan and Iraq, or, as transpired in 2005, sent to CIA-run secret prisons in, for example, Eastern Europe. Further details regarding the treatment of the detainees surfaced, compounding the domestic and international fallout over new US counterterrorism practices. Inter alia, high-ranking detainees were subjected to interrogation techniques such as waterboarding, a practice that simulated drowning.[65] The practice was revived after 9/11 to obtain information deemed useful for the prevention of future attacks. The congressional Gang of Eight was briefed on these practices as early as 2002,[66] and additional checks and balances kicked in two years later, even if they remained inconclusive at times: The Supreme Court began issuing a series of rulings in 2004, establishing its jurisdiction in Guantanamo;[67] determining that US enemy combatants had writ of habeas corpus rights;[68] and requiring a statutory mandate for the military commissions.[69] Congress scrambled to pass the Military Commissions Act of 2006 in response, validating most of the Bush regime. The rulings were also inconclusive in that they confirmed the administration's right to detain individuals until the end of the war on terror as well as military commissions.[70]

The practice of extraordinary renditions was started during the Reagan administration and has been utilised by every administration since; however, Congress did pass the Detainee Treatment Act in 2005, outlawing waterboarding and any 'cruel, inhuman, or degrading treatment or punishment' of any prisoner of the US government.[71] The law further required military interrogations to be performed according to the US Army Field Manual and thus conform to US and international law standards. At the same time, Congress represented a crucial part of an insurmountable obstacle to President Barack Obama's efforts to close Guantanamo. Congress in June 2010 passed a law that banned the transfer or incarceration of detainees from Guantanamo to US prisons and has since blocked all funding for the transfer of any Guantanamo detainees into the United States.[72]

Germany: Germany was among the chief critics of the US prison regime in Guantanamo; US torture practices; as well as extraordinary renditions. Over time, details of German involvement in some of these controversial activities surfaced. For example, members of the BfV and BND conducted interrogations in Guantanamo starting in 2003.[73] A June 2006 report by the Council of Europe concluded that Germany was among 14 European governments which colluded with the CIA over the transport of terror suspects around the world; specifically, Germany provided 'staging posts' for rendition operations.[74] Inter alia, German authorities facilitated the abduction of Abu Omar, an Egyptian-born cleric in Italy who was taken from Milan, Italy, flown to a base in Germany and then on to Egypt, where he was tortured. Bavarian prosecutors responded to reports about the rendition of a German citizen, Khaled el-Masri, by indicting 13 alleged CIA operatives for his abduction in Macedonia, transport to Afghanistan, and torture.[75] The indictment resembled no more than a paper tiger; the German legal system does not allow for *in absentia* trials and the German government did not officially request their extradition.

However, in the case of another German citizen, Mohammed Haydar Zammar, German authorities facilitated his extra-legal rendition by forwarding Zammar's travel details to the CIA and also sending counterterrorism officials to Syria for interrogations. At the time, Zammar was under investigation for his involvement in planning the 9/11 attacks but German authorities lacked sufficient evidence to arrest him.[76] Against this backdrop, a special Bundestag committee of inquiry was convened, from 2006 to 2009, to investigate BND involvement in the Iraq war and double-dealings with regard to extraordinary renditions.[77] While the parliamentary system thus allowed for some scrutiny of secret participation in the American war on terror, this occurred after the fact, with the German government claiming executive privilege.[78] The inquiry also did not have any bearing on the counterterrorism services under supervision of the Chancellery and BMI and subject to oversight of the Parliamentary Control Committee (Parlamentarisches Kontrollgremium, PKG) tasked with checking the activities of all federal intelligence services.[79] A closer look at the PKG illustrates the inherent conflict of interest built into parliamentary systems: the chancellor and coalition parties always constitute a majority among committee members, greatly blurring the separation of powers and system of checks and balances.

NSA Surveillance

United States: In 2013, revelations by NSA whistle-blower Edward Snowden triggered another major transatlantic crisis: his documents revealed information about wiretaps on the German chancellor; the NSA gaining access to email address books, contact lists, and the cloud storage system of Google and Yahoo; as well as PRISM, a system the NSA used to gain access to the private communications of users of nine popular internet services, including Yahoo, Google, Facebook, Skype and Twitter.[80] PRISM access was governed by Section 702 of the Foreign Intelligence Surveillance Act, passed in 1978 and reformed in 2008. The FISA governs foreign intelligence collection in the US and established the FISA court, which is responsible for issuing surveillance and search warrants as part of foreign intelligence investigations in the US. Section 702 of FISA allowed senior Obama administration officials to 'authorize' the 'targeting of persons reasonably believed to be located outside the United States'.[81] PRISM was thus overseen by the FISA court and therefore also by Congress. So there was oversight, but this arrangement did not help Germans – the programme is designed to specifically target foreign users of internet platforms. The USA Freedom Act, passed in 2015 mostly to reform the Patriot Act, did nothing to limit the NSA's foreign operations involving non-Americans.

Germany: While German law also does not restrain foreign intelligence activities of German services, the public outcry over NSA surveillance had to be addressed: the German parliament tasked another special committee with investigation of the NSA spying scandal; the extent of foreign spying in Germany; as well as German involvement in NSA surveillance. The committee started its work on 20 March 2014, with the final report slated for June 2017.[82] Similar to the parliamentary BND inquiry, operational realities that transpired from the special inquiry indicate that German intelligence services not only benefited from NSA activities – various terrorist attacks were prevented by means of these partnerships – but also cooperated with the NSA. In the absence of any Bundestag G10 Commission intervention, German security services assisted NSA intelligence collection after 2007, for example, with the BND accepting selectors' search terms (for phone numbers and email addresses) from the NSA and monitoring them for NSA use.[83] According to Snowden documents, German domestic and foreign intelligence services relied on spy software provided by the NSA, allowing them to engage in bulk collection and sharing with the American service.[84] This collusion intensified once German authorities sought to prevent Germans joining ISIL, starting in 2013.[85] The G10 Commission most likely approved of the data collection taking place inside Germany – similar to the American FISA court, the rubber-stamping panel has traditionally rejected only a minuscule percentage of all surveillance measures.[86] Even though the G10 Commission seems better equipped to veto surveillance measures than the PKG – the G10 committee is not made up of members of parliament and, therefore, not beholden to the government – it suffers from a severe lack of staff and expertise.

Summary

After 9/11, the US government launched a series of international programmes and measures; some of which existed in secret and/or arguably in violation of both US and international law. Most of these counterterrorism responses abroad were drawn up by the executive branch. However, Congress provided more or less extensive oversight, via standard committees or the Gang of Eight, and, with the exception of Guantanamo detention and extraordinary renditions, also took steps to rein in executive excesses like the 2005 NSA surveillance programme and torture practices.

German involvement in US counterterrorism operations was generally secret and not known to the German public. While military operations remain strictly vetted and circumscribed by parliament, the Parliamentary Control Committee and G10 Commission of the German Bundestag – assuming they were aware of all counterterrorism practices – did not veto rendition flights and surveillance programmes, arguably in violation of German law, and thereby allowed for extensive collaboration between the BND, BfV, and NSA. At the end of the day, Germany's parliamentary government features offered the Chancellery and Interior Ministry extensive unilateral freedoms, with parliamentary scrutiny occurring 'after the fact' – once the information became public knowledge and special inquiries convened.

CONCLUSION

Despite some hiccups, Germany and the United States have worked closely together since 9/11, both at home and abroad. Even though Germany did not suffer an attack on 9/11, Jihadi terrorism has been viewed as the primary security threat since then. German security concerns were further compounded by subsequent attacks in Spain, the UK, and more recently France and Germany, as well as the large number of ISIL fighters originating from Germany and other European neighbours since 2013.

German government structures were instrumental for the formulation of domestic counterterrorism responses. Through their representation in the Bundesrat, the German Länder were dealt a strong hand in legislative decision-making processes, allowing them to protect and expand their own counterterrorism powers and prevent a more centralised federal counterterrorism apparatus. Government structures also significantly shaped US counterterrorism responses. Despite fears of executive overreach, starting in 2002 Congress emerged as a central player in counterterrorism policy formulation, by creating new counterterrorism institutions, intensifying oversight of executive programmes, and forcing corrections of executive branch initiatives deemed extra-legal.

German checks and balances largely remained in place when it came to formulating domestic counterterrorism measures. Germany did not suffer a direct attack and German responses were more restrained than those of the United States. However, German counterterrorism services also violated German and international law, mostly when it came to international activities conducted unilaterally by Chancellery- and BMI-supervised intelligence agencies and in tandem with US services. While US programmes, measures, and actions, both at home and abroad, far exceeded those of Germany, they were regularly overseen by select lawmakers or entire congressional committees. In the German fusion of power system, parliamentary oversight of intelligence actions was more blurred and arguably less robust[87] – a circumstance the 2016 reform of the Parliamentary Control Committee also sought to address.[88]

DISCLOSURE STATEMENT

No potential conflict of interest was reported by the author.

NOTES

1. On this point, see also Dorle Hellmuth, *Counterterrorism and the State* (Philadelphia: University of Pennsylvania Press, 2015), p.274.
2. Prominent members of the structural school include Samuel Huntington, *The Common Defense: Strategic Programs in National Politics* (New York: Columbia University Press, 1961), and Kenneth Waltz, *Foreign Policy and Democratic Politics: The American and British Experience* (Boston: Little Brown, 1967). See also Stephen Krasner, 'Are Bureaucracies Important?', in G. John Ikenberry (ed.), *American Foreign Policy: Theoretical Essays* (Glenview, IL: Scott, Foresman and Company, 1989), pp.419–33; see also Hellmuth, *Counterterrorism*, pp.1–2.
3. For major contributions, see Graham T. Allison, *Essence of Decision: Explaining the Cuban Missile Crisis* (New York: Harper Collins, 1971); Morton H. Halperin, *Bureaucratic Politics and Foreign Policy* (Washington, DC: Brookings, 1974); Amy Zegart, *Spying Blind: The CIA, the FBI, and the Origins of 9/11* (Princeton, NJ: Princeton University Press, 2007).
4. On this point see also Hellmuth, *Counterterrorism*, pp.124, 274.
5. The article distinguishes between domestic and international responses as the former involves significant civil liberty considerations and legislative branch involvement, whereas the latter does not.
6. Richard Russell, 'American Military Retaliation for Terrorism: Judging the Merits of the 1998 Cruise Missile Strikes in Afghanistan and Sudan', *Georgetown Institute for the Study of Diplomacy Case Study* 238 (2000), p.7.
7. Stefan Malthaner and Peter Waldmann, 'Terrorism in Germany: Old and New Problems', in Marianne van Leeuwen (ed.), *Confronting Terrorism: European Experiences, Threat Perceptions and Policies* (The Hague: Kluwer Law, 2003), pp.112–13.
8. For more details on US reforms, see also Hellmuth, *Counterterrorism*, chapter 2.
9. Mike De Bonis, 'House Passes Bill to Tighten Flow of Syrian Refugees over Obama's Objections', *Washington Post*, 19 November 2015.
10. Michael O'Hanlon, 'Border Protection', in Michael d'Arcy, Michael O'Hanlon, Peter Orszag, Jeremy Shapiro, and James Steinberg (eds), *Protecting the Homeland, 2006/2007* (Washington, DC: Brookings Institution Press, 2006), pp.96–113.
11. Michael Shear and Adam Liptak, 'Supreme Court Takes Up Travel Ban Case, and Allows Parts to Go Ahead', *New York Times*, 26 June 2017.
12. Stephen Flynn, *America the Vulnerable* (New York: Harper Collins, 2004), chapter 5.
13. Dorle Hellmuth, 'Countering Jihadi Radicals and Foreign Fighters in the United States and France: Très Similaire!', *Journal for Deradicalization* 4 (Fall 2015), pp.2–21.
14. See also Hellmuth, *Counterterrorism*, chapter 3.

15. 'Ausbildung im Terrorcamp wird strafbar', *Zeit Online*, 28 May 2009, http://www.zeit.de/online/2009/23/justiz-terror-strafen (accessed 20 June 2017).
16. Jenny Gesley, 'Germany: New Anti-Terrorism Legislation Entered Into Force', 10 July 2015, *Library of Congress*, http://www.loc.gov/law/foreign-news/article/germany-new-anti-terrorism-legislation-entered-into-force/ (accessed 20 June 2017).
17. 'Anti-Terror-Gesetze erneut verschaerft', *Zeit Online*, 1 June 2016, http://www.zeit.de/politik/deutschland/2016-06/terrorismus-bundesregierung-anti-terror-paket (accessed 20 June 2017).
18. Dorle Hellmuth, 'Countering Islamist Radicalization in Germany', *Combating Terrorism Center Sentinel* (at West Point) 6/1 (Jan. 2013), pp.13–16.
19. Hellmuth, *Counterterrorism*, pp.100, 126.
20. 'Legislative Background: Recent Action on the USA Patriot Act', *Congressional Digest* 84/7 (Sept. 2005), p.201.
21. Sheryl Gay Stolberg, 'Senators Left Out of Loop Make Their Pique Known', *New York Times*, 19 May 2006.
22. Eric Lichtblau and David Johnston, 'Court to Oversee U.S. Wiretapping in Terror Cases', *New York Times*, 18 Jan. 2007.
23. 'A Better Surveillance Law', *Washington Post*, 20 June 2008.
24. Ellen Nakashima, 'Congressional Action on NSA is a Milestone in the Post-9/11 World', *Washington Post*, 2 June 2015.
25. See also Hellmuth, *Counterterrorism*, p.76.
26. Ibid., p.75.
27. George Archibald, 'Panel Ties Funding to Ridge Testimony', *Washington Times*, 22 March 2002; George Archibald, 'White House Mollifies House Panel', *Washington Times*, 23 March 2002; 'Stampede on Intelligence', *Washington Post*, 2 Sept. 2004.
28. John Lancaster and Jonathan Krim, 'Ashcroft Presents Anti-Terrorism Plan to Congress', *Washington Post*, 20 Sept. 2001; John Lancaster, 'Senate Passes Expansion of Electronic Surveillance', *Washington Post*, 12 Oct. 2001.
29. Greta Wodele and John Stanton, 'Compromise Clears Way for Intelligence Overhaul Vote', *GovExec. com*, 7 Dec. 2004. See also Hellmuth, *Counterterrorism*, pp.52–53.
30. Hellmuch, *Counterterrorism*, pp.163–65, 175–76.
31. Bundesministerium des Innern, 'Informationen zum Terrorismusbekämpfungsergänzungsgesetz', *Pressemitteilung*, 11 July 2006.
32. See also Hellmuth, *Counterterrorism*, pp.71–72, 125–26.
33. Steven Brill, *After: How America Confronted the September 12 Era* (New York: Simon & Schuster, 2002), pp.285–87.
34. Richard Posner, *Preventing Surprise Attacks: Intelligence Reform in the Wake of 9/11* (Lanham, MD: Rowman & Littlefield, 2005), p.56.
35. Robin Toner and Neill A. Lewis, 'Bill Greatly Expanding Surveillance Power in Terrorism Fight Clears the Senate', *New York Times*, 12 Oct. 2001; E.J. Dionne, Jr., 'Why the Democrats Caved', *Washington Post*, 10 Aug. 2007; Alison Mitchell, 'New Antiterrorism Agency Faces Competing Visions', *New York Times*, 14 June 2002.
36. 'Lawmakers Say Bush, Cheney Need to Lobby', *Washington Post*, 22 Nov. 2004.
37. Hellmuth, *Counterterrorism*, p.125.
38. Stefan Krempl, 'Der Neue Otto-Katalog ist da', *Telepolis*, 1 Nov. 2001.
39. Bundesrat, 'Beschluss the Bundesrates', *Drucksache* 860/08 (Beschluss), 28 Nov. 2008.
40. Klaus Brummer, 'The Bureaucratic Politics of Security Institution Reform', *German Politics* 18/4 (2009), p.515.
41. Hellmuth, *Counterterrorism*, p.126.
42. 'Eigensinn der Länder lähmt Terrorbekämpfung', *Süddeutsche Zeitung*, 18 March 2004; 'Innenminister beschließen Islamisten Datei', *Die Welt*, 9 July 2004; 'Zentral gegen den Terror', *Süddeutsche Zeitung*, 15 Sept. 2004.
43. 'Islamisten-Datei und ein zentrales Lage- und Analysezentrum', *Frankfurter Allgemeine Zeitung*, 9 July 2004.
44. Hellmuth, *Counterterrorism*, p.185.
45. See, for example, Charles Babington, 'Congress Votes to Renew Patriot Act, with Changes', *Washington Post*, 8 March 2006.
46. Shailagh Murray, 'Obama Joins Fellow Senators in Passing New Wiretapping Measure', *Washington Post*, 10 July 2008.
47. Military Order of November 13, 2001, Detention, Treatment, and Trial of Certain Non-Citizens in the War Against Terrorism, 66 Fed. Reg. 57,833 (16 Nov. 2001).
48. *Authorization for Use of Military Force*, PL 107-40, 107th Cong., 1st sess. (18 Sept. 2001).

49. Louis Fisher, 'NSA Eavesdropping: Unchecked or Limited Presidential Power', in Ralph Carter (ed.), *Contemporary Cases in U.S. Foreign Policy*, 4th ed. (Washington, DC: CQ, 2011), pp.229–58.
50. Ibid.; 'Obama's Speech on Drone Policy', *New York Times*, 23 May 2013.
51. Authorization for Use of Military Force Against Iraq Resolution of 2002, Pub.L, 107–243.
52. Kathleen McInnis, 'Coalition Contributions to Countering the Islamic State', *Congressional Research Service Report*, 24 Aug. 2016.
53. New America Foundation, 'America's Counterterrorism Wars', https://www.newamerica.org/in-depth/americas-counterterrorism-wars/ (accessed 20 June 2017).
54. See, for example, German Ministry of Defence, *Defence Policy Guidelines*, 18 May 2011, p.1.
55. The Federal Government, *White Paper 2016*, 13 July 2006, p.34.
56. Federal Ministry of Defence, *White Paper 2006*, 18; *2016 White Paper*, p.4.
57. *2016 White Paper*, p.4.
58. *2006 White Paper*, pp.9, 55.
59. NATO, 'ISAF Placemats Archive', http://www.nato.int/cps/en/natolive/107995.htm (accessed 19 March 2017).
60. NATO, 'Resolute Support Mission', http://www.nato.int/nato_static_fl2014/assets/pdf/pdf_2017_01/20170126_2017-01-RSM-Placemat-new.pdf (accessed 1 Feb. 2017).
61. 'German Cabinet Agrees to Send Troops to Train Iraqi Kurds', *DW.com*, 17 Dec. 2014, http://www.dw.com/en/german-cabinet-agrees-to-send-troops-to-train-iraqi-kurds/a-18136604 (accessed 19 March 2017).
62. Noah Barkin and Sabine Siebold, 'Germany to Support Military Campaign against IS after French Appeal', *Reuters*, 26 Nov. 2015.
63. *Rasul v. Bush*, 542 U.S. 466 (2004).
64. Linda Cornett and Mark Gibney, 'The Rights of Detainees: Determining the Limits of Law', in Ralph Carter (ed.), *Contemporary Cases in U.S. Foreign Policy*, 4th ed. (Washington, DC: CQ, 2011), pp.444–69.
65. Julie Tate, 'The CIA's Use of Harsh Interrogations', *Washington Post*, 9 Dec. 2014.
66. Joby Warrick and Dan Eggen, 'Hill Briefed on Waterboarding in 2002', *Washington Post*, 9 Dec. 2007.
67. *Rasul v. Bush*, 2004.
68. *Hamdi v. Rumsfeld*, 542 U.S. 507 (2004).
69. *Hamdan v. Rumsfeld*, 548 U.S. 557 (2006).
70. *Boumediene v. Bush*, 553 U.S. ___ (2008).
71. Michael John Garcia, 'Interrogation of Detainees: Requirements of the Detainee Treatment Act', *Congressional Research Service Report*, 26 Aug. 2009.
72. Marina Koren, 'Obama's Last Guantanamo Pitch to Congress', *The Atlantic*, 23 Feb. 2016.
73. 'Ready to Go to the Island', *Spiegel*, 24 Nov. 2003.
74. Council of Europe Parliamentary Assembly, 'Alleged Secret Detentions and Unlawful Inter-state Transfers involving Council of Europe Member States', 7 June 2006.
75. Craig Whitlock, 'Germans Charge 13 CIA Operatives', *Washington Post*, 1 Feb. 2007.
76. Craig Whitlock, 'In Another CIA Abduction, Germany Has an Uneasy Role', *Washington Post*, 5 Feb. 2007.
77. Peter Carstens, '3 Jahre, 140 Zeugen und 3500 Seiten später', *FAZ.net*, 19 June 2009.
78. Council of Europe Parliamentary Assembly', Secret detentions and illegal transfers of detainees involving Council of Europe member states: second report', Doc. 11302 rev., 11 June 2007.
79. 'Parliamentary Controller Says Secret Service Is 'Out of Control', *Deutsche Welle*, 18 Dec. 2006. See also Florian Geyer, 'Fruit of the Poisonous Tree: Member States' Indirect Use of Extraordinary Rendition and the EU Counter-terrorism Strategy', *Center for European Policy Studies Working Paper 263* (April 2007).
80. Timothy Lee, 'Here's Everything We Know About PRISM to Date', *Washington Post*, 12 June 2013.
81. Ibid.
82. Deutscher Bundestag, '1. Untersuchungsausschuss: ("NSA")', https://www.bundestag.de/ausschuesse18/ua/1untersuchungsausschuss (accessed 24 June 2017).
83. 'Waiting for Schindler's list', *Economist*, 6 June 2015, p.41.
84. 'Secret Links between Germany and the NSA', *Spiegel*, 22 July 2013.
85. Greg Miller, 'Backlash in Berlin over NSA Spying Recedes as Threat from Islamic State Rises', *Washington Post*, 29 Dec. 2014.
86. Russell Miller, 'Intelligence Oversight – Made in Germany', in Zachary Goldman and Samuel Rascoff (eds), *Global Intelligence Oversight* (New York: Oxford University Press, 2016), pp.269–70; Rachel Stern, 'Fiercely Critical of NSA, Germany now Answering for its Own Spy Practices', *Christian Science Monitor*, 22 May 2015.

87. On this point, see also Miller, 'Intelligence Oversight', p.258; Jan-Hendrik Dietrich, 'Of Toothless Wind-bags, Blind Guardians and Blunt Swords: The Ongoing Controversy about the Reform of Intelligence Oversight in Germany', *Intelligence and National Security* 31/3 (2016), pp.397–415.
88. Deutscher Bundestag, 'Ausschuesse: Parlamentarisches Kontrolgremium', https://www.bundestag.de/ausschuesse18/gremien18/pkgr/einfuehrung/248044 (accessed 24 June 2017).

Index

Printed in the United States
by Baker & Taylor Publisher Services